Information Search Pattern In Electronic Environment

M. Bavakutty
Rekha Rani Varghese

Ess Ess Publications

4837/24, Ansari Road, Darya Ganj,
New Delhi-110002
✆ : 23260807, 41563444
Fax : 011-41563334
E-mail: info@essessreference.com
url:http://www.essessreference.com

Ess Ess Publications
4837/24, Ansari Road,
Darya Ganj,
New Delhi-110 002.

Tel.: 23260807, 41563444
Fax: 41563334
E-mail: info@essessreference.com
www.essessreference.com

First Published - 2007

ISBN: 81-7000-512-4 (10 Digit)
978-81-7000-512-4 (13 Digit)

Published By Ess Ess Publications and printed at Salasar Imaging Systems

PRINTED IN INDIA

Preface

The technology for electronic transfer of information has advanced so rapidly that it is now possible for electronic publishing, electronic storage, processing and delivery of information including text and images. Libraries, in particular, have benefited from these developments. Former barriers between libraries and their users have dissolved creating a "library without walls". Through these advances, users enjoy increased access to library resources and services and libraries benefit from enhanced resource sharing. Electronic information environment facilitates enhancement in the speed of service, number of users served, the quantum and exhaustiveness of information provided.

The web has introduced millions of people to the concept and capabilities of Information Retrieval (IR) systems. The large, general search engines are the main tools of resource discovery. Many search engines such as Google, Alta Vista and Yahoo now provide access to Internet based documents covering the breadth of human knowledge. Directory services, subject specific search engines, lists and "hear-say" (learning URLs from other people or from other types of media) cover only a tiny part of the Web. The World Wide Web is the fastest growing information medium today. The exponential growth of the Web has drastically changed the availability of electronic information, but, somewhat paradoxically, this success has also made it increasingly difficult to find and organize information. It is a well-known fact that users often become overwhelmed by the number of items retrieved by a simple query in a search engine, and that the precision of those results is in many cases fairly inadequate, resulting in low effectiveness. Electronic searches vary in complexity. Broad generalized topics are easier to search, as they are more likely to retrieve a number of core references. Topics which are more specific, such as those with three or more structured search concepts, requires more structured search patterns, as the likelihood of finding suitable references significantly decreases. Users' problem solving with the Web are dependent on some information searching factors such as knowledge about the Internet search tools and the ability in the use of appropriate search methods. As a result, libraries are facing new challenges, new competitors, new demands, new expectations and a variety of information services from users tailored to their wants and needs.

The information search patterns of the users are different depending upon their personal attributes and environment. The main aim of the case study is to examine the information search pattern of the science doctoral students in the electronic environment. How researchers search information, the type of information needed, the services they used and their priorities in searching for information are highly relevant, because they provide a basis for reorganizing libraries and information centers and reshaping their information support activities.

The first chapter of this work provides a brief description of the information search tools. In the second chapter the recent developments in computer, storage, communication and wireless technologies are discussed. Chapter three gives the review of related studies on the information search in the electronic environment. Chapter four furnishes a case study of the information seeking behaviour of the science doctoral students in the universities. And chapter five summerises the findings of the case study, followed by suggestions for improving the access and use of electronic information resources and the conclusion.

The application of high technology has become the order of the day to catch up with the developed world and to meet the challenges of 21st century. The technological developments in recent years particularly in the area of computer, telecommunication and storage technologies have significantly changed the way we generate, collect, organize, present, disseminate, share and use information. The role of the librarian would change to accommodate their changing work environment. Librarians would need to be familiar with multi-platform systems in order to serve and aid their clientele. Their knowledge of organizing and indexing information for the researcher will have intrinsic value, especially for the end-users when they search the system. But they will need a deep understanding of the developing search engines and technologies for multimedia. In an era of continuous technological developments in conjunction with information overload, information search pattern studies continue to be a vital tool enabling information professionals to improve both their understanding of information use and hence information delivery. This study, we hope will help librarians and other information managers in India and other developing countries to develop Information and Communication Technology based library system. Many libraries are taking steps to switch over from their traditional roles into technology enabled service-centered roles; in this context the present study will be of great help to plan and develop a well automated Information and Communication Technology enabled library system.

We are grateful to our professional colleagues in the University of Calicut for their suggestions in the preparation of this book and the science doctoral students in the universities studied for promptly providing the required data. We are thankful to Mr. Sumit Sethi, Managing Director, Ess Ess Publications for the sincere efforts he has taken to get this book published with in a short period.

Calicut University Campus **Prof. M. Bavakutty**

25th May 2007 **Dr. Rekha Rani Varghese**

Contents

Preface 5

1. Introduction **11**

1. Information Search Tools
2. Information Search Methods
3. Online Search
4. Conclusion

References

2. Electronic Information Environment **22**

1. Developments in Computer Technology
2. Developments in Storage Technology
3. Developments in Communication Technology
4. Networking
5. Intranet and Extranet
6. Wireless Technology
7. Mobile Technologies
8. Digital Libraries
9. Electronic Publishing
10. Conclusion

References

3. Studies on Information Search Pattern in Electronic Environment: A Review **63**

1. Information Search Pattern
2. Use of Internet
3. Electronic Information Services
4. Information Seeking Behaviour
5. Information Needs and Use Studies

References

4. Information Search Pattern in Electronic Environment : A Case study 135

1. General Information
2. Places of Accessing electronic information resources
3. Frequency of Accessing Electronic Information Resources
4. The Ways of Identifying Electronic Information Resources for Research
5. Methods of Learning Internet
6. Frequency of Use of Internet Tools and Resources
7. Time Spent for Using Internet Tools and Resources
8. Internet Facilities Used for Communication
9. Frequency of Use of Internet Search Engines
10. Purpose of Conducting Electronic Information Searches
11. Search Methods Used
12. Use of Advanced Search Methods
13. Difficulties in Obtaining Information from Online Search
14. Ability in Using Electronic Information Resources
15. Impact of Electronic Information Resources on Research
16. Use of Printed Documents While Using Electronic Information Resources
17. Characteristics of an Ideal Search Engine
18. Conclusion

5. Summary 283

1. Major findings of the case study
2. Suggestions for Improving the Access and Use of Electronic Information Resources
3. Suggestions for Further Research
4. Conclusion

***Questionnaire* 324**

***Select Bibliography* 332**

***Web References* 348**

***Index* 355**

1
Introduction

FAST ADVANCES in information technology have unleashed forces, which are shaping and affecting the basic structure of our society. Large-scale computerizations, and enormous growth of electronic information coupled with global access to information via telecommunication infrastructure, are some of the underlying factors of the present transformation process. Information is emerging as a critical resource for user activities at all levels, education, research and development, advancing the frontiers of knowledge, competitiveness in business and industry, economic and social development, improving the quality of day-to-day life etc. Anyone, anytime, anywhere, any information, any format will be the feature of coming society. With more and more emphasis towards right to access, any information should become available to any individual on the planet. It is clear that information will occupy a centre stage position governing human life in the coming years making a profound impact on society and economy.

Assimilation of scientific and technological information is an essential precondition for progress in developing countries. Most of the world's scientific and technological activity is centered in the industrialized world, with less than ten percent of the world's research work taking place in developing countries. Not surprisingly, the bulk of the world's scholarly communication is generated and exchanged among industrialized countries. Thus, at least for scientific and technical information, developing countries are necessarily dependant upon sources in industrialized countries to keep abreast of technological developments. With the explosion in the use of information technology that has provided scientists, researchers, and private citizens with unprecedented access to information. The Internet has brought data communications and information exchange into a new level, providing the means to access a wide variety of databases and information repositories throughout the world. Anyone with a computer and a link to a network can access an astonishing array of information resources located throughout the world. The technology for electronic transfer of information has advanced so rapidly that it is now possible for electronic publishing, electronic storage, processing and delivery of information including text and images. Libraries, in particular, have benefited from these developments. Former barriers between libraries and their users have dissolved creating a "library without walls". Through these advances, users enjoy increased access to library resources and services and libraries benefit from enhanced resource sharing. Electronic information environment facilitates enhancement in the speed of service, number of users served, the quantum and exhaustiveness of information provided. The features of electronic information environment are[1]:

* Provide access to very large information collections including access to primary and complete information, not merely surrogates or indexes.
* Support multimedia content
* Network accessibility
* User friendly interfaces

* Unique referencing of digital objects
* Multi use and refer various areas in the same time
* Current information services
* Advanced search and retrieval
* Support both formal and informal learning
* Remote access
* Online discussions and commands
* Accessibility from anyone, anywhere, anytime, during travel, hotel etc., supporting, opportunity to publishing, annotation and integration of new information.

The Internet and more specifically the web have introduced hundreds of millions of people to the concept and capabilities of Information Retrieval (IR) systems. The large, general search engines are the main tools of resource discovery. Many search engines such as Google, Alta Vista and Yahoo now provide access to Internet based documents covering the breadth of human knowledge. Directory services, subject specific search engines, lists and "hear-say" (learning URLs from other people or from other types of media) cover only a tiny part of the Web. The World Wide Web is the fastest growing information medium today. The exponential growth of the Web has drastically changed the availability of elcctronic information, but, somewhat paradoxically, this success has also made it increasingly difficult to find and organize information. It is a well-known fact that users often become overwhelmed by the number of items retrieved by a simple query in a search engine, and that the precision of those results is in many cases fairly inadequate, resulting in low effectiveness. Electronic searches vary in complexity. Broad generalized topics are easier to search, as they are more likely to retrieve a number of core references. Topics which are more specific, such as those with three or more structured search concepts, requires more structured search patterns, as the likelihood of finding suitable references significantly decreases. Users' problem solving with the Web are dependent on some information searching factors such as knowledge about the Internet search tools and the ability in the use of appropriate search methods. As a result, libraries are facing new challenges, new competitors, new demands, new expectations and a variety of information services from users tailored to their wants and needs.

1. INFORMATION SEARCH TOOLS

In the last ten years, the world has seen a truly amazing amount of growth in the Internet as well as the advent and growth of the World Wide Web. Today so much information is available on-line that user is put in the sometimes enviable—but often frustrating—position of having too much information. Many librarians and researchers see the Web as a monster that has grown out of control and yearn for a managed, maintained, and friendlier source of information. The major tools available to search online information are the following:

1.1. Internet Search Engines

For finding information on the Internet, online search is carried out with the use of "search engines." Search engines are built by computer robot programs ("spiders") and a computer algorithm ranks all pages. The search engines will search for Internet sites containing the words that designate as a search term. It provides results back in the form of links to those sites that have the term(s) looking for. Factors that influence results include the size of the database, the frequency of updating, and the search capabilities. There is no single online search tool, which has an index to the entire contents of the Internet. Each search engine uses different search techniques and various software tools to collect and catalog indexes of the Internet. Search engines also differ in their search speed, the design of the search interface, the way in which they display results, and the amount of help they offer. Search Engine has three basic parts[2]:

* **Spider (crawler, link finder) :** a computer program that harvests web links from page to page
* **Index :** a database that is organized and searchable of the Spider's harvested results
* **Search and retrieval mechanism :** Software that allows users to search the Index and return results in a predetermined order.

Search engines do not search the Internet itself, but instead search a database of information about the Internet. Thus, when a document is placed on the Internet, it will only be found by a search engine if information about that document has been recorded in the search engine's database. There are at least two ways a search engine finds out about a document. One way is for the publisher of the document to register it with the engine. The second way that documents get registered is if the search engine company finds it as part of its research routines. Some search engines use "spiders" or search robots to search the Internet and gather information, which is subsequently recorded in the engine's database. Some search engines index not only the World Wide Web, but also Usenet newsgroups. Many search engines are now becoming reference sites, which contain much more than just search capability. They may also have news, weather, free software, picture indexes, ratings of web sites, and other features. There are several hundred-search engines, but they fall into a handful of types[3]:

* Global search engines, typified by Google, Fast Search, Northern Light, HotBot, AltaVista, and others, reads pages from all over the world in many languages. These engines may index more than a billion pages.
* Regional search engines are limited geographically.
* Targeted search engines limit themselves to one subject, like biography, medicine, graphics, art, fishing,

and so forth.

* Reference search engines provide information from a set of reference works, such as an encyclopedia.

1.2. Meta Search Engines

The growth in the number of search engines has led to the creation of "meta" search tools, often referred to as multi-threaded search engines. These search engines allow the user to search multiple databases simultaneously, via a single interface. While they do not offer the same level of control over the search interface and search logic, as do individual search engines, most of the multi-threaded engines are very fast. Recently, the capabilities of meta-tools have been improved to include such useful features as the ability to sort results by site, by type of resource, or by domain, the ability to select which search engines to include, and the ability to modify results. These modifications have greatly increased the effectiveness and utility of the meta-tools.

1.3. Subject Directories

Subject directories are hierarchically organized indexes of subject categories that allow the Web searcher to browse through lists of Web sites by subject in search of relevant information. They are compiled and maintained by people and many include a search engine for searching their own database. Subject directory databases tend to be smaller than those of the search engines, which mean that result lists tend to be smaller as well. However, there are other differences between search engines and subject directories that can lead to the latter producing more relevant results. While a search engine typically indexes every page of a given Web site, a subject directory is more likely to provide a link only to the site's home page. Furthermore, because their maintenance includes human intervention, subject directories greatly reduce the probability of retrieving results out of context. Because subject directories are arranged by category and because they usually return links to the top level of a web site rather than to individual pages, they lend themselves best to searching for information about a general subject, rather than for a specific piece of information.

Now specialized subject directories are available due to the Web's immense size and constant transformation, keeping up with important sites in all subject areas is humanly impossible. It is a guide compiled by a subject specialist to important resources in his or her area of expertise to produce relevant information and is usually more comprehensive than a general guide. Such guides exist for virtually every topic.

2. INFORMATION SEARCH METHODS

Information is of vital importance for scientific development of an individual, organization, state or country. Although lots of information are published everyday yet it is well established fact that many of them crate noise/pollute the information or cause information overload. Many search engines by default offer a keyword search, but this kind of search will find all pages that contain any of the words specified. Moreover, the search will find the words in any order and in any location. The amount of information available in the electronic information sources especially on the Internet is so vast, it's important to have a very clear idea of the various search methods to widen or narrow the search results. The various advanced search methods used for information search are:

2.1. Boolean Search

Boolean operators, also known as logical operators, are used to separate keywords to construct more complex searches. They help to make a search more accurate. The Boolean logic consists of three operators: 'AND', 'OR' and 'NOT'. The operator 'AND' used to find documents containing all of the specified words in the search strategy. However, this type of search normally retrieves fewer results than if it is searched for one of the terms on its own. The 'OR' operator retrieves all works that contain any or the entire search terms it separates. This type of search retrieves more results than if one of the terms searched for on its own. The 'NOT' operator retrieves all works that contain the first search term but not the second. In searching, 'NOT' is used to get rid of unwanted concepts. Each of these operators can be visually described using Venn diagrams as shown below:

Operator	***Example search***	***The search will find***	***Venn diagram (The dark portion shows the result)***
AND	Internet and research	Items containing "Internet" and "research" AND narrows a search, resulting in fewer hits.	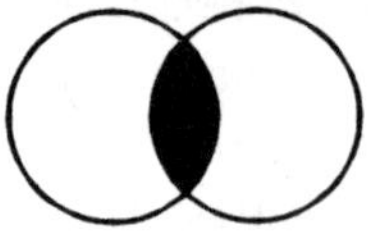
OR	Internet or research	Items containing either "Internet" or "research" or both. OR broadens a search, resulting in more hits.	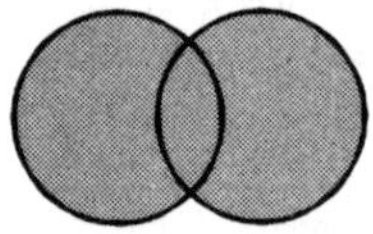
NOT	Internet not Intranet	Items containing "Internet" but not "Intranet"	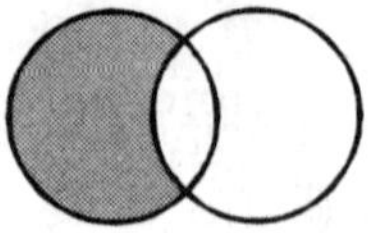

Fig. 1. Boolean Operators

In Internet search engine, the use of Boolean operators may be manifested in three distinct ways[4]:

* Full Boolean logic with the use of the logical operators.
* Implied Boolean logic with key word searching.
* Predetermined language in a user fill-in template.

2.2. Truncation of Search Terms

Truncation allows search for variant spelling and expansion of word stem using any one of the key board symbols such as *, ? and #. The symbols may be placed at the beginning or at the end of a word. There are three types of truncation searches such as: Open Truncation, Restricted Truncation and Internal Truncation.

2.3. Proximity Search

Proximity search means search for two or more words that occur within a specified number of words (or fewer) of each other in the databases. The proximity operators are WITH, NEAR, ADJ or ADJACENT and a number (to specify the number of words)[5]. The proximity operator is placed between the words that are to be searched. Adding a number following WITH requires the terms to occur with up to that number of other words between the two terms in the order typed. Adding a number following NEAR requires the terms to occur with up to that number of other words between the two terms in either the order typed or the reverse order. ADJ is usually equivalent to WITH in requiring the search terms to be adjacent to each other in the order typed.

Proximity searching is used with a keyword or Boolean search. Combine words or phrases using proximity operators to ensure that search terms occur reasonably close to each other in a full text search. The operators usually can be used to specify the exact number of words between search terms and the order in which the search terms occur in the document Proximity operators are especially useful in full text systems (such as Lexis-Nexis) or in systems that default to keyword searching with the 'AND' Boolean operator (such as First Search).

2.4. Phrase Searching

Phrase searching is used to search for words as phrases. That is, the words must be side by side and in the given order. More than one keyword, in phrase searching terms is searched exactly as keyed (all terms required to be in documents, in the order keyed). Enclosing keywords in quotations (" ") forms a phrase in many databases. By using phrase searching fewer results are retrieved.

2.5. Field Searching

A field is a section of an electronic record. When the search engines retrieve information from Web pages around the world, they sort the information into various categories or fields. The main fields that can be accessed in field searching are: Title, URL (Uniform Resource Locator) and Domains. Almost all search engines in CD-ROM or online library products and the more sophisticated Web search engines allow users to search for terms appearing in a particular field. This can help immensely when looking for a very specific item

There are a number of advanced search methods such as fuzzy searching, meta searching, concept searching, etc. All these search methods will help to retrieve more relevant information from online searches.

3. ONLINE SEARCH

The online search process calls for user's awareness of system capabilities. How successful a searcher will be at the terminal, is almost depending entirely upon the various factors such as[6]:

* Coverage of databases
* User's ability to verbalise his/her requirements
* Awareness of search methods
* Ability of the vocabulary to describe concepts of interests to user
* User ability to search systematically

4. CONCLUSION

The application of high technology has become the order of the day to catch up with the developed world and to meet the challenges of 21st century. The technological developments in recent years particularly in the area of computer, telecommunication and storage technologies have significantly changed the way we generate, collect, organize, present, disseminate, share and use information. The role of the librarian would change to accommodate their changing work environment. Librarians would need to be familiar with multi-platform systems in order to serve and aid their clientele. Their knowledge of organizing and indexing information for the researcher will have intrinsic value, especially for the end-users when they search the system. But they will need a deep understanding of the developing search engines and technologies for multimedia. In an era of continuous technological developments in conjunction with information overload, information search pattern studies continue to be a vital tool enabling information professionals to improve both their understanding of information use and hence information delivery.

REFERENCES

1. Gopal, Krishan. (2000) Digital libraries in electronic information era. Delhi, Authors Press, pp. 14-15.
2. Franklin, Curt. How Internet search engines work [Internet] Available from: <http://www.howstuffworks.com/search-engine.htm/printable> [Accessed September 20th 2005]
3. The best search engines [Internet] U. C. Berkeley. Available from : <http://www.lib.berkeley.edu/TeachingLib/Guides/Internet/SearchEngines.html > [Accessed July 10th 2005]
4. Boolean searching on the Internet university libraries. [Internet] University at Albany. Available from : <http://library.albany.edu/internet/boolean.html> [Accessed July 10th 2005]
5. Electronic searching: Guide to library research. (2003) [Internet] Duke University Library. Available from: <http://www.lib.duke.edu/libguide/adv_searching.htm> [Accessed October 10th 2005]
6. Kumbar, I. N. (1999) Online services and their use in the library. IN: Library vision 2010: Indian libraries and librarianship. Sardana, J. L., ed. ILA, Delhi, pp. 379-389.

2
Electronic Information Environment

THE LAST DECADE has witnessed a growing competition to deliver new digital information services to millions of new users. The Internet, as a leading communication system, was -up to a few years ago - the only and ultimate channel for providing sophisticated data information services. Several Internet technologies were developed and tested, leading to the introduction of new techniques for distributing data. Web technologies such as Java, TCP/IP, XML and HTML became the de-facto solutions for distributing data over the Internet. Along with new tools, new flexible ways of creating applications were developed. When compared to the traditional Client/Server paradigm (based on data transmission) the mobile code model has shown enormous potential: not only is the data transmitted but also the logic for interpreting the data itself. Nowadays, the increasing advances in network technology are pushing the information revolution towards new Telecommunication systems, offering even more sophisticated digital channels than the Internet; side by side with the traditional (audio and video) content, new data services (such as eCommerce, digital archives, games, etc.) can be delivered over these broadcasting and mobile phone networks. A very aggressive competition is developing among these newer digital systems to deliver flexible, cheap and ubiquitous data services. In such a moving world, the objectives of the content providers are constantly being revised, so new solutions have to be implemented at a very fast pace.

The knowledge is admitted as a key piece in the socioeconomic relations established by the societies, the organizations and the countries. The knowledge of the technologies of information and communication is specially important because it refers to an area of the knowledge generated by the man and that has been produced to make viable some exchange forms and of relations; they are a fundamental support of the process of the current globalization that leads to the knowledge society. It seems that electronic information systems is to blame in large part for the "speed up" of modern society - everything has to get done faster, be there sooner, and be available immediately. It is not hyperbolic to say that the information explosion and Information Technology (IT) revolution has led to the emergence of the electronic information environment.

Today on the Web, information is fetched by browsing documents. Tomorrow on the Web, information could be found by searching repositories. In the new millennium beyond the Web, analysis environment technology would allow for the correlation of information across repositories to solve problems. Internet information resources are fast seeping into the common consciousness of academia, taking their place alongside traditional academic resources in core research assignments. Information Technology had a profound effect on every aspect of modern society, including research. The electronic media has provided many possibilities and opportunities for providing faster and quicker access to information at the global level. For the meaningful use of electronic information sources a researcher should have the Digital Information Fluency (DIF). Digital Information

Fluency is the ability to find, evaluate and use digital information effectively, efficiently and ethically. DIF involves knowing how digital information is different from print information; having the skills to use specialized tools for finding digital information; and developing the dispositions needed in the digital information environment.

1. DEVELOPMENTS IN COMPUTER TECHNOLOGY

Today computers and computer oriented technology have come as a boost to nations which are struggling to either remain in the forefront of or are trying to restructure their economy to create wealth. The major developments in the area of computer technology are:

1.1. Input Devices

As computers and software get more sophisticated so do input devices. An input device is a peripheral device that converts symbols that people understand into bits that computers can process. An input device includes a keyboard, a terminal, a touch screen, a mouse, a scanner, etc. Today, more data and instructions are entered a CPU of microcomputers directly using direct input devices used to provide a more natural user interface. These entry devices reduce users' typing errors. While direct input is an advanced fourth generation data entry form, voice input (speech input) is the mode of next generation input technology. There are many forms of direct input devices such as Mouse, Touch screen, Light Pen, Graphics Tablet, Scanner, Bar-code readers, Magnetic Entry, and Voice-Input Devices.

1.2. Output Devices

An output device is any peripheral device that converts machine-readable information into people-readable form such as a monitor, printer, and plotter output device. On the output side, there have been interesting changes too. The trend in Laser printers is to look for those with postscript. The advantage of post script is that any piece of software having postscript can work with postscript printer. Recently a new technology of Liquid Crystal Shutter (LCS) and voice output device are added to the field

1.3. Artificial Intelligence (AI)

Artificial Intelligence is a branch of science which deals with helping machines find solutions to complex problems in a more human like fashion. This generally involves borrowing characteristics from human intelligence, and applying them as algorithms in a computer friendly way[1]. In the 1940's Alan Turing said "a machine has Artificial Intelligence when there is no discernible difference between the conversation generated by the machine and that of an intelligent person"[2]. Machines that exhibit AI appear to demonstrate human intelligence and behaviour. They are said to be concerned with manipulation of knowledge rather than mere data. Artificial intelligence has many applications, but the most famous aspects are: automation control, Robots, Expert systems (ES), processing of natural languages and simulation systems.[3] Artificial intelligence systems have also been developed and used in libraries to carry out activities such as indexing and cataloguing. These activities rely on experts who know and understand complex rules, but who also rely on decision-making processes based on previous experience and examples, making them suitable processes for experiments with artificial intelligence. Attempts have also been made to deliver reference and online information retrieval using artificial intelligence systems.[4]

1.4. Expert Systems

Expert Systems are computer programs that embody a substantial amount of knowledge of some topic and use that knowledge to answer questions and solve problems that are traditionally solved by human experts[5]. Expert systems have been described as the most significant practical project to emerge from 30 years of A.I research. The main components of expert system are a knowledge base, an inference mechanism and a user interface. The knowledge base is comparable to a data base; the inference mechanism to an algorithm. The user interface is self-explanatory. This knowledge is of two types, facts and heuristics. The facts comprise information that is widely shared and acknowledged by experts in the field. Heuristics are rules of thumb or any other devices, that limit the range of search solutions for problems and indicate which among several courses of action is to be preferred. Expert systems attempt to mimic the problem solving activities and performance of an expert. Typically they are used for problems dealing with complex diagnosis, scheduling forecasting, monitoring and control or data analysis and interpretation[6]. The development of expert systems coupled with increasing availability of low cost computers provides new potential for dissemination of expert knowledge in a digestible form direct to the users.

1.5. Virtual Reality (VR)

Virtual reality means, the simulation of reality through real time, three-dimension modeling, position tracking and stereo audio and video techniques[7]. The advantage of Virtual Reality is that it can immerse people in an environment that would normally be unavailable due to cost, safety, or perception restrictions. A successful Virtual Reality environment offers users immersion, navigation, and manipulation. Virtual Reality encompasses a range of interactive computer environments, from text-oriented on-line forums and multiplayer games to complex simulations that combine audio; video, animation, or three-dimensional graphics; and scent. Some of the more realistic effects are achieved using a helmet like apparatus with tiny computer screens, one in front of each eye and each giving a slightly different view so as to mimic stereoscopic vision. Sensors attached to the participant (e.g., gloves, bodysuit, footwear) pass on his or her movements to the computer, which changes the graphics accordingly to give the participant the feeling of movement through the scene. Computer-generated physical feedback adds a "feel" to the visual illusion, and computer-controlled sounds and odors reinforce the virtual environment[8]. Virtual Reality systems break away from the convention of the user/screen interface, and surround users with a realistic computer generated environment. Users can directly participate in simulations of processes at any scale, calling up linked hypermedia information and explanation when they need it. Virtual Reality is used in some electronic games, in amusement-park attractions, in military exercises, and to simulate construction designs. Experimental and envisioned uses include education, industrial design, surgical training, and art.

1.6. Multimedia

Multimedia, in personal computing, software and applications that combine text, high-quality sound, two- and three-dimensional graphics, animation, photo images, and full-motion video. i.e. *Multimedia* is the use of several different *media* to convey information. The integration of various media on a single platform and use of these media to improve the quality of the interface between the machine and its user are the most exciting aspect of multimedia. As the information is presented in various format, multimedia enhances user experience and helps grasping information better and faster.

Chowdhury[9] has quoted Ching-Chihchen, that multimedia refers to synthesis of text, data, graphics, animation, optical storage, image processing and sound. Now multimedia technology is being used in many areas such as[10]:

* Information and education
* Personal management and training
* Leisure and entertainment
* Research and development

* Maintenance and repair
* Banking and finance
* Crime records and analysis
* Marketing and sales
* Home science and cookery
* Production and manufacturing
* Industry specific applications (such as tourism)

It is conventional to describe multimedia as lying at the convergence of three or four separate industries viz., computing, telecommunications, entertainment and publishing.

2. DEVELOPMENTS IN STORAGE TECHNOLOGY

Although magnetic media have proved faithful and reliable, there has always been a quest for a media with higher storage capacities. One of the major media to enter the market place is the optical or laser discs which offer high storage capacities. Optical disk is a disk written and read by laser beam. This optical disk has a great impact on today's storage technology. Optical disk does not spin, does not need to move access arms and read/write heads, because a laser beam can be moved electronically. The capacity of the storage is considerably greater than magnetic disk counterparts, and optical disk storage may eventually replace all magnetic tape and disk storage.

2.1. CD-ROM

CD-ROM (Compact Disk Read Only Memory) is an optical disk storage that contains text, graphics and hi-fi stereo sound. CD-ROM is a 4.75-inch optical disk storage that can store around 650 MB of data. CD-ROM is a read-only disk that cannot be written on or erased by the user. Compact discs were the successor to compact cassette tapes and they are still going strong. In CD-ROM standard, data (text or pictures) cannot be viewed with audio play simultaneously. CD-ROM XA standard can do.

Nwali[11] has pointed out that the potential value of CD-ROM as follows:

* It has enormous storage capacity
* Stored information is not affected by power cuts;
* Disc cannot be damaged by magnetic or microwave scanning;
* On line charges not required in the case of CD-ROMs.
* Telecommunication links are not necessary; and
* It is user friendly.

A number of encyclopedias, directories, back volumes of periodicals and other electronic documents are available in this medium.

2.2. CD-Re Writable (CD-RW)

The CD-Re Writable disk is a new type of CD disk that enables information to be written on to it in multiple sessions. The CD-RW disk will store up to 650 MB of information compared with the typica1 1.4 MB capacity of a floppy disk and can be overwritten thousands of times[12]. CD-RW drives and optical disks can be treated just like a floppy or hard disk, writing data onto it multiple times. CD-RW builds on the existing benefits of CD technologies and will be able to read CD-ROMs and write onto today's CD-R disks.

2.3. CD- Recorder (CD-R)

Compact disc was developed originally in the audio environment and made its debut in two ways: CD-R, the technology that enables the user to archive images and documents and Photo CD. Photo CD was one alternative to high-end scanning, but its propriety format and difficulty in achieving colour fidelity prevented it from becoming an industry standard. CD-R, on the other hand, is rapidly gaining popularity as an extremely flexible and reliable storage medium. And, because there are no propriety concerns, it is accessible to all. CD-R is superior to magnetic or optical storage or digital audio tape (DAT) tape in many respects. Chief among its many advantages is the ability to maintain data integrity for many years because it is not susceptible to magnetic fields, radiation or most normal physical abuse. With a disc storage capacity of 650 MB, CD-R is one of the most efficient and the most affordable storage media.

The most appropriate applications for CD-R take advantage of the medium's unique attributes, including

* high storage capacities with instant random access
* ability to add unalterable data in multiple recording sessions over time
* resistance to degradation of media and stored data over time
* ISO 9660 standard, which ensures broad compatibility
* extensive (and growing) installed base of CD-ROM drives
* Compact size for ease of use and distribution.

Access to CD's over a local area network (LAN) has been possible for some years. The use of CD-ROM in conjunction with Intranet is emerging as a viable option for users working on a limited budget or without access to Internet services.

2.4. DVD (Digital Versatile Disc or Digital Video Disc)

DVD, the Digital Versatile Disc, is a high capacity CD-size disc for video, multimedia, games and audio applications. The digital videodisc is the new standard for optical digital storage and is being hailed as the successor to CD audio, CD-ROM, VHS tape and laserdisc. A DVD disc is the same size as a CD disc but holds 25 times more information and is up to 9 times faster. This increased capacity enables DVD to store high quality video and higher quality than current CD audio. A single sided single layer DVD disc will hold two hours of video and a double sided, double layer disc eight hours of video. DVD is essentially a bigger, faster CD that can hold cinema-like video, better-than-CD audio, still photos, and computer data. DVD aims to encompass home entertainment, computers, and business information with a single digital format. It has replaced laserdisc, is well on the way to replacing videotape and video game cartridges, and could eventually replace audio CD and CD-ROM. There are six recordable versions of DVD: DVD-R for General, DVD-R for Authoring, DVD-RAM, DVD-RW, DVD+RW, and DVD+R. DVD-R and DVD+R can record data once, like CD-R, whereas DVD-RAM, DVD-RW, and DVD+RW can be rewritten thousands of times, like CD-RW.

DVD-R uses organic dye technology, like CD-R, and is compatible with most DVD drives and players. DVD-RW (formerly DVD-R/W and also briefly known as DVD-ER) is a phase-change erasable format. Developed by Pioneer based on DVD-R, using similar track pitch, mark length, and rotation control, DVD-RW is playable in many DVD drives and players. DVD-RW uses groove recording with address information on land areas for synchronization at write time (land data is ignored during reading). Capacity is 4.7 billion bytes. DVD-RW discs can be rewritten about 1,000 times. DVD-RAM, with an initial storage capacity of 2.58 billion bytes, later increased to 4.7, uses phase-change dual (PD) technology with some magneto-optic (MO) features mixed in. DVD-RAM is the best suited of the writable DVD formats for use in computers, because of its defect management and zoned CLV format for rapid access. However, it's not compatible with most drives and players.

The main features of the DVD formats are[13]:

* Up to 4.7 GB read-only capacity per layer, 8.5 GB per side maximum

* Backwards compatibility with current CD media. All DVD hardware will play audio CDs and CD-ROMs
* Physical dimensions identical to compact disc but using two 0.6 mm thick substrates, bonded together.
* Single-layer/dual-layer and single/double sided options.
* Designed from the outset for video, audio and multimedia, not just audio All formats use a common file system (UDF).
* Digital and analogue copy protection for DVD-Video and DVD-Audio built into standard.

The latest developments in storage technology is Hybrid formats such as DVD Plus (also known as 'Dual Disc'), which combine a DVD layer with a CD layer.

3. DEVELOPMENTS IN COMMUNICATION TECHNOLOGY

Information society dominated by computers and communications is in front of us. In this society, the strategic resource is knowledge and information, and the movement through the information pathway will increase the value of that resource. A communication network is the pathway that allows information, data, and knowledge to be spread. Thus, the mainstream of the information age is communication. Communications involve many technologies. In addition, many new communication technologies are being incorporated into the fabric of the information society as fast as people can learn how to maintain and use the technologies.

3.1. Electronic Data Interchange (EDI)

Electronic data Interchange is basically computer-to-computer communication, involving the interchange of standard formulated data between the computer application systems of partners with minimal manual intervention. With EDI, standards are required to define the contents of message and the techniques for assembling message, in order that they can be read by the receiving system and processed automatically. These EDI standards cover five interrelated areas such as messages, segments, data elements, and syntax and message design guidelines[14]. There are three major sets of EDI standards. *UN/EDIFACT* is the only international standard (infact, a United Nations recommendation) and is predominant in all areas out side of North America. *ANSI ASC X12* and Uniform Communication Standard (UCS) are popular in *North America* and are very similar to each other. Despite being relatively unheralded, in this era of technologies such as *XML* Services, the *Internet* and the *World Wide Web*, EDI is still the engine behind 95 percent of all *electronic commerce* transactions in the world. Advanced countries have successfully implemented Electronic Data Interchange services for effective information management and communications.

3.2. Facsimile Transmission (Fax)

Fax is a means of transmitting a copy of a page of text or graphics to a remote location via telecommunication links. Fax is one possible technology for electronic document delivery. The main advantage of fax is that it transmits text, graphics, diagrams, etc easily as it treats them all as still pictures. Faxes operate with or without paper; in the latter case faxes are sent directly from the computer using a fax modem. This is a useful system in the current stage of transition for communicating with the world of atoms from the world of bits. However these are badly used bits; as it is not possible to edit or alter the fax we receive, change its format or its fonts, unless it is digitized by means of some OCR (Optical character recognition) system. The fax ties us to the sender rather than releasing us, as is the case with electronic mail, where the bits are at our disposal, allowing us all kinds of manipulation and editing. The fax will gradually disappear as the use of paper as documentation declines.

3.3. Video text

Videotext has been defined as a system for the widespread dissemination of textual and graphic information by wholly electronic means for display on low cost terminals under the selective control of the recipient using control procedure easily understood by the users[15]. Traditional videotext systems are limited to menu-oriented applications, in which information is selected from hierarchically arranged menus and displayed in fixed frames. Newer technologies allow greater interactivity and scroll the information across the viewing screen. There are two forms of videotext systems. One-way teletext systems permit the selection and display of such general information as airline schedules, traffic conditions, and traditional newspaper content. View data systems are more specific and provide for two-way, or interactive, communication[16]. Videotext system is useful in disseminating general information. Current application of videotext in libraries is mainly for two purposes.

* To provide community information
* To supply bibliographical information

3.4. Broadband Wireless

Broadband wireless (BW) is an emerging wireless technology that allows simultaneous wireless delivery of voice, data, and video. BW is considered a competing technology with Digital Subscriber Line (DSL). It is generally implemented in metropolitan areas and requires clear line of sight between the transmitter and the receiving end. BW comes in two flavors: *Local multi-point distribution service (LMDS)* and *Multi-channel multi-point distribution service (MMDS)*. Both operate in FCC-licensed frequency bands. LMDS is a high bandwidth wireless networking service in the 28-31 GHz range of the frequency spectrum and has sufficient bandwidth to broadcast all the channels of direct broadcast satellite TV, all of the local over-the-air channels, and high speed full duplex data service. Average distance between LMDS transmitters is approximately one mile apart. MMDS operates at lower frequencies, in the 2 GHz licensed frequency bands. MMDS has wider coverage than LMDS, up to 35 miles, but has lower throughput rates. Broadband wireless still involves costly equipment and infrastructures. However, as it is more widely adopted, it is expected that the service cost will decrease.

3.5. UWB Technology

Ultra-wideband (UWB), is a *radio modulation* technique based on transmitting very-short-duration pulses, often of duration of only *nanoseconds* or less, whereby the occupied bandwidth goes to very large values. Ultra-wideband or UWB is a developing *communication technology* that delivers very high-speed network *data exchange rates* across relatively short distances with a low power source. Ultra-Wideband technology (UWB) brings the convenience and mobility of wireless communications to high-speed interconnects in devices throughout the digital home and office. Specifically, UWB is defined as any radio technology having a spectrum that occupies a bandwidth greater than 20 percent of the center frequency, or a bandwidth of at least 500 MHz[17]. Designed for short-range, wireless personal area networks (WPANs), UWB is the leading technology for freeing people from wires, enabling wireless connection of multiple devices for transmission of video, audio and other high-bandwidth data. UWB, short-range radio technology, complements other longer range radio technologies such as *Wi-Fi* and cellular wide area communications. It is used to relay data from a host device to other devices in the immediate area (up to 10 meters, or 30 feet). Modern UWB systems use other modulation techniques, such as Orthogonal Frequency Division Multiplexing (OFDM), to occupy the extremely wide bandwidths. In addition, the use of multiple bands in combination with OFDM modulation can provide significant advantages to traditional UWB systems. UWB's combination of broader spectrum and lower power improves speed and reduces interference with other wireless spectra.

4. NETWORKING

The conglomeration of computers, databases and telecommunications has led to the creation of network. Networking concerns itself with mutual co-operation and co-ordination between systems of information for exchange of resources, services, facilities etc. Khan[18] defines network as "group of individuals or organizations that are interconnected. The linking must include a communication mechanism, and many networks exist for the purpose of facilitating certain types of communication among their members". In the library world, institutions form networks primarily to achieve sharing of resources consisting of bibliographic information and of collections and better service to patrons. The networks allow users to collect data and information from and transmit these to powerful central computers or terminals. The objectives of communication networks are:

* To offer more timely interchange of information and data among users.
* To reduce the effort and cost required to collect and transmit data and information.
* To support better performance of tasks and improved management control over an organization especially with several remote locations.
* Networks can help standardize policies, procedures, and practices among network users.

Modern networks are intelligent carriers that provide effective information interchange among attached centers. Computer networks can also overcome isolation in developing countries, and allow increased information access and resource sharing. The use of information and networking technology, however, has lagged far behind in developing nations. There are many obstacles to the use of information technology in developing countries which include a lack of access to computers and software; few locally produced databases; a lack of adequately trained personnel; a chronic lack of willingness to cooperate among librarians; legal and regulatory issues; difficulties in arranging access to the databases in industrialized countries; and economic constraints

4.1. Internet

The international community has enthusiastically seized the opportunities by the Internet and has connected hundreds of information services and resources to the networks. Internet offers access to a wealth of information that includes library catalogues, citation databases, electronic conferences, electronic journals and newsletters, satellite images, full text articles, anonymous FTP sites containing archives of text, images and software, and a growing number of sophisticated resource discovery tools such as WAIS, Archie, Gopher and World Wide Web.

Internet has made profound effects on the way in which the doctoral students are finding and searching information due to the astounding increase in the amount of information available online and the diversity of information management tools. Now Internet acts as a global information super highway and becoming the mechanism of distribution of three fourth of the specialized books and journals as well as research information. Electronic mail is the most commonly supported service across the diverse set of networks that are connected or gateway to the Internet. Electronic mail supports a number of information-related services which include: personal communication, electronic conferences, electronic publishing, ILL messaging, and email-based FTP. File transfer service, supported by FTP (File Transfer Protocol) on the Internet, involves the exchange of computer files between computers. FTP supports the transmission of both binary and ASCII files. TELNET, remote login service within the TCP/IP protocol suite, allows a user to connect to a remote computer and interact with it as though his or her local computer were a terminal of that remote machine. TELNET provides users with the capability of connecting to any system on the Internet. The USENET news service, supported by NNTP (Network News Transfer Protocol) on the Internet, provides access to a large number of electronic conferences and news. Internet Gopher is a simple, but powerful system that provides easy, menu-driven access to many network resources. A useful component of the Internet gopher is Veronica, a system that allows keyword searching of menus of all registered gophers around the world. Veronica provides an efficient method of finding information in gophers on specific topics. World Wide Web (WWW) provides an easy-to-use interface to a number of Internet resources. WWW, however, uses a combination of hypertext and text retrieval to provide access to these resources[19]. A specific interface for World Wide Web, called Mosaic, is the latest Internet tool to become popular. It allows users to browse through hypertext, multimedia documents that are located throughout the Internet. The concept of the "deep" or "invisible" Web has emerged in recent months. This refers to content that is stored in databases accessible on the Web but not available via search engines. The best way to access information on the invisible Web is to search the databases themselves. The distribution of web sites according to their type of content [20] is displayed in Fig. 2.1.

4.2. Video Conferencing

Video conferencing is an electronic meeting in which geographically separated groups communicate using interactive audio and video technology. Codec's (coder-decoders) are the critical component of digital conferencing, converting analog video signals into digital form, then using

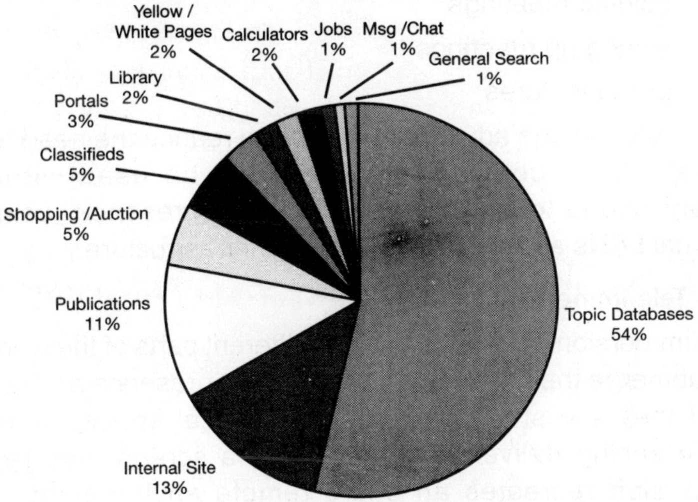

Fig. 2.1. Distribution of Web sites by Type of Content

coding techniques to reduce signals bandwidth to allow transmission over standard digital telephone lines. The technological advances in codec's, in cameras and in audio systems and displays, slash reduction in and recent decrease in the cost of telecommunications networking have accelerated the growth of video conferencing[21]. Basically, using a network, a camera and a headset with videoconferencing people can interact as if they were talking face to face in a room. There are two types of video conferencing. One is called point to point conferencing which basically is a communication link between any two locations. Another is multipoint conferencing which is a link between a variety of locations (more than two). Multi point conferences can further be classified as two types, LAN and MCU (Multi Control Unit). Lan provides links between different locations, groups etc. In a Multi Control Unit environment, audio and video signals are automatically switched during conferencing. Video conferencing can be used for :

* conducting interviews

* holding meetings
* setting up meetings
* giving lectures

And has the advantage that it can reduce the need for travel. Video conferencing can also be used within organisations to provide immediate telepresence, using internal LANs as the communications infrastructure.

4.3. Tele Immersion

Tele immersion will allow people in different parts of the world to submerge themselves in one another's presence and feel as if they are sharing the same physical space. Video conferencing delivers flat images to a screen, but Tele immersion recreates an entire remote environment. In addition to high-speed networks, Tele-immersion will require supercomputers to perform the trillions of calculations that are needed to portray environments in 3D. Virtual reality allows people to move around in a pre-programmed representation of a 3D environment, whereas Tele-immersion is more like photography. It's measuring the real world and conveying the results to the sensory system. Such technology would enable researchers to collaborate in fields such as architecture, medicine, astrophysics and aero plane design.[22]

4.4. Internet Relay Chat (IRC)

Internet Relay Chat is a form of instant communication over the Internet. It is mainly designed for group (many-to-many) communication in discussion forums called channels, but also allows one-to-one communication. IRC is an open protocol that uses TCP and optionally SSL. Today there are several thousand running IRC networks in the world. They run various implementations of IRC servers, and are administered by various groups of IRC Operators, but the protocol exposed to IRC users is very similar, and all IRC networks can be accessed by the same client software.

IRC has changed much over its life on the Internet. New server software has added a multitude of new features.

Services: Network-operated bots to facilitate registration of nicknames and channels, sending messages for offline users and network operator functions.

Extra Modes: While the original IRC system used a set of standard user and channel modes, new servers add many new modes for such features as removing color codes from text, or obscuring a user's hostmask ("cloaking") to protect from denial of service attacks.

Proxy Detection: Most modern servers support detection of users attempting to connect through an insecure (misconfigured or exploited) proxy, which can then be denied a connection.

Additional Commands: New commands can be such things as shorthand commands to issue commands to Services, to network operator, only commands to manipulate a user's hostmask.

Encryption: For the client-to-server leg of the connection SSL might be used. For client-to-client communication, SDCC (secure DCC) can be used.

Ident: Provides identification to the IRC server.

IRC can be connected to via IPv4, the current standard version of the Internet Protocol, or by IPv6, the next-generation version of the Protocol.

4.5. VoIP (Voice over Internet Protocol)

Voice over IP- that is, voice delivered using the Internet Protocol is a term used in IP telephony for a set of facilities for managing the delivery of voice information using the Internet Protocol (IP). This means sending voice information in digital form in discrete packets rather than in the traditional circuit-committed protocols of the public switched telephone network (PSTN). A major advantage of VoIP and Internet telephony is that it avoids toll charges by ordinary telephone service[23]. In addition to IP, VoIP uses the real time protocol (RTP) to help ensure that packets get delivered in a timely way.

4.6. Internet2

Internet2 is a consortium being led by 207 universities working in partnership with industry and government to develop and deploy advanced network applications and technologies, accelerating the creation of tomorrow's Internet. Internet2 is recreating the partnership among academia, industry and government that fostered today's Internet in its infancy. The primary goals of Internet2 are to[24]:

* Create a leading edge network capability for the national research community
* Enable revolutionary Internet applications
* Ensure the rapid transfer of new network services and applications to the broader Internet community.
* Prompt experimentation with the next generation of communications technologies.
* Catalyze partnerships with governmental and private sector organizations.
* Encourage transfer of technology from Internet 2 to the rest of the Internet.

Internet2 collaborators plan to use Quality-of-Service (QoS) tools so that participants can reserve and use bandwidth for special events or in certain time periods.

5. INTRANET AND EXTRANET

An Intranet is a private network that is contained within an enterprise. It may consist of many interlinked local area networks and also use leased lines in the wide area network. Typically, an Intranet includes connections through one or more gateway computers to the outside Internet. The main purpose of an Intranet is to share organization information and computing resources among employees. An Intranet can also be used to facilitate working in groups and for teleconferences. Intranets allow people to work together more easily and more efficiently. An Intranet uses TCP/IP, HTTP, and other Internet protocols and in general looks like a private version of the Internet. Typically, larger enterprises allow users within their Intranet to access the public Internet through firewall servers that have the ability to screen messages in both directions so that company security is maintained.

An Extranet is really just an Intranet that connects the organization to clients, customers, and partners - all within a private, secure network. The Extranet uses Internet protocols so users can navigate with a browser, but resides on the organization's private server rather than on a public Internet server. Extranet access from the Internet can be controlled through various architectures that are password or username specific. In other words, areas of the Extranet will be available according to password credentials[25]. This limits users to extranet pages relevant to the business they might be conducting, while keeping other areas of the Extranet private and secure.

One very valuable application for an Extranet is customer service. Online patches, upgrades, download, knowledge bases, and an interactive Help Desk are just a few examples of ways to serve a client base using an Extranet. Extranet chat boards where customers help each other with company products can also build customer confidence and brand loyalty, while saving valuable human resources. Chat boards are also a rich source for potential future product and support development. Another resource an Extranet can provide is the ability to create secure areas for interaction between an organization and its partners. Development, dissemination of marketing information and tools, data sharing, research, sales reports and more are all possible using an Extranet environment. An Extranet can also connect to other Extranets through the common language of Internet protocols. This makes it invaluable to organizations involved in collaborative efforts and opens the door to greater creative opportunities. In the past, geography was a significant hindrance to collaboration, but Extranet technology bridges that gap effortlessly and virtually cost-free. Extranets can revolutionize the way an organization works, improve the bottom line, enrich the customer base, and create opportunities that remain out of reach without an Extranet.

6. WIRELESS TECHNOLOGY

The term wireless refers to telecommunication technology, in which radio waves, infrared waves and microwaves, instead of cables or wires, are used to carry a signal to connect communication devices. These devices include pagers, cell phones, portable PCs, computer networks, location devices, satellite systems and handheld digital assistants. Wireless technology is rapidly evolving, and is playing an ever-increasing role in the library and information services throughout the world. Wireless technology enables users to physically move while using an appliance, such as a handheld PC, paging device, or phone. Without the physical connection of cables or wires, this technology allows users to the immediate access of digital resources. It is very useful when employees must process information on the spot, directly in front of customers or share real-time information. There is a wide-range of wireless devices that implement radio frequency (RF) to carry the communication signal. Some wireless systems operate at infrared frequencies, whose electromagnetic wavelengths are shorter than those of RF fields. Wireless systems can be divided into fixed, portable, and IR wireless systems[26].

A Fixed wireless system uses radio frequencies requiring a line of sight for connection. Unlike cellular and other mobile wireless systems, they use fixed antennas with narrowly focused beams. Fixed wireless systems can be used for almost anything that a cable is used for, such as high-speed Internet connection, and satellite television connection. Technology has brought higher radio frequencies with broader bandwidth that can carry more information, and require smaller antennas, resulting in lower costs and easier to deploy systems. A Portable wireless system is a device or system, usually battery-powered, which is used outside the office, home, or vehicle like handheld cellular phones, portable computers, paging devices, and personal digital assistants (PDAs), which operate through microwaves and radio waves. An IR wireless system uses infrared radiation to send signals within a limited-range of communication. These systems are commonly used in television remote-control boxes, motion detectors, and cordless computer keyboards and mice. With progressing new technologies, IR wireless systems can now connect notebook computers and desktop computers used within the same local area network (LAN) workstation, which will heavily impact the way we conduct meetings, presentations, and daily business, at the office.

6.1. Wireless Networking

Increased use of laptop computers within the enterprise, and increase in worker mobility has fuelled the demand for wireless networks. Up until recently, wireless technology was a patchwork of incompatible systems from a variety of vendors. The technology was slow, expensive and reserved for mobile situations or hostile environments where cabling was impractical or impossible. With the maturing of industry standards and the deployment of lightweight wireless networking hardware across a broad market section, wireless technology has come of age. The term wireless networking refers to technology that enables two or more computers to communicate using standard network protocols, but without network cabling. With wireless networking users can access shared information without looking for a place to plug in, and network managers can set up networks without installing or moving wires. Compared with wired networking, wireless capability offers more timeliness, affordability, and efficiency.

An ad-hoc or peer-to-peer wireless network consists of a number of computers each equipped with a wireless networking interface card. Each computer can communicate directly with all of the other wireless enabled computers. They can share files and printers this way, but may not be able to access wired LAN resources, unless one of the computers acts as a bridge to the wired LAN using special software. A wireless network can also use an access point, or base station. In this type of network the access point acts like a hub, providing connectivity for the wireless computers. It can connect (or "bridge") the wireless LAN to a wired LAN, allowing wireless computer access to LAN resources, such as file servers or existing Internet Connectivity.

6.2. Bluetooth

Bluetooth is a technology specification that utilizes the 2.4 GHz Industrial, Scientific, and Medical (ISM) frequency band in order to achieve wireless connectivity among devices. The technology is aimed at small mobile devices because the components are small, require very little power, and are inexpensive. Bluetooth wireless technology revolutionizes the personal connectivity market by providing freedom from wired connections - enabling links between mobile computers, mobile phones, portable handheld devices, and connectivity to the Internet. Bluetooth technology is an industry wireless specification standard for use in various devices for short-range communications[27]. As a radio-based technology it allows devices to share information over a maximum range of 10 meters. Bluetooth will enable users to connect to a wide range of computing and telecommunication devices without the need to buy, carry or connect cables. Bluetooth enabled devices give the user more flexibility, security, reduced power consumption, and becoming affordable for everyone. Bluetooth technology is not meant to replace wireless networks but to complement it. Some of the benefits Bluetooth technology are:

* Enhances users experience
* Connecting devices without the need for cables
* Becoming more integrated within laptops, mobile phones, handhelds, and many other devices
* Reduced power consumption
* Industry wireless communications standard
* Becoming more affordable for everyone.

Bluetooth enables information between devices to be automatically synchronized with no action required by the user. Thus, contact information on one's cell phone or PDA can be updated automatically when within range of a Bluetooth-enabled PC. Bluetooth is also going to be important for machine-to-machine communications - one of the largest growth areas in telecommunications. Bluetooth has the potential to redefine the way we perceive and experience connectivity. However, with limited penetration and availability, Bluetooth won't start to gain serious momentum until a few kinks are worked out.

6.3. Infrared

Infrared is a cable replacement technology similar to blue tooth wireless technology. It uses infrared-a faster wave frequency that is closer to visible light. Infrared technology transmits data in a point-to-point configuration, there is no multilingual capacity. In infrared communication an LED transmits the infrared signal as bursts of non-visible light. At the receiving end a photodiode or photoreceptor detects and captures the light pulses, which are then processed to retrieve the information they contain. Some common applications of infrared technology are: Augmentative communication devices, Car locking systems, Computers, Emergency response systems, Environmental control systems, Home security systems, Navigation systems , Signage, Telephones and TVs, VCRs, CD players, stereos. The advantages infrared technologies are[28]:

* **Low power requirements:** therefore ideal for laptops, telephones, personal digital assistants
* Low circuitry costs
* **Simple circuitry :** no special or proprietary hardware is required, can be incorporated into the integrated circuit of a product
* **Higher security :** directionality of the beam helps ensure that data isn't leaked or spilled to nearby devices as it's transmitted
* Portable
* **Few international regulatory constraints :** IrDA (Infrared Data Association) functional devices will ideally be usable by international travelers, no matter where they may be
* High noise immunity

6.4. HyperLAN Technology

High Performance Radio Local Area Network (HyperLAN) is a Wireless LAN standardised by the European Telecommunication Standardisation Institution. HyperLAN runs in the 5 GHz ISM band, and has a theoretical maximum speed of 54 Mbps. HyperLAN is a competitor to 802.11a technology[29]. HIPERLAN/ 2 (High Performance Radio Local Area Network type 2) is a flexible Radio LAN standard designed to provide high speed access to a variety of networks including 3G mobile core networks, ATM networks and IP based networks, and also for private use as a wireless LAN system. It supports two basic modes of operation: centralised mode and direct modes. HiperLAN2 supports different Quality of Service (QoS) for different connections. QoS support allows the transmission of a mix of different types of information (e.g. voice, video or other data). HiperLAN2 also provides unicast, multicast and broadcast transmissions.

6.5. Wireless LAN

A Wireless Local Area Network (WLAN) is a flexible data communication system implemented as an extension to or as an alternative for, a wired LAN. It uses a high speed, radio frequency (RF) network access technology to transmit data. It links computers to each other or to networks for shared access to network and Internet based information. Thus wireless LAN's combine data connectivity with user mobility. Wireless LAN is based upon the 802.11 standard for wireless communications[30]. Most WLANs operate in the 2.4 GHz license-free frequency band and have throughput rates up to 2 Mbps. There are three physical layers for WLANs: two radio frequency specifications (RF - direct sequence and frequency hopping spread spectrum) and one infrared (IR). WLANs requires setting up a small radio tower that connects to a high-speed Internet connection via DSL, T1, etc. The WLAN access point is then able to provide wireless Internet access to anyone within a 300-foot radius of the base station. WLAN provides the benefits of high-speed data rates and the freedom of mobility with the ability to access broadband data anywhere within the local area network. The important technologies used in WLAN are Narrowband Technology, Spread Spectrum Technology and Infrared Technology.

6.6. WiMax

WiMax is a Wireless Metropolitan Area Network (MAN) technology that will connect 802.11(Wi Fi) hotspots to the Internet and provide a wireless extension to cable and DSL for last mile (last km) broadband access[31]. The technology also provides shared data rates up to 70 Mbit/s, which, according to WiMax proponents, is enough bandwidth to simultaneously support more than 60 businesses with T1-type connectivity and hundreds of homes at DSL-type connectivity.

WiMax has the potential to enable even more millions to access the Internet wirelessly, cheaply and easily. The WiMax wireless coverage is in square km (miles) while that of WiFi is in the medium range. A WiMax base station would beam high-speed Internet connections to homes and businesses in a radius of up 50 km (30 miles); these base stations will eventually beam to an entire metropolitan area, making that area into a WMAN and allowing true wireless mobility within it, as opposed to hot-spot hopping required by Wi Fi. The proponents are hoping that the technology will eventually be used in notebook computers and PDAs. Although true roaming cell-like wireless broadband is IEEE standard 802.20, which is compatible with WiMax. WiMax is referred to as "WiFi on steroids". WiMax does not conflict with Wi Fi but actually complements it.

6.7. WWAN

Wireless Wide Area Network (WWAN) technologies enable users to establish wireless connections over remote public or private networks. Some of the current WWAN technologies based on second-generation (2G) systems have limited roaming capabilities and are incompatible with each other. Still in development are the third-generation (3G) technologies that will follow a global standard to provide worldwide roaming capabilities.

6.8. Digital Audio Broadcasting (DAB)

Digital Audio Broadcasting is a broadcast wireless digital network with the capability of delivering high-quality audio streams and digital data content to a wide range of personal devices: from desktop PCs to laptops, from PDAs to electronic kiosks. The DAB system has tremendous potentialities for providing both traditional and modern content in an advanced digital format. The main features offered by DAB are[32]:

Broadcasting : DAB is a suitable medium for delivering wide-interest content (streaming audio programmes, as well as data services such as news, traffic reports, weather forecasts and financial information). It is cheaper than the UMTS wireless system. Because of its high scalability, one DAB transmitter can serve an infinite number of wireless receivers.

Wireless : DAB is a wireless system; when used with other wireless systems (GSM, UMTS) to provide so-called feedback channels, it can provide tremendous interactive data services to mobile wireless devices: PDAs, electronic kiosks etc. The mobile capabilities of DAB make it the perfect system for developing location-based data service.

Real time / best quality : The data transmitted using the DAB system (both high-quality streaming audio and data applications) can be updated in real time.

7. MOBILE TECHNOLOGIES

With recent advances in compression and communication technologies and the growing uptake of 3G technologies, mobile technologies are gaining tremendous ground. Enabling 3G technologies have been instrumental in helping mobile applications become widely available and affordable enough to suit a variety of budgets. The whole world is going mobile. Phones, computers and media devices now fit in the users' pockets and can connect to a variety of information sources and enable communication nearly everywhere they go. With respect to technologies, 'mobile' generally means portable and personal, like a mobile phone. The major developments in the mobile technology are:

7.1. WAP (Wireless Application Protocol)

WAP is an application communication protocol used to access

services and information, inherited from Internet standards for handheld devices such as mobile phones[33]. WAP is a protocol designed for micro browsers. WAP specifies architecture based on layers.

WAP's application layer is the Wireless Application Environment (WAE). WAE directly supports WAP application development with Wireless Markup Language (WML) instead of HTML and WMLScript instead of JavaScript. WAE also includes the Wireless Telephony Application Interface (WTAI, or WTA for short) that provides a programming interface to telephones for initiating calls, sending text messages, and other networking capability. WAP's session layer is the Wireless Session Protocol (WSP). WSP is the equivalent to HTTP for WAP browsers. WAP involves browsers and servers just like the Web, but HTTP was not a practical choice for WAP because of its relative inefficiency on the wire. WSP conserves precious bandwidth on wireless links; in particular, WSP works with relatively compact binary data where HTTP works mainly with text data. Wireless Transaction Protocol (WTP) prevents duplicate copies of packets from being received by a destination, and it supports retransmission, if necessary, in cases where packets are dropped. In this respect, WTP is analogous to TCP. WTP is essentially a pared-down TCP that squeezes some extra performance from the network. Wireless Transaction Layer Security (WTLS) provides authentication and encryption functionality analogous to Secure Sockets Layer (SSL) in Web networking. Like SSL, WTLS is optional and used only when the content server requires it. Wireless Datagram Protocol (WDP) implements an abstraction layer to lower-level network protocols; it performs functions similar to UDP. WDP is the bottom layer of the WAP stack, but it does not implement physical or data link capability[34]. To build a complete network service, the WAP stack must be implemented on some low-level legacy interface not technically part of the model. These interfaces, called bearer services or bearers, can be IP-based or non-IP based. WAP supports dial-up networking using IP and Point-to-Point Protocol (PPP) as the bearer interface underneath WDP. It also supports Short Message Service (SMS) and General Packet Radio System (GPRS).

7.2. General Packet Radio Service (GPRS)

The General Packet Radio Service (GPRS) is a new nonvoice value added service that allows information to be sent and received across a mobile telephone network. GPRS is a packet-based wireless data communication service that promises continuous connection to the Internet for mobile phone and computer users. GPRS bridges the gap between 2G and 3G systems by providing a continuous connection to the Internet for mobile phone and computer users. GPRS provides enormous advantages to the end user, with burst speeds up to 115 Kbps, a data rate that is significantly faster than a GSM circuit-switched data connection. GPRS users should initially have an average peak data rate of 53.6 Kbps for downloading data, which rivals dialup wire line modems today and is clearly superior to the previous single-digit connection speeds[35].

GPRS supplements today's Circuit Switched Data and Short Message Service. GPRS facilitates instant connections whereby information can be sent or received immediately as the need arises, subject to radio coverage. No dial-up modem connection is necessary. This is why GPRS users are sometimes referred to be as being "always connected". Immediacy is one of the advantages of GPRS (and SMS) when compared to Circuit Switched Data. High immediacy is a very important feature for time critical applications such as remote credit card authorization where it would be unacceptable to keep the customer waiting for even thirty extra seconds. GPRS will fully enable the Internet applications used to on the desktop from web browsing to chat over the mobile network. Other new applications for GPRS, profiled later, include file transfer and home automation- the ability to remotely access and control in-house appliances and machines

Because of its synergy with the Internet, GPRS would allow mobile users to participate fully in existing Internet chat groups rather than needing to set up their own groups that are dedicated to mobile users. Since the number of participants is an important factor determining the value of participation in the newsgroup, the use of GPRS here would be advantageous. GPRS will not however support point to multipoint services in its first phase, hindering the distribution of a single message to a group of people.

7.3. Mobitexs

Mobitex is similar to the digital cellular technology used for today's mobile telephone systems. The network consists of interconnected cells, each of which is served by a radio base station that provides wireless access to the network for mobile users. However, despite these basic similarities, Mobitex is unique in several key respects: it is a narrowband, data-only network; it uses packet switching; and it is based on an open international standard. Mobitex technology is best suited for applications that send and receive short messages; the communications channels in a Mobitex network have a bandwidth of 12.5 KHz, meaning that it is a narrowband radio technology. Raw data throughput is 8 Kbps, but actual throughput after protocol overhead is about half this rate, and round trip delays usually range from 4 to 6 seconds. All active users in the operating area of the base station share the channel.

7.4. CDMA

CDMA (Code Division Multiple Access) is a wireless technology developed by Qualcomm that uses unique coding for each call or data session; this allows mobile device to disregard other transmissions on the same frequency. In effect, CDMA lets everybody in the area use the same piece of spectrum, and separates the calls by encoding each one uniquely.

7.5. Cellular Digital Packet Data (CDPD)

CDPD provides wireless access to the Internet and other public packet-switched networks over CDMA cellular systems. CDPD is a packet-data wireless technology developed by AT&T Wireless Services and other cellular carriers based on Internet Protocol (IP) networking; it is deployed as an overlay to analog cellular networks. As a data network, CDPD is used to access the Internet and e-mail, and also supports point-of-sale transactions, credit card authorizations, dispatch services, alarm monitoring, telemetry, remote control, and numerous other applications. Although 2.5G networks provide similar capabilities, an advantage of CDPD today is an always-on connection to the Internet. CDPD service has a data rate of 19.2 Kbps; however, some of this capacity is used for error correction and system overhead.

7.6. Packet radio

Packet radio technology is the application of packet switching techniques to radio. Packet radio has the potential to provide some connectivity solutions in developing nations where land-based communications are unreliable or absent. Packet radio applies packet communications to a radio channel rather than wire-based media, enabling wireless data communications. This technology can be used to create local area networks that link terminals, microcomputers, and large mainframes, as well as provide gateways to other network systems and databases[36]. Thus, packet radio provides an opportunity to extend the benefits of networking and computer connectivity to developing nations, thereby increasing access to library services and enhancing resource sharing. Recent technological advances have made packet radio communications more effective and affordable, and thus a candidate for use in developing countries. There are many types of packet radio that can be used to transmit data and create computer networks: 1) line-of-site (LOS) terrestrial packet radio where stations must "see" each other; 2) high frequency terrestrial packet radio where stations can be over the horizon; 3) packet radio using geostationary satellites; 4) packet radio using low earth orbit (LEO) store and forward satellites; and 5) packet radio using LEO constellations.

7.7. Cellular Radio

Another method of data communication is to use the cellular telephone systems that have spread across most industrialized countries. Although these systems are based largely on analogue rather than digital technology, they have the advantage of an installed base of cellular transmitters, and relatively inexpensive cellular radio modems. Data communication through the cellular network is much like using the regular phone system. All that is needed is a telephone—in this case a cellular telephone—and one of the many commercial cellular modems and adapters that plug into it. The cellular modems are more sophisticated, however, than standard wire-based modems because of the special characteristics of the cellular system. Specifically, the cellular system works by covering a geographic area with a blanket of contiguous "cells" about eight miles in diameter—the radio range of a transmission tower. As a caller moves along, the signal must be passed off from cell to cell as the caller moves into and out of range of the transmission towers. Cellular modems are designed to compensate for this environment by using techniques such as error correction, data compression, as well as variations in transmission speed and packet sizes.

8. DIGITAL LIBRARIES

The digital library is an integration of digital contents and various advanced information technologies built on high performance computing and communication. A digital library is an infrastructure of standardized electronic information that allows for distributed data storage, searching, and retrieval over a wide geographical region through links and operations transparent to the end-user. It is a storehouse of information available through the Internet. They are an extension and enhancement of information storage and retrieval systems that manipulate digital data in any medium (text, images, sounds; static or dynamic images) and exist in distributed networks[37]. The content of digital libraries includes data, metadata that describe various aspects of the data (e.g., representation, creator, owner, reproduction rights), and metadata that consist of links or relationships to other data or metadata, whether internal or external to the digital library.

Digital libraries are the digital face of traditional libraries that include both digital collections and traditional, fixed media collections. So they encompass both electronic and paper materials. Digital libraries are being pursued because they allow for a wide distribution of a vast amount of data and because they provide new ways of interacting with information and manipulating data. Most of the technology for digital libraries exists and is in active use on the Internet and the World Wide Web (WWW). A digital library could potentially change the library from a community-based institution to a more active part of a global system. The majority of a library's holdings would no longer be printed text, but would incorporate large amounts of multimedia information as well.

9. ELECTRONIC PUBLISHING

One of the outstanding and exciting developments of 20th century is the publication of the documents in the electronic form. The electronic media has provided many possibilities and opportunities for providing faster and quicker access to information at the global level through communication networks thereby making the whole world a global village. The conventional books as carriers of information are not suited for providing faster, quicker and speedy access to information at the global level. But now with the emergence of electronic media the potential to store large quantities of information has increased, with an advantage of accessing and transferring it to any place and from anywhere in the world through electronic means using advanced network facilities.

The publications in the electronic form offer substantial advantages over paper books in providing aids for connectivity, audio-visualisation, dynamics, customizability, interactivity and rapid information retrieval. Electronic information sources provide greater opportunities for transfer of information from one location to another location easily, and the information can be automatically searched in order to locate items of interest and facilitate better and faster access to information through networking. The searching options for an item in electronic environment are easier and simplified if one is familiar with the structure, organization and search facilities. The electronic media, by their very nature and characteristics, provide new and exciting opportunities for doctoral students in finding the information related to their investigation.

10. CONCLUSION

The world is rapidly changing; computers have gone from mainframes to palmtops. Radio communications has gone from lunchbox sized to cigarette-pack-sized micro-cellular telephone technology. The wireless world is accelerating. 3G is quickly moving on to 3.5G, 3.9G and 4G and is changing the way the world communicates. The evolution of wireless technologies including GPRS and CDMA allow development of new wireless devices that combine voice, Internet, and multimedia services. The latest advancement in computer and communication technologies, storage technologies, explosive growth of Internet and wireless technologies have several effects on time and the timeliness of information. As more information is being made available on the Web, its use is becoming both more fruitful and more cumbersome Many users (including researchers and librarians) are beginning to see the Web as a disorganized, unmanaged monster, without a way to verify on-line information, and without more than elementary search tools. The shift to electronic publication wouldn't be possible in the absence of a social organization that enables scientific communities to compensate for features of print discourse that are lost in the transition. The next chapter provides a review of literature related to the science doctoral students information search pattern in the electronic environment.

REFERENCES

1. Champandard, Alex J. Artificial Intelligence [Internet] Available from: <http://ai-depot.com > [Accessed October 4th 2004].
2. Artificial Intelligence [Internet] Available from: <http://www.e-consultancy.com/knowledge/glossary/48/artificial-intelligence.html> [Accessed October 14th 2004].
3. Salem, Shawky. (1997) Artificial Intelligence (AI) and Expert Systems (ES) tools for development. IN: Library and Information Science parameters and perspectives. Prasher, R.G., ed. New Delhi, Concept Publishing, p. 91.
4. Expert systems [Internet] Available from: <http://www.slais.ubc.ca/courses/libr500/2000-2001-wt1/www/a_olsen/expert.htm> [Accessed June 20th 2005]
5. Coggan, Donald A. Knowledge base sets expert systems apart [Internet] Available from: <http://www.cs.utexas.edu/users/porter/Courses/expertSystems.html > [Accessed December 20th 2004]
6. Martin, William J. (1995) The global information society. England, Aslib Gower, p. 48.
7. Kawatra, P.S. (2000) Text book of information science. New Delhi, APH Publishing Corporation, p.282.

8. Virtual reality, computers and computing [Internet] Available from: <http://reference.allrefer.com/encyclopedia/V/virtreal.html> [Accessed March 22nd 2004]

9. Chowdhury, G. G. (1999) Introduction to modern information retrieval. London, Library Association Publishing, p.286.

10. Ibid, 290.

11. Nwali, L.O. (1991) Potential value of CD - ROM in Nigerian libraries and information centers. Journal of Librarianship and Information Science, 23(3), p. 156.

12. CD-ROM technology analysis [Internet] Available from: <http://www.educationau.edu.au/.htm> [Accessed August 2nd 2005]

13. DVD frequently asked questions and answers [Internet] DVD demystified. Available from: < http://www.dvddemystified.com/dvdfaq.html >[Accessed October 8th 2005]

14. Martin, William J. Op.cit. p. 78.

15. Swaroop Rani, B.S. (1992) Digitizing libraries with today's information technology. IN: Proceedings of the Thirty Eighth All India Library Conference on Library and Information Technology: In Pursuit of Excellence. Delhi, ILA, p.51.

16. Videotex [Internet] Available from: <http://www.encyclopedia.com/html/v1/videotex.asp> [Accessed July 12th 2005]

17. Ultra-Wideband (UWB) Technology [Internet] Intel. Available from: <http://www.intel.com/technology/comms/uwb> [Accessed July 2nd 2005]

18. Khan, M.T.M., (1997) Information organization and communication. New Delhi, Ess Ess Publications, pp.5-6.

19. Lehnert, Wendy G. (2001) Internet 101. Singapore, Addison Wesley Longman, p. 293.

20. Web content analysis [Internet] Available from: <http://www.brightplanet.com/deepcontent/tutorials/DeepWeb/index.asp > [Accessed April 8th 2005]

21. Martin, William J. Op.cit. p. 79

22. Ananthaswamy, Anil. Tele immersion [Internet] Available from: < www.newscientist.com> [Accessed December 2nd 2004].

23. VoIP (Voice over Internet Protocol) [Internet] The Concise Tech Encyclopaedia. Available from: <http://www.tech-encyclopedia.com/VoIP-5.htm> [Accessed October 5th 2005].

24. Saunders - McMaster, Laverna. (1997) Internet 2: an overview of

the next generation of the Internet. Computers in Libraries, March, p. 57.

25. What is an Extranet [Internet] Available from: <http://www.wisegeek.com/what-is-an-extranet.htm > [Accessed October 5th 2005].

26. Wireless Technologies [Intranet] Available from <http://www.cisco.com/univercd/cc/td/doc/cisintwk/ito_doc/wireless.htm> [Accessed October 5th 2005].

27. Mohammed Haneefa, K. & Bavakutty, M. (2001) Wireless networking in Libraries: a conceptual introduction. IN: Proceedings of the National Seminar on Library Co-operation in a Networked World. 25-26 May, University of Calicut. New Delhi, Ess Ess Publications, p.135.

28. Kaine-Krolak, Maureen & Novak, Mark E. An Introduction to Infrared Technology [Internet] Available from: <http://trace.wisc.edu/docs/ir_intro/ir_intro.htm> [Accessed June 20th 2005].

29. HyperLan [Internet] Protocol & Testing Competence Center. Available from: < http://www.etsi.org/ptcc/ptcchiperlan.htm> [Accessed June 20th 2005].

30. How WiFi Works [Internet] Available from: <http://www.howstuffworks.com/wireless-network.htm> [Accessed June 20th 2005].

31. WiMax [Internet] Bamboo web Dictionary. Available from: <http://www.bambooweb.com/articles/w/i/WiMAX.html> [Accessed August 12th 2005].

32. Barletta, Antonio. (2001) Java Applications in Digital Audio Broadcasting. EBU Technical Review [Internet] September (1 / 14). Available from: <http://21cif.imsa.edu/resources/materials/difcore/ > [Accessed December 12th 2005].

33. WAP Introduction [Internet] Available from: <http://www.w3schools.com/wap/wap_intro.asp> [Accessed June 20th 2005].

34. What is WAP? [Internet] Available from: <http://www.gsmworld.com/technology/wap/intro.shtml> [Accessed August 12th 2005].

35. GPRS auto-configuration in Wireless Wide Area Networks [Internet] Available from: <http://www.microsoft.com/whdc/device/network/wireless/GPRS.mspx> [Accessed October 10th 2005].

36. Packet radio: applications for libraries in developing countries. (1993) [Internet] IFLANET. Available from: <http://www.ifla.org/VI/

5/reports/rep5/53.htm> [Accessed October 10th 2005].

37. Mischo, William H. (2005) Digital libraries: challenges and influential work. D-Lib Magazine [Internet] 11(7/8).Available from: <http://www.dlib.org/dlib/july05/mischo/07mischo.html > [Accessed October 10th 2005]

3

Studies on Information Search Pattern in Electronic Environment: A Review

THE AVAILABILITY of information in the electronic media has created an opportunity for global access to information. As the web, the digital libraries, and information retrieval (IR) systems become a major form of information access for many doctoral students, it is necessary to learn more about their interactions with IR technologies during the information search process. In this chapter a detailed survey of recent studies conducted in India and abroad on information search pattern and its related aspects in the electronic environment, with a view to justify the need and relevance of the present study. This facilitates to gain a better understanding of the complexity and diversity of the subject. It also helped to formulate a sound design and tools for the successful completion of the case study. This chapter contains reviews of related studies on the following topics :

1. Information Search Pattern
2. Use of Internet
3. Use of Electronic Information Services
4. Information seeking behaviour

5. Information need and use

1. INFORMATION SEARCH PATTERN

The human society is undergoing a transformation due to the rapid development and diffusion of information technology in all walks of life. The application of computer and communication technologies in storage, retrieval and dissemination of information has brought new possibilities of automatic indexing and free text searching. Electronic information environment facilitates enhancement in the speed of service, number of users served, the quantum and exhaustiveness of information provided. The way in which scientists search information to support research, teaching and creative activities is changing as new technologies and information delivery systems emerge. So the libraries and information centers are compelled to plan, organize and disseminate the huge information according to the needs of users with the help of information and communication technologies. It needs a good understanding and assessment of users' interaction with information retrieval technologies during their information search as well as evaluation of electronic information sources.

Charles and Clark (1990)[1] conducted a study to evaluate the feasibility of providing an online updating service to end-user searching CD-ROM databases. The objectives of the study were: to determine if patrons searching Agricola on CD-ROM would be willing to use an online updating system to obtain more current citations and to measure the level of satisfaction experienced after searching both Agricola on CD-ROM and the online updating system. For collecting data, end user searching strategies were noted. Data were also collected through questionnaire. Analysis revealed that majority of the respondents was eager to update their CD-ROM Agricola search with an online search. The respondents found problems in the formulation of the search strategy because majority of the respondents did not understand the basic concepts of searching such as selection of search terms, use of Boolean operators, truncation and limiting. The study revealed that end users were interested in the availability of a low – cost, hybridized CD-ROM/online updating systems.

Jakobovits and Nahl-Jakobovits (1990)[2] studied skills in three domains of search behaviour (affective, cognitive, sensori motor) at three levels of competence (basic, intermediate, advance). A computer based education system known as PLATO was used to test an online interactive measure of information searching competence on three populations of university students. The concept of affective library search errors recognizes that users' freedom of access to information was restricted by irrational fears or unreasonable frustrations. The wide spread practice of focusing almost exclusively on cognitive skills relies on the individuals' own initiative to supply the affective and to keep up with the sensori motor. Bibliographic instruction helped to address affective errors or impediments to skill acquisition in many searches.

Marshall (1990)[3] analysed the value of diffusion of innovation theory for predicting the level of implementation of end user online searching. Data were collected from 124 Canadian health professionals, using questionnaire method. The results show that three perceived attributes of the innovation were the strongest predicators of implementation level: relative advantage, compatibility and complexity. These perceived attributes predict thirty per cent of the variance in a global implementation measure, which includes amount, and frequency of use. The attributes also predicted forty eight per cent of a personal commitment to the innovation. The results showed a wide variation in the level of implementation achieved by end-users and confirmed the predictive value of the perceived attributes from diffusion of innovation theory in accounting for this diversity.

Olepors (1990)[4] conducted a study focused on users' information seeking habits and use of online searching in county libraries of Aabenraa and Horsholm. The study was intended to find out: users' purpose of library visit; the kind of materials users want; user activities; and the terminal users' use of the card catalogue and their search performance. Data were collected through questionnaire, interview and observation. The investigator found that most of the users visited the library for getting knowledge about the subjects. The specific purpose of library visit was for borrowing materials in a specific subject and only 10 per cent of the respondents from Aabenraa used online searching possibilities when they had the option.

Marghalani and Hafez (1993)[5] investigated the awareness of faculty members at King Abdulaziz University (KAAU) towards online search services in the Jeddah main campus. The study was specifically conducted to: evaluate the demand of the faculty members from different faculties and institutions; find out the subject areas for which more search requests were made; and propose a set of guidelines for further improvements. Administering a specially designed questionnaire to all the chairmen of departments, each faculty collected the data for this study. Personal interview were also conducted with the library staff responsible for the online search service at the KAAU Central Library. The analysis of data indicates that forty five per cent of the respondents used online search service to conduct personal searches. The largest number of requests was found to be made by the faculty of engineering. In regard to the subject distribution of online searches, medicine was found to be most prominent. Fifty four per cent of the respondents stated that they know about the online search service through a colleague. Most of the department chairmen were appeared to be more involved in online searches than other groups.

Sprague (1994)[6] examined the information searching patterns of university administrators and non-faculty professional staff members in the Ohio State University. The research questions were: 1.What information providers do they use in work situations, 2.Why do they use them and 3. How do they perceive the institutions library as an information provider? Data were collected through questionnaire method. The results of the study indicated that administrators and non-faculty professional staff members preferred interpersonal providers and convenient print materials. Respondent's value accurate, current and understandable information, but less concerned about its cost. Most of the respondents reported using print materials and few used access tools such as the online catalogue or electronic databases. Most of the respondents complained about the library regarding decentralization of materials, the disorder of materials and the lack of relevant materials.

Siddiqui (1996)[7] analysed online searches conducted for faculty, graduate students, and researchers, in King Fahd University of Petroleum and Minerals (KFUPM) Library during a six-year period, July 1988 – June 1994. The purpose of the study was to review and measure the effectiveness of the online search service, besides determining the future trend of online search keeping in view the availability of CD-ROM searching since July 1991. Data were collected through online search form, which was filled by the users before conducting the search. During the period of study, a total of 1,267 online searches were conducted, out of which 352 (28 per cent) online searches were conducted through DIALOG and ORBIT search services, while 915 or seventy two per cent online searches were conducted using KACST databases. The study shows that majority of the online searches, 155 (44 per cent) were conducted for the engineering departments, while science departments accounted for 82 (23 per cent) online searches. The civil engineering department ranked first with

59(17 per cent) online searches. Faculties requested the largest number of online searches followed by graduate students. During the study period, a total of 241(68.5 per cent) patrons preferred broad search, and 111(31.5 per cent) patrons preferred narrow search.

Chaya Devi (1997)[8] assessed the attitudes of the users of the National Ship Design Research Center (NSDRC) towards on-line information search and retrieval. The investigator was intended to find out: the methods of access to information (manual/online); whether online retrieval method is preferable over the manual method and experience of any difficulties with online search; formulation of search strategy; use of databases and types of databases used. The questionnaire was used for data collection, which were distributed to 40 employees of NSDRC, India. The results of the study were: 1. Majority of the end users preferred to search the information through on-line than that of manual method due to the reasons of immediate and global accessibility to information. 2. Most of the end-users had the previous experience in the use of on-line technology. 3. The end-users preferred to search the information by subject / keywords and natural language search was preferred more than controlled vocabulary. 4. Most of the respondents opined that bibliographic databases were most convenient source to access information and 5. Majority of the end-users agreed that the experience with time made them expert in getting access to information through online. The investigator concluded the study with the suggestion that the end users should be taught the search strategies and the use of controlled vocabulary to make the online search process easier.

Ray and Lang (1997)[9] conducted a replicative study to analyze the search styles of patrons and staff of two university libraries-University of Pacific and Adelphi University. Data were collected through transaction logs. The most intriguing aspect of the study was the discovery of the rise in student use of online periodical databases and the subsequent impact on catalogue searches. The online indexes were the primary cause of the decrease in total searches in catalogue. The investigators pointed out that there was an increase in subject searches and diminish in key word searches, and the labeling of individual search option had an impact on search style. It was found that University of Pacific users were more successful in conducting searches than Adelphi users.

Wood, Wallingford and Siegel (1997)[10] reported the results of a customer survey conducted by National Library of Medicine. The study was intended to find out the Internet access and use; the computer equipment platforms used for Internet access, and searching behavior and patterns. In the survey ,2,500 NLM users were randomly selected from a population of 15,372 U.S users who conducted searches during the months of April to June 1995. The questionnaire method was used for data collection. The analysis reveals that seventy per cent of the respondents had access to the Internet at the time of the survey and ninety two per cent of the respondents who had access to the Internet also had Web access. The most common means of access was a commercial service such as America Online, Prodigy or CompuServe, and then comes a dial-up modem connecting directly to NLM followed by an Ethernet, Novell or other local area network. E-mail was the service used by the largest per centage of respondents. Most of the respondents (81 per cent) used IBM – compatible equipment for Internet access. For searching NLM database majority of the respondents used the Grateful Med software, and Office was listed as the primary search location. NLM identified the Internet as the source of one of its major opportunities to improve service delivery, especially for information dissemination.

Adeniran (1999)[11] studied the library software use in Southern Africa. The study examines the various search engines, facilities to modify or fine tune preset database structure, import and export facilities, the operating environments and other tools available on all off-the-shelf packages in the region. Data were collected through questionnaire method.728 questionnaires were sent to libraries in Botswana, Lesotho, Mozambique, Namibia, South Africa, Swaziland and Zimbabwe. The major findings of the study were: 1.The leading search engines on software in the region were browse (79.3 per cent), Boolean (75.9 per cent), keyword-in-title (75.9 per cent) and term proximity (65.2 per cent) searches. 2. Software ranked number one by search engine site availability count were Erudite, In magic plus, Caudra Star, URICA, BIBLIOS and STYLIS. 3. Numeric ranking of database structure fine-tuning tools were: report generators (65.5 per cent), printing formats (58.6 per cent), ability to add, amend and delete fields in a database (55.2 per cent) and design and creation of new database (55.2 per cent). 4. Sixty five per cent of software operates in real time, of which nine packages can also be made to run in batch mode too. 5. Interface facilities on the software were SA MARC (41.1 per cent), ASCII (37.9 per cent), UK MARC (27.6 per cent), Windows (27.6 per cent), and LC MARC (24.1 per cent). 6. Leading operating systems on which software runs were Dos, UNIX, VAX, IBM and Novell. The investigator suggested that the institutions with serious research interests should have software with online thesaurus term switch search facility.

Voorbij (1999)[12] examined the searching of scientific information on the Internet by the students and academics in Netherlands. The scope of the study was limited to thirteen universities in Netherlands. A detailed questionnaire was distributed among 1000 members of the academic community and three focus group interviews were held with faculty members. 499 valid responses were analysed statistically, using SPSS. Pearson Chi – square analysis was performed on each question to determine the significant differences (PLO.05) existed according to discipline or status of the respondents. The study reveals that the majority of the academic community was using the Internet for study or work related purposes and e-mail was the most popular facility. The World Wide Web was being used primarily to search general, factual, ephemeral or very specific information. Academics regard World Wide Web as an extra facility, not as a facility that replaces printed information. The most severe problem in subject searches on World Wide Web was large amount of irrelevant hits. The study shows that a major reason for not using the Internet was lack of skills. The most used search engine was Alta Vista followed by Yahoo and the frequency of use of advanced search facilities was low. The investigator concluded that the Internet may have conquered a place for itself, but it has not pushed aside traditional printed and other information resources.

Jansen (2000)[13] studied the effects of query structure on retrieval by Web search services. Fifteen queries were selected from the transaction log of a major Web search service in simple query form with no advanced operators (e.g., Boolean operators, phrase operators, etc.) and submitted to five major search engines - Alta Vista, Excite, FAST Search, Info seek, and Northern Light. The results from these queries became the baseline data. The original 15 queries were then modified using the various search operators supported by each of the five search engines for a total of 210 queries. Each of these 210 queries was also submitted to the applicable search service. The results obtained were then compared to the baseline results. A total of 2,768 search results were returned by the set of all queries. In general, increasing the complexity of the queries had little effect on the results with a greater than seventy per cent overlap in results, on average. The search engines Excite, FAST Search, and Infoseek returned on average 7 to 9 results exactly the same regardless of whether the query was simple or complex. Alta Vista and Northern Light means were slightly lower at six. This research indicates that the typical Web searcher was adhering to a very reasonable course of action by entering simple queries. The results imply that Web search engine designers are doing a proper job of designing Web interfaces and ranking algorithms that accommodate the searching patterns of their customers.

Pajarillo (2001)[14] studied the use and evaluation of three search databases by professional nurses. The purpose of the study was to identify strong and positive features of the databases and recommend suggestions to enhance their effectiveness and use by novice and inexperienced users. Data were collected through interview. Three search databases: Yahoo, AskJeeves and MEDLINE were evaluated. The analysis shows that MEDLINE was superior in terms of scope of retrieval features and utility, and second for user friendliness. AskJeeves was placed second for retrieval and usefulness and first for user friendliness, while Yahoo was consistently third in retrieval features, utility and user friendliness. The features such as natural language (in AskJeeves), subject trees (for Yahoo) and pull-down menus for search categories and limiting factors (for MEDLINE) were important and practical. The respondents were generally pleased with the utility of the search results generated from MEDLINE and MEDLINE appears to be the expected choice for nurses since it was a health specific database.

Debowski (2001)[15] conducted a survey to assess inexperienced information searchers working with the Silver Platter bibliographic database on CD-ROM, and the error-prone behaviours, which resulted. A total of forty eight first year undergraduate students from two Western Australian universities were recruited to demonstrate their search skills. Search behaviours were assessed using the stored search histories of each participant. The study reveals that on average, participant's spent 27.71 minutes on their search, with approximately 8.15 keywords entered and 7.77 connectors employed. The investigator found that search quality scores of respondents were low (Mean 22.74, SD>1.91) and search breadth was the best aspect of quality search executed by the participants, with a mean of 4.96. It was found that the major cause that affects search quality was the capacity to search at sufficient depth and with a satisfactory search sequence of commands. The investigator suggested for developing a search template for online searching, this would allow users to be guided through the search model, and enable them to undertake more complex searching.

Zhang (2001)[16]evaluated user search performance of the students using group consensus method. The study was designed to test the effect of four user characteristics on search performance: educational level, academic background, native language, and computer experience. The participants of the study were fifty six students from the University of Toronto and a public school in Toronto. The data were collected through questionnaire and transaction log methods. MANOVA, ANOVA, and Tukey tests were used for statistical analysis. The study reveals that academic background had a significant effect on search performance measures. The science/engineering students achieved a much higher relevance score on search questions than that obtained by the social science students. The educational level was found to have a significant influence on search performance measures, however no significant difference was found between different language groups. It is pointed out that there was no significant effect by computer experience on users' search performance measures.

Cothey (2002)[17] studied World Wide Web users information searching behaviour in a higher education institution in UK. The aim of the investigation was to detect whether or not there was any change in an individual's web information seeking behaviour as that individual gains experience. Data were collected through web transaction log. Web information seeking behaviour of 206 college students over a 10-month period were taken for analysis. Analysis reveals that users access the web less often, which was more sporadically, as they become more experienced. Users' relied more on a passive link clicking or browsing style of information searching. The study shows that users' web host conformance-both mean conformance and aggregate conformance decreased i.e. users individually reduced their requests to the most popular web hosts across the user sample. The findings have implications for the design of future web information retrieval tools.

Wolfram and Xie (2002)[18] investigated the end user searching and response to a General Audience Digital Library (GADL). The study was intended to find out: the user characteristics; access to and interaction with GADL; and user searching and viewing behaviour. Data were collected from a web based end-user survey and data logs of resource usage for a web based GADL .The analysis revealed that: 1.EBSCO host most used by dial up users. 2. Libraries and educational institutions were the primary means by which respondents learned about badger link. 3. Respondents used Badger link for a variety of purposes, primarily related to research, education, work and personal information. Majority of the respondents used the service to search for specific information. 4. Respondents viewed Badger link as a non-stop search environment, instead of as a supplementary resource to print – based published resources, and expected to find everything they needed online and 5. Familiarity with databases was the most frequently cited reason (54.3 per cent) in selecting databases available through Badger link. The implications for the development and evaluation of future General Audience Digital Libraries to accommodate a variety of user needs and expectations are also discussed.

The impact of query term and operator usage on Web search results was examined by Lucas and Topi (2002)[19]. Data were collected via a web-based survey, enabling the subjects to choose the location and time best suited to their needs for participating. The results showed that the difference in the number of terms between expert and non expert searches, the per centage of matching terms between those searches, and the erroneous use of non supported operators in non expert searches explain most of the variation in the relevancy of search results. The findings highlight the need for designing search engine interfaces that provide greater support in the areas of term selection and operator usage.

The multitasking information seeking and searching process was studied by Spink, Ozmutlu and Ozmutlu (2002)[20]. The objectives of the study were: to determine the prevalence of multitasking seeking and searching over multiple studies in different information environments; analyse the characteristics of the multitasking information seeking and searching process; compare the characteristics of the multitasking search sessions with single-topic search sessions; and determine any factors that may indicate a topic change during a user search session. The data analysed in the study were taken from four studies of user behaviour during their information seeking and searching process. The studies were: 1. Survey responses from 11 excite web search engine users. 2. One hundred and fourteen search sessions by Excite web search engine users. 3. Four mediated on line searches and 4. Thirteen university library users. The data from each study was analysed separately. The results of the study were: 1. Total of 114 Excite user sessions from an analysis of a data set of 1,000 Excite user sessions included multi tasking searching. 2. Out of 246 topic changes, 63 changes were within the same category, where as 183 were among categories. 3. Many multitasking search sessions included one or two or three topic changes, with a mean of 2.1 topic changes per session. 4. Multitasking information seeking and searching was a common human behaviour. 5. Mean number of topics per web search ranged of one to more than ten topics with a mean of 2.11 topic changes per search section and 6. Information retrieval multitasking search sessions were longer than single topic sessions.

Spink. et al. (2002)[21] presented the results of a study on the progress of mediated information retrieval searching during human information seeking process. In the study the investigator was intended to find out: successive mediated search topics; frequency of successive mediated searches; reasons for successive mediated searches; and characteristics of successive mediated searches. The study had involved observational, longitudinal data collection in the United States and the United Kingdom. Three questionnaires were used for pre and post search interviews: reference interview; information seekers post search, and search intermediary post search questionnaires. A total of 198 information seekers participated in a mediated online search. The analysis reveals that search topics ranged across the Physical Science, Social Science, Humanities and Medical issues, and successive searches were generally spaced over time with some information seekers requesting a second or third mediated search within a week and some within a month. The major reason for conducting successive searches was the information searcher's need to refine or extend the first search, based on their evaluation of the previous search results or due to changes in their information problem including the need to search different databases or use different search terms to find more information. It was found that the mean number of search terms per search did not change significantly between first, second or third searches and the successive searches may not necessarily lead to a decrease in the mean number of items retrieved per search as the number of successive searches increases. The findings of the study have implications for the design of IR systems, the development of interactive IR models, and the training and searching practice of end users and search intermediaries.

Ford, Miller and Moss (2002)[22] investigated the links between web search strategies and retrieval effectiveness. The research questions were: 1. There any links between high or low relevance scores, and use of Boolean, best-match and combined approaches; use of advanced search features; other features of strategy? 2. To study whether there any association between strategies and low relevance scores due to errors in the use of the strategies, as opposed to the strategies themselves? The sample of the study consists of 64 students at the Department of Information Studies, University of Sheffield. For collecting data a Java script front-end (search data) was built which interfaced with the AltaVista search engine. Multiple regression and factor analysis were applied to the data using SPSS. The study reveals that: 1. Boolean – only was associated with poor retrieval. 2. Boolean - only performed worse than best match and combined. 3. Best match plus Boolean (i.e. combined) performed worse than best-match on its own and 4. There was no evidence that such effects were due to the number of errors, terms or any interaction between these, in Boolean as opposed to best match or combined.

The characteristics of certain popular search engines among the Internet users of Madurai Kamaraj University were studied by Ally Sornam and Dhandapani (2004)[23]. Data were collected through the questionnaire method. Out of the 100 questionnaires distributed, 72 questionnaires were received back and analysed. The findings of the study were: 1. Sixty six per cent of the respondents were belonged to science and technology disciplines and forty four per cent of them belonged to Humanities and Social sciences. 2. In addition to Internet, majority of the respondents were aware of ERNET (40 per cent), NICNET (23 per cent), SIRNET (12 per cent) and INFLIBNET (11 per cent). 3. The most frequently used search engine among the respondents was AltaVista (61 per cent) followed by Google (35 per cent), Yahoo (27 per cent) and Lycos (22 per cent). 4. Forty five per cent of the respondents were spending one hour per day for using Internet and 43 per cent of them were spending two hours per day on Internet, and 5. The search engine features such as accessibility, user friendliness, currency of information and relevance were indicated as very good by majority of the respondents.

Wouters, Helsten and Leydesdorff (2004)[24] studied the internet time and reliability of search engines. The investigators were intended to find out the set of methodological problems encountered when using search engines to gather data and construct time series. For the study the investigators used the search engines of AltaVista and Google comparatively and for searches at different moments in time. The study reveals that search engines constantly overwrote the past in the Internet. This affects the numbers of results as well as the actual Web pages that the search engines retrieve. Search engines not only lose information quantitatively, but they also erase the structure entailed in the relationships between words in the titles of the Web pages. The search engines AltaVista and Google systematically relocate the time stamp of Web documents in their databases from the more distant past into the present and the very recent past. They also delete documents from the year they were initially assigned to. This leads to the loss of information in the historical record on the Web as represented in the search engine databases. It was also found that information also gets lost in the sense of loss of structure in the semantic networks. Both Google and AltaVista "shed structure" as the consequence of the differential frequencies with which documents get their time–stamps updated. In short, search engines are unreliable tools for data collection for research that aims to reconstruct the historical record or for research that aims to analyze the structure of information at a particular moment in history

There are 24 studies on Information Search Pattern and related topics reviewed in this section. Among these, 22 studies were conducted abroad and 2 in India. The review of these studies reveals that the information search pattern studies in the electronic environment not gained much momentum in India. It is found that most of the user groups studied lack proper knowledge regarding the use of various search methods to retrieve information from the electronic information sources. The reviews indicated that there is a need for the development of interactive IR models, and the training and searching practice of end users and search intermediaries.

2. USE OF INTERNET

Internet is an exciting and intellectually stimulating social medium of communication and information. Effective search and discovery over open and hidden digital resources on the Internet remains a problematic and challenging task. The difficulties are exacerbated by today's greatly distributed scholarly information landscape. This distributed information environment is populated by silos of: full-text repositories maintained by commercial and professional society publishers; preprint servers and Open Archive Initiative (OAI) provider sites; specialized Abstracting and Indexing (A & I) services; publisher and vendor vertical portals; local, regional, and national online catalogs; Web search and meta search engines; local e-resource registries and digital content databases; campus institutional repository systems; and learning management systems. In order to redesign the library and information center services it is necessary to study the impact and use of Internet resources among the scientific community. This section reviews the use of internet based resources.

Moyo (1996)[25] conducted a study to determine the training needs of Internet users in an academic environment. The specific objectives of the study were to assess the: 1. Level of net awareness among academic staff of University of Botswana, 2. Extend of usage of the Pegasus mail, 3. Areas of application of the Internet in academic works such as teaching, research and publication, 4. Existing IT skills among academic staff, 5. Nature and magnitude of impact of current use of facility on academic work and 6. Perceptions of Internet/e-mail among the academic staff. Data were collected through questionnaire, which was mailed to a sample of 200 academic staff, among which 164 questionnaires were returned and analysed. The analysis shows that 71.3 per cent of the respondents subscribed and used e-mail facility. The investigator found that there were under utilization of existing facility (i.e. usage of a limited number from a range of available features and limited areas of application) because basic IT skills were lacking among the academic staff and help provided by computer center laboratory staff at present was neither adequate nor effective in assisting staff to learn about the existing facility. Overall impact of the facility on academic work in University of Botswana was generally very low.

Lazinger, Bar-Ilan and Peritz (1997)[26] investigated the Internet use by faculty members in various disciplines in the Hebrew University of Jerusalem. The primary focus of the investigation was on the differences in usage, training, and perceived importance of the Internet between two major groups of faculty members-those in the sciences and agriculture and those in humanities, social sciences or law. Questionnaires were sent to faculty members in all departments and professional schools of The Hebrew

University for collecting data. Data were analysed statistically using SPSS. The results of the study were: 1.The faculty members in the science and agriculture group used the Internet more intensively than faculty members in humanities and social science group. 2. All Internet users used e-mail extensively, primarily for correspondence with colleagues about research issues, and judge it the most important Internet service. 3. Other Internet services – file transfer, list serves/news groups and search interfaces were used in descending order by all faculty members surveyed, with higher percentages of use and perceived need in the science and agriculture group than in humanities and social science group. 4. Most of the Internet users learned to use the Internet services without the aid of a course, but more than half of these users would be interested in taking a course to learn more about the Internet. 5. Faculty members in all disciplines perceived the primary influence of Internet use on their professional life to be the increase in co-operation with colleagues with improved access to databases and research updates seen as the next important influence.

Obst (1998)[27] conducted a survey on the use of Internet resources by German medical professionals. The study was aimed to find out: intensity of Internet usage; preferred services and resources; and advantages of using the Internet. Questionnaire was used for data collection, which was mailed to 19 German Internet discussion groups related to medicine (two mailing lists and 17 news groups). The number of recipients of the mailing lists was estimated to be approximately 250. Nearly 300 questionnaires were posted in the 17 targeted news groups. Ninety-six questionnaires were returned out of which ninety completed questionnaires were analysed. The analysis reveals that majority of the respondents (83.7 per cent) used the Internet from one hour a week to two hours a day. All the respondents used e-mail and 85.6 per cent used news groups. The third most popular service was the Web followed by file transfer protocol, Gopher, Archie, Telnet, Veronica and the interactive services like Internet relay chat / multiple user dimensions (MUD). The suggested Internet library services were: 1.Presentation of Internet resources. 2. Internet introduction courses. 3. Evaluation of the Internet resources. 4. Database via Internet. 5. OPAC via Internet and 6. ILL via Internet. The survey documented that the Internet resources in the United States like electronic discussion and mailing lists and the resources of the NLM, the NIH and various universities were well known by German medical professionals.

Zhang (1999)[28] studied the library and information science researchers use of Internet based electronic resources. The major objectives of the study were: 1.To examine in detail the frequency of use of various Internet tools and protocols, 2.To assess the ways of accessing various Internet tools and applications, 3.To find out the strategies for locating e-sources for research, 4.To know the opinions on citing e-sources and 5. Evaluation of Internet based sources for research. Questionnaire was used for data collection, which was sent via e-mail and also U.S post. 179 researchers responded to the survey request, out of which 156 completed replies were analysed. The findings of the study were: 1. Most frequently used Internet tool was e-mail (93.6 per cent), followed by web browsers, mailing lists and Internet search engines. 2. More than 80 per cent of the respondents had access to Internet based e-sources from their work place. 3. The most used strategy to locate e-sources for research purpose was Internet search engine. 4. Timeliness was rated as the best feature of e-sources and 5. Most of the researchers were not satisfied with the current state of Internet based e-sources for their research. The investigator pointed out that the quality; reliability and stability of e-sources were the major problems in using e-sources.

Savolainen (1999)[29] investigated the role of Internet

among other sources and channels in information seeking. The study was aimed to find out: the motives for starting network use; current patterns of service utilization in job related and non-work contexts; major problems of use; and the issues concerning the place of network services in everyday life. Both qualitative and quantitative methods were used for data collection. The author conducted 23 theme interviews in Tampere, Finland and the data of the National survey on the use of information technology at Finnish house holds conducted in 1996, based on the interviews of 2360 persons, aged 10-74 years were utilized. The study reveals that only three per cent of Finns had utilized the Internet in order to seek information about new jobs, time tables etc. Males were more active than females in the search for practical information. The seeking of orienting information which serves the needs to stay up to date or to monitor daily events was somewhat more frequent than searches for practical or problem – specific information. The respondents were preferred networks because of its easiness of use and the speed of data transmission and e-mail was the most frequently used network tool for communication. Tele text service accessible through the remote control device on a television was used relatively often even though not very actively in problem-specific information seeking. Most of the informants already had experiences of the electronic versions of newspapers.

The uses and perceptions of the World Wide Web were analysed by Dalgleish and Hall (2000)[30]. The study examines how under graduate students view their acquisition in terms of open resource model, where the web was accessed to retrieve information from diverse sources which may, or may not, be educationally based. The data were collected through interviews. The analysis shows that a key factor in students' use of the WWW as an information resource was time, and the students were not at ease with the information retrieval process from the WWW. Students used the WWW to provide a different perspective on the subject they were searching through the availability of links to related information. The investigators found that most of the students have only a vague understanding of the way search engine works which resulted in a poor exploitation of their facilities. The students have a clear desire for better indexing of WWW sites and better descriptions to be provided of each sites contents so that only relevant links would be followed allowing them to quickly obtain the information they wanted. Students regarded that WWW resources were more up to date than traditional sources but they placed less trust in contents.

The student use of web resources was investigated by Grimes and Boening (2001)[31]. The purpose of the research project was to determine whether students were using unauthenticated web resources; whether they are evaluating their web resources; and whether there was a gap between the quality of resources expected by instructors and the quality of resources used by students. Using case study methodology the investigators interviewed instructors and students and analysed web resources cited in research papers in two English composition classes. The analysis shows that students were evaluating web resources only superficially and they were indeed using unauthenticated web resources. None of the students took advantage of availability of databases or web guides provided by the library. There was a gap between what instructors expect and what students were actually doing with web resources.

Byerly and Chambers (2002)[32] analysed non-visual user's accessibility and utility of web-based library databases. The study examines the accessibility of two popular web based abstracting and indexing services - periodical abstracts offered by OCLC First Search, and Gale Group's Expanded Academic ASAP, when accessed by blind users using screen reading programs. Two screen reading programs: JAWS (Job

Access With Speech) for Windows 3.1 and Window Eyes 4.1 were selected to test each database. In addition to testing each database, a short questionnaire was sent to representatives of OCLC First Search and the Gale Group. The study measured accessibility based on guidelines from the amended section of the Rehabilitation Act of 1973 and on the web content Accessibility Guidelines issued by the WWW consortium. The investigation reveals that OCLC First Search and the Gale Group Info Trac search engines provided a high degree of accessibility. The investigators discovered that both databases appear to meet most of the guidelines in the amended Section 508 of the Rehabilitation Act of 1973. Investigators pointed out that there was a need for web developers to conduct usability testing of commercial databases with people who rely on screen readers for access to the web and the librarians must be cognizant of accessibility issues and demand assurance from database vendors that their products were accessible.

D'Elia et al. (2002)[33] studied the public's use of the library and Internet. The main aim of the study was to investigate the characteristics of the current consumer market for public library services and Internet services. The specific objectives were: to describe why people use the library and to determine if use of the Internet affects the reasons why people use the library; to describe why people use the Internet and to determine if use of the library affects the reasons why people use the Internet; to identify the decision criteria that people used when choosing between the library and the Internet and to describe how the library compares to the Internet on these decision criteria; to describe why people do not use the library; to describe why people do not use the Internet when they have access to it; and to describe the information requirements of people who do not use the library and who do not have access to the Internet. Data were collected through a national Random Digit Dialing (RDD) telephone survey of 3,097 English and Spanish speaking adults, 18 years of age or older. The study shows that 75.2 per cent of the Internet users also used the library and 60.3 per cent of the library users also used the Internet. Library users and Internet users were both significantly younger than library and Internet non-users. The mean age of library users was 43.9 years and that for Internet users was 40.1 years. While the mean age of library non-users was 47.1 and has Internet non users was 50.6 years. Respondents rated library service characteristics were highly, especially on those characteristics such as cost, accuracy, privacy and helpfulness of librarians. Internet in contrasts to the library ranks highly on such factors as availability and currency of information and lower for accuracy, privacy and cost. The main reason for non-use of library was lack of time (55.6 per cent) and reason for not having Internet access was its cost (51.6 per cent). The authors pointed out that some differentiation between the library and the Internet was taking place, which may very well have an impact on consumer choices between the two.

Nicholas, Hunbington and Williams (2002)[34] compared the use of two consumer health web sites– NHS Direct Online and Surgery Door. The aims of the research were to demonstrate and refine measures to enable valid comparisons to be made between the uses made of web sites from the abundant data that was present in access log files. In addition to the ubiquitous visitors and hits the metrics trailed were: 1. Average time spent viewing a page. 2. Average number of pages viewed per user or visitor. 3. Re-visits to the site. 4. Search session types and number of sessions under taken. 5. Time spent on a search session and 6. Pages viewed per search session. Data were collected through web logs that recorded user activity on a real time and continuous basis. The findings of the study were: 1. The Surgery Door site attracted about half the number of users attracted by

NHS Direct. Surgery Door attracted 20,611 users and NHS Direct attracted 41,510 users. 2. The NHS site attracted proportionality more daytime commercial users while Surgery Door tended to attract evening (home) users who had logged on via an Internet provider. 3. The architecture of the site was found to have a significant impact on the metrics of page views and the number of pages viewed in a session. 4. Surgery Door users were found to conduct sessions that lasted approximately 18 per cent longer than users of NHS Direct and 5. Users of Surgery Door undertaking a far higher proportion of single page sessions than NHS users. NHS users were far more likely to undertake multiple sessions in a day, forty two per cent as compared with twenty one per cent of Surgery Door.

The use of Internet resources and services in Gulbarga town was studied by Maheswarappa and Ebnazar (2003)[35]. The objectives of the study were to identify the: 1. Demographic background of Internet users such as environment, occupation, educational qualifications, age and gender. 2. Computer background of Internet users such as knowledge of computers, place of access to computers, type of computers that they were using, operating system and the software/s that they were familiar with and the purpose/s of using computers. 3. Use of Internet resources and services in Gulbaraga city, specifically to know: since how long they have been using and their overall ability in using Internet; the place/s of accessing Internet and how often they access; the time spend, the purpose, the frequency of use of resources and tools and place/s of access; the frequency of use of different file formats and the place/s of access; the subject/s on which they search websites and the web pages/home pages created by them (if any); the search engines most often used and the steps taken after accessing and retrieving information; the opinion about Internet facility and the extent of its usefulness as a tool for communication and as a source of information; and the difficulties in accessing and using the Internet. Data were collected through questionnaire from one hundred and twenty three Internet users in private and public sectors covering forty seven users from cyber cafes and seventy six users from university and college environment. The results of the study were: 1. Most of the respondents used computers at work place, nearly all using Pentium systems and familiar with windows 98 and MS office. 2. Majority using Internet since last six months and half of them have an average ability. 3. Ninety three per cent of the respondents were using Internet for sending e-mails followed by visit to websites (78.1 per cent). 4. Most frequently used resources and tools of Internet were e-mail (55.3 per cent), web browser (22.8 per cent) and search engines (10.6 per cent). 5. Majority of the respondents was frequently using document file formats. 6.The subject areas of web sites visited are diverse. 7. WWW.Yahoo.com, WWW.rediff.com, WWW.usa.com and WWW.hotmail.com are the most used websites. 8. Most frequently used search engines are Yahoo, rediff, msn and Lycos. 9. Majority of the respondents prefers to read instantly on the monitor and search the Internet on their own. 10. Seventy per cent of the respondents have not received any instructions in the use of Internet and felt the need for training. 11. A large majority (69.9 per cent) was not satisfied with the facilities available for surfing Internet in Gulbarga city and 12. Slow accessibility, getting connectivity and lack of training were the main difficulties faced in the use of Internet.

Kumbar and Shirur (2003)[36] conducted a study to elicit opinions from the users of Sree Jayachamarajendra College of Engineering (SJCE) regarding the exploitation of Internet resources. The investigators intended to find out: the purposes for which the academic community in SJCE was using the Internet; the relation between prior computer experience and the use of Internet in SJCE; how far Internet services has been utilized; from which channels users were getting latest information about websites/search engines; most used Internet services; the problems faced by the users using various Internet services; the satisfaction level of users regarding working hours, infrastructure facilities etc. The data were collected through questionnaire method, which were distributed among 100 Internet users of SJCE, Mysore out of which 79 members have responded. The study reveals that: 1. Most of the respondents had started using Internet for more than one year. 2. Thirty per cent of academic community used the Internet 2-3 times in a week (students 33.33 per cent, researchers 20.83 per cent and faculty members 45.83 per cent). 3. Most of the users (39.24 per cent) learned Internet through the assistance of colleagues and friends. 4. Ninety seven per cent Internet users indicated that they were using Internet for e-mail service, while 55.7 per cent used to obtain copies of articles. 5. Out of seventy-nine respondents' 44.3 per cent of users acquainted with the search engines through colleagues and friends followed by 17.7 per cent through professional books and journals. 6. Fifty three per cent users have got sufficient results at the time of searching the information on Internet. 7. Thirty nine per cent of the respondents indicated that they were facing difficulties in browsing the Internet, and thirty six per cent of the respondents indicated that they were not facing any problems in Internet use.

Vaughan and Thelwall (2003)[37] investigated the factors that influence the creation of links to journal websites. The investigators try to find out: the impact of the journal websites within the scholarly community; journal website content level; and journal website age. Data were collected using online tools: The Way Back machine, the Internet Archive and commercial search engine AltaVista. The two disciplines chosen for a disciplinary comparison were Library and Information Science and Law. From the study it was found that both site age and site content was significant factors for the disciplines studied. Scholars and publishers were aware that richer content on a journal's website tends to generate links and thus the traffic to the site. The investigators pointed out that LIS journal web sites attracted more in link pages than their law counterparts that have the same journal impact factors. In web site age there was no difference between law and LIS. The investigators suggested that site age were a complicating factor and that should be taken in to consideration for comparing the web sites.

Among the 13 studies reviewed in this section, 11 are reported from abroad and 2 are from India. This shows that users are well favoured to the internet based resources, but the quality, reliability and stability of the sources were the major problems in using these sources.

3. ELECTRONIC INFORMATION SERVICES

The availability of information in the electronic media has created an opportunity for global access to information. Electronic information environment facilitates enhancement in the speed of service, number of users served, the quantum and exhaustiveness of information provided. The electronic media, by their very nature and characteristics, provide new and exciting opportunities for doctoral students in finding the information related to their investigation

Winship (1986)[38] examined various aspects of use, operation and effects of online services in libraries attached to universities, polytechnics and other institutions of higher education in the United Kingdom. Data were collected through questionnaire. 96 questionnaires were distributed and 63 were returned. The study reveals that in a typical library six to eight staff carryout search per year, mostly to provide a comprehensive literature survey, using five host systems and at a cost of $ 7000. Most libraries make a charge to some or all of their users, usually at a subsidized rate, but the cost of services was seen as a barrier to more extensive use, especially for students. Most of the respondents used online services for identifying publications rather than to retrieve information. It was found that most used online system was DIALOG (98 per cent), followed by BLAISE (83 per cent) and science and technology was the most popular subject area. The investigator concluded that the availability of online searching has not led to any wide spread cancellation of printed abstracts, and online and manual searching was seen as complementary.

Abels, Liebscher, and Denman (1996)[39] conducted a study to explore factors that influence the adoption and use of electronic networks and network services by science and engineering faculty in small universities and colleges. The data were collected through the mail survey, followed by interviews with faculty members and administrators. Six small colleges and universities in the South Eastern United States were selected for the study. The analysis reveals that accessibility appears to be a key factor influencing the adoption of the electronic network. No significant correlation was found between workstation availability and intensity of use or number of services. The investigators pointed out that there was a relationship between users' perceived expertise and the number of network service used, and majority of network users were using the services for research and teaching. E-mail, electronic databases, run programs and file transfer were considered most useful for research and e-mail was the most used service among the respondents. The investigators indicated that providing networked workstations to the faculty members in their offices could maximize the network adoption rate among faculty at small colleges and universities.

McMurdo and Meadows (1996)[40] investigated the acceptance and use of computer-mediated communication (CMC) by information students. The study was aimed to find out: levels and patterns of use of e-mail; categories of CMC information found useful: and attitudes towards computing and CMC. Data were collected through questionnaire, which was distributed, electronically to 121 students of the departments of Communication and Information studies at Queen Margaret College, Edinburgh. The investigation reveals that most of the students used e-mail 1-7 times per week, and majority of them used it for sending messages to other students. Students' expectations of CMC increase with time. Increasing popular awareness of the Internet, World Wide Web and information superhighway may reinforce this. Students main concern was to get course related information. Interaction with, and access to staff via CMC may empower students. The investigators found that CMC was complementary rather than substitution.

Philip (1996)[41] investigated the current use of automated chemical information systems by academic chemists in the U.K. The objectives of the study were to: identify the type and range of systems currently used by academics; study the impact of information systems on academic chemists and especially to see if there was a relationship between the research prowess of departments and the use of such systems; investigate and gauge the existence of a usability gap; examine the factors which are inhibiting the wide spread use of Leading-edge systems by academic chemists. Data were collected through questionnaire, which was distributed, to academic chemistry staff at 16 British Universities. The results of the study shows that use of computers was common among academic chemists, with a large majority using micros (86 per cent) followed by main frames (44 per cent), minis (36 per cent), super computers (14 per cent) and other types of systems (6 per cent). The most used information system by the chemist academics was bibliographic databases. Most used leading-edge information system among academic chemists was

Cambridge Structural Database (CSD). Majority of the users' access chemical information systems through telecommunication networks, probably because of the free access made available by EPSRC. The investigator found that research prowess was correlated with progressive use of leading-edge information systems. The reasons for not using leading-edge systems were: 1.Unawareness of systems, 2. Expensiveness and 3. Hard / software constraints.

Liebscher, Abels and Denman (1997)[42] investigated the factors influencing the adoption and use of electronic networks by Science and Engineering faculty in six small universities in the South Eastern US. The study was intended to find out the use of network and network- based services. Data were collected through questionnaire, followed by interview with faculty members and administrators. Questionnaires were sent to 371 faculty members from six universities, out of which 216 completed and usable questionnaires were analysed. The results of the study were: 1. The majority of the respondents (65 per cent) used the electronic network. 2. Almost all respondents who reported using the network were users of electronic mail (97.9 per cent). Besides e-mail, file transfer and interactive remote databases were also fairly well used. 3. Most of the electronic mail users (60.3 per cent) both send and received between one and 20 messages in a typical workweek. 4. Majority of the users of electronic discussion groups, subscribed to one or two discussion groups. 5. Majority of the respondents (65.2 per cent) accessed remote databases for teaching, research and current awareness and 6. Network file transfer was used by 65 per cent of the respondents. The investigators found that a connection to the Internet was an important communication tool for faculty members on small campuses

Tomney and Burton (1998)[43] assessed university academics attitude towards electronic journals and examines the current level of use of these publications in a British

University. The investigators were proposed to find out: the use of electronic journals; reasons for non use of electronic journals; advantages of electronic journals; and disadvantages of electronic journals. Questionnaire was used for data collection. Ten departments were selected from five faculties in a British University. They were Department of Physics and Applied Physics and Department of Pharmaceutical Sciences from Faculty of Science; Department of Electrical and Electronic Engineering and Department of Civil Engineering from Faculty of Engineering; Department of History and Department of English from Faculty of Arts; Department of Economics and Department of Law from Faculty of Business school and Department of Social work and School of Further Education from Faculty of Education. Analysis reveals that the use of e-journals was highest among the Business, Science and Engineering Faculties. Both users and non-users of e-journals made use of other electronic information resources, especially Internet. The two main sources of information about electronic journals were browsing on the Internet and from colleagues within the university. The quality of articles in e-journals was considered by most of the users (71.4 per cent) to be the same as in print publications. The investigator found that the main reason for the non-use of electronic journals was the lack of awareness. Accessibility and the ability to read the material from the desktop were considered as the biggest advantages of e-journals and most of the respondents believed that electronic publication was not 'real' publication. The investigator pointed out that most of the academics were aware of the materials available in electronic medium.

The impact of local factors on the use of electronic journals was studied by Pullinger (1999)[44]. The objectives of the study were: 1. Identifying the key aspects of e-journals expressed as needs by the prospective users, 2. Developing e-journals service to match the needs in as far as possible,

3. Monitoring the use made of the journals and 4. Identify the local factors that affect the use of electronic journals. Questionnaire method was used for data collection. Thirteen academic institutions involved as test sites. The study shows that three universities, Sussex, De Mont fort and Warwick, have lack of range of journals in the holdings. Twenty Eight per cent of the use of e-journals was out of office hours with office hours defined as being from 9 AM to 6 PM. According to the investigator the local factors, which affect the use of e-journals were: 1.Holdings of print journals, 2.Accessibility of the library, 3.Distance to the library, 4. Opening hours, 5.Promotion of available e-journals, 6.Technical infrastructures, 7. Training and support for information retrieval and 8. User authentication.

Costa and Meadows (2000)[45] examined the effects of using information technology on the communication of research by social scientists in Brazil. Two disciplines were studied- Economics and Sociology-via both interviews and a questionnaire survey. The results indicate that major changes in communication habits were occurring. More economists than sociologists thought that networked computers would make collaborative work easier. Differences have been found between economists and sociologists, with the former more active in their use of electronic facilities. Investigators pointed out that along with such discipline related differences; the developments also appear to be influenced, in part, by pressure from the research community and from the institutional environment. According to the investigators one significant impact of information technology seems to be an increasing democratization of the international research community.

Monopoli and Nicholas (2000)[46] conducted an evaluation of Social Science Information Gateway (SOSIG). The study was intended to find out the frequency of SOSIG uses; reasons for using SOSIG; and search or browse options used. An online questionnaire was used for data collection. The questionnaire was made available on the SOSIG Website for a period of one month. One hundred and thirty one SOSIG users responded to the survey. The analysis shows that majority of the respondents were regular Internet users. Ninety three per cent of women used the Internet on a daily or weekly basis while the figure for men was ninety one per cent. Regarding occupation, the largest group of respondents proved to be information scientists, accounting for thirty per cent of the sample. The occasional use of the SOSIG was indicated by forty six per cent of the respondents and research was the main reason for using the service. The most popular search method was direct searching-fifty per cent of the respondents preferred this method. The online help function seemed to have been used by all occupation groups, but mostly by information scientists. The investigators pointed out the need for providing training and guidance in using the information system.

Belecis. et al (2001)[47] studied the use of web based information resources. The study was intended to find out: the variability of International Coalition of Library Consortia's (ICOLC) data elements over time; the ratios of queries per session for searchable databases; and use of e-journal collections. To gather data, the investigators either drew on statistical reports sent regularly by vendors or retrieved data from password –protected websites provided by vendors. From the study it was found that: 1. Electronic resource use exhibited a great deal of variance over time, 2. Ratios of queries per session showed more stability over time than individual ICOLC elements, 3. Use per hour, which documented remote use but confirmed that most use occurred during regular library hours, and 4. Use of electronic journal collections, which was more scattered than the classic 80/20 distribution.

Music scholars' use and perceptions of the helpfulness

of e-mail and electronic discussion groups were studied by Brown (2001)[48]. Diffusion of innovations theory was used to describe and assess the music scholars' level of agreement with statements concerning the relative advantages and compatibility of e-mail and electronic discussion group use within the context of the research process. Data were collected via interviews and a survey administered to music scholars in Canada and the United States. Music scholars rated e-mail as consistently more helpful than discussion groups for selected activities in the research process. Scholars who found discussion groups not helpful in their research reacted by periodically unsubscribe, a pattern of intermittent discontinuance consistent with diffusion theory. These modes of computer-mediated communication were found to play marginal roles in the music scholar's research process.

Cooper (2001)[49] investigated the usage patterns of a web based catalogue that can be accessed through Internet. Transaction log method was used for data collection. During the study period of 479 days, about 2.5 million sessions were recorded and these consisted of 3.6 million pre search activities, 7.4 million searches, 13 million display requests, 11 million other requests and only about 60,000 help requests. Of the 2.5 million sessions analysed, about twenty seven per cent were from spiders, eleven per cent from tourists and sixty two per cent were real sessions. During the study period, the average search session lasted about five minutes and 16 months later it was increased to about ten minutes. An average search consisted of about 1.5 pre search actions lasting about 25 seconds, about 5.3 display actions, and 2.5 searches per session. The investigator found that there were major differences in usage (number of searches, search time, number of display actions and display time), depending upon the databases accessed.

Monopoli and Nicholas (2001)[50] evaluated the use of

ADAM – a Subject Based Information Gateway in the Art, Design, Architecture and Media information. The objectives of the study were: to find out the use of online information service (ADAM) by calculating the number of users and establishing their identity regarding their age, gender and occupation; to evaluate user satisfaction with the services. The scope of the study was limited to the Institute of Art and Design based in Surrey, which hosts ADAM. An online questionnaire was used as the main data-gathering medium. The questionnaire was made available on the ADAM website for a period of two months from 1st May until 30th June 2000, was aimed only academic end users – research staff, teaching staff and students. The questionnaire was divided into two sections; the first section entitled 'personal questions' was intended to obtain personal information on the user. The second part entitled 'ADAM use' was meant to obtain information on reasons for and frequency of ADAM use, the search methods and services provide, and users opinions on various issues such as the advantages and disadvantages of ADAM. Eighty four users responded to the survey, of which 53.6 per cent were under graduate, post graduate or research students, 3.6 per cent were research fellows or assistance and 16.7 per cent were lectures, senior lectures, professors or heads of departments, 13.1 per cent librarians and 13.1 per cent others. The investigator found that more than thirty eight per cent of the respondents gained access to ADAM from the university and writing up a term paper or a thesis was their main reason for using the service. The most popular search method among the respondents was direct searching. The search strategy most favoured was 'simple search,' 74.1 per cent of the respondents mentioned it, and ADAM browser was the browse strategy with the highest proportion of use.

Rogers (2001)[51] investigated the electronic journal usage at Ohio State University. The study was intended to find out: the awareness and use of electronic research and reference databases and e-journals and printed journals provided by the library; the advantages and disadvantages of e-journals; and the frequency of use of electronic journals and databases. Data were collected through computer assisted telephone interview. The analysis reveals that 24-hour availability and easy access were the primary advantage of electronic journals. In the study period (1998-2000) the number of faculty respondents reporting daily, weekly or monthly use of e-journals increased from 36.2 per cent to 53.9 per cent. The number reporting the similar use of printed journals decreased from 74.3 per cent to 65.6 per cent over the same period. There was no statistical correlation between age and frequency of use. The study showed that there was significant progress in the acceptance and use of e-journals with more than half of the faculty and graduate students at Ohio State University.

Pettigrew, Durrance and Unruh (2002) [52] studied how public libraries were using on-line community networks to facilitate public's information seeking and use in everyday situations. The study was intended to find out: 1.How the pubic is using networked community information systems and the Internet for daily problem solving, 2. The barriers encountered by the users and 3.The benefits for individual and physical communities from the public library-community networking initiatives and the emergence of information communities. Data were collected using on-line surveys, field observation, in depth interviews and focus groups with Internet users, human service providers and library staff. The major findings of the study were: 1. Networked community information systems were used by the respondents for many different types of situations, including work related and those of a personal nature, 2. Barriers to using community information systems were: technological; economic and geographic; search skills; psychological and cognitive, 3. Respondents used the community network as a personal gate way to websites located throughout the world, while people far beyond the network's physical home were using it to obtain local information and 4. Community networks had provided: greater confidentiality protection and greater comfort in asking sensitive questions; greater skill and confidence building; employment and educational gains; increased knowledge of community; and value for family friends and neighbourhood. The investigators pointed out that the Internet was responsible for the strong emphasis on employment opportunities, health information and other international community information as well as the emergence of new community information categories.

Monopoli. et al. (2002)[53] evaluated the use of the electronic journals service of the library and information service of the university of Patras, Greece. The investigators were proposed to find out: the number of users; personal characteristics of users (age, gender and occupation); frequency of use; purpose of use; search method and service provided; obstacles preventing users accessing a digital library; and preferred form of subscription to a journal title – electronic or print. An on-line questionnaire was used to collect the data on electronic journals use. A total of 246 e-journals service users responded to the survey. The study reveals that the e-journals service appears to be used by all age ranges, although the majority (61.8 per cent) was under thirty-five. Majority of the respondents were used the service on a weekly basis. Those aged 25-34 and postgraduate students were the highest proportion of users, who used the service on a daily, weekly or monthly basis. Investigators found that 93.3 per cent of the respondents used the service for writing up of a paper for publication, and the most popular search method was keyword. The online help function had been used by all the occupational groups, but was most used by research associates/visiting lectures (53.8 per cent). More than two-thirds of the respondents (69.5 per cent) considered the electronic version as the most favourable method of reading a journal title, and the most common reason for not reading an e-journal was the lack of enough information relevant to the users' interests.

Hewitson (2002)[54] studied the awareness and extent to which academic staff at Leeds Metropolitan University (LMU) use and assimilate electronic information services into their work. The study was based on the four questions: 1.How do academic staff at LMU obtains information for their work, 2. What they do with information they obtain, 3. Awareness of electronic information sources by academic staff at LMU and 4. Barriers in using electronic information sources. Data were collected through questionnaire method to a random stratified sample of 200 university staff (of which 101 were returned) and an interview. The investigation reveals that Internet was the most extensively used electronic information source by university staff (71.3 per cent). Majority of the staff were using the electronic information sources, to keep up to date in their own subject area. Often staff, especially those with low level IT skills, used the Internet because it was easy to access and provides instant results. The investigator pointed out that most of the respondents were aware of at least one of the major abstracting and indexing or electronic journal services and the level of staff's IT skills had a major influence on their take-up of electronic information sources.

Franklin and Plum (2004)[55] examined the library usage patterns in the electronic information environment. Data were collected from Web-based surveys of more than 15,000 networked electronic services users in the United States between July 1998 and June 2003 at four academic health sciences libraries and two large main campus libraries serving a variety of disciplines. Results from the Web-based surveys showed that at the four academic health sciences libraries, there were approximately four remote networked electronic services users for each in-house user. This ratio was even higher for faculty, staff, and research fellows at the academic health sciences libraries, where more than five remote users for each in-house user were recorded. At the two main libraries, there were approximately 1.3 remote users for each in-house user of electronic information. Sponsored research (grant funded research) accounted for approximately 32 per cent of the networked electronic services activity at the health sciences libraries and 16 per cent at the main campus libraries. Sponsored researchers at the health sciences libraries appeared to use networked electronic services most intensively from on-campus, but not from in the library. The purpose of use for networked electronic resources by patrons within the library was different from the purpose of use of those resources by patrons using the resources remotely.

All the 17 studies on the use of various electronic information services reviewed in this section are from abroad. This confirmed that there is a significant progress in the acceptance and use of electronic information sources abroad. But situation in India is just opposite, which strongly advocate the need for wide use of electronic information sources in the country and providing training and guidance to the user communities in using the electronic information system.

4. INFORMATION SEEKING BEHAVIOUR

In the electronic environment, the studies, which are conducted in order to find out the mode of interaction of the user community with the information system, are very important. The information seeking behaviour means the manner in which a user conducts himself in relation to a given information environment. These studies play a vital role in planning, designing and introducing new information services and their utilities. This section contains reviews on the information seeking behaviour studies in the electronic environment.

Wiberley and Jones (1989)[56] surveyed information

seeking pattern of humanities scholars. Data were collected from eleven humanities scholars from seven departments: Anthropology, English, History, History of Art, Philosophy, Political Science, and Women's Studies. The study reveals that most of the respondents had begun to use computers recently within the past two or three years. Investigator found that most of the respondents ignore online and seldom consult reference librarians, but they do rely on archivists and special collections librarians. The number of respondents using the e-mail for communication was very few. Most of the respondents limit use of formal bibliography to one or two sources and employ it intensively only when exploring new topics.

Berger and Hines (1994)[57] studied the characteristics of user groups and their current information seeking behaviour, including non-library resources used in the Duke University. Data were collected through questionnaire method. The analysis shows that only about twenty two per cent of the respondents were used the library for browsing, socializing, non-academic research, and casual reading. Most of the respondents regularly use online catalogues, computerized indexes and computerized access beyond the libraries. The kinds of resources most of the respondents would like to get via computer access were journal articles, catalogues, bibliographies, newspapers, conterence proceedings and books. The respondents suggested for providing more computers, improving computer searches and offering many online services.

Hsieh-Yee (1996)[58] investigated the information seeking behaviour of students at the American University (AU) and the University of the District of Columbia (UDC). The study was intended to find out: 1.The information channels used by college students when they work on course related projects, 2.The factors which affect the selection of information channels, and 3.The use of ALADIN, an augmented catalogue that provides access to the holdings of the Washington Research Library Consortium and several commercial databases by the students. Data were collected through a questionnaire survey, out of 258 questionnaires sent, 157 were returned resulting in a response rate of sixty one per cent. Students identified "convenience" and "quality of data" as the top two factors in their choice of information channel. Not many students accessed the online catalogue remotely. Most conducted keyword and subject searches, but few seemed to have understood the differences between them. Students searched the online catalogue file and databases containing the most recent literature more frequently than other databases, and had positive views about searching the system. Analysis of selected characteristics of students showed that race, school, and economic background contributed to their information seeking behaviour. The study affirms the value of librarians and of formal information channels and suggests way to augment the online cataloguing and reminds librarians that equal access to information technology does not necessarily lead to equal use.

Curtis. et al. (1997)[59]analysed the information seeking behaviour of the teachers of Health Science faculty including their use of new information technologies. A survey was administered to all faculties in medicine, nursing and pharmacy at the University of Illinois at Chicago. The analysis reveals that faculty used electronic resources in higher per centages and used a wider variety of electronic resources. From the study it was found that 68 per cent of the faculty accessed MEDLINE through electronic means while 30.5 per cent continued to use print index Medicus. Faculty continues to rely heavily on personal journal subscriptions as a source of journal articles, and the most used Internet service was e-mail, followed by World Wide Web, Gopher, FTP and Telnet. Health science faculty used a wide variety of databases in addition to MEDLINE. The study concluded that the training preferences of faculty needed to be further explored

Information seeking behaviour of securities analysts was studied by Baldwin and Rice (1997)[60]. The investigators were intended to find out the influence of individual characteristics on the use of information sources and communication channels, and the influence of information sources and communication channels on outcomes. The data for the study were collected through a telephone survey administered to a random sample of 100 securities analysts from forty of the largest investment banking firms in the United States and the United Kingdom. The analysis shows that more than three quarters of analysts were using commercial databases and e-mails. The investigator pointed out that individual characteristics have a little influence on the information sources and communication channels used by analysts, and there by do not have a significant influence on the out comes of analysts information activities. Institutional resources do have a significant influence on the information sources and communication channels analysts used, but also have a direct influence on outcomes, and there by play a significant role in analysts' information activities.

Pelzer, Wise, and Leysen (1998)[61] studied the library use and information seeking behavior of Veterinary Medical students in the electronic environment. The study was aimed to find out: students' activities in veterinary medical library; resources used to find current information on a topic; and use of indexes / electronic resources. Data were collected through the questionnaire. Three hundred twenty eight questionnaires were returned from a total of 398 enrolled students in the ISU College of Veterinary Medicine. The analysis of the study reveals that most of the students used the library to seek specifically assigned reading or reserve materials and to seek information related to course work or research. The resources used to find current information on a topic were handbooks, textbooks, computerized indexes, library's online catalogue, World Wide Web / Internet and print indexes. Most of the students (82 per cent) indicated the use of computerized indexes VETCD, MEDLINE and BEASTCO. Analysis shows that majority of the respondents were aware of at least one of the following electronic resources: 1.Computer services: NOAH – The American Veterinary Medical Associations Network of Animal Health; VIN – Veterinary Information Network. 2.Websites: Net Vet and Electronic Zoo. 3. E-mail lists: VETSTU-L; VETMED-L; VET PLUS-L. 4.Veterinary news groups. The investigators noticed that in the electronic environment most of the students were interested in using computerized products included the use of the Internet for finding current information.

Jange and Maheswarappa (1998)[62] analysed the information seeking behaviour of physical scientists in the Gulbarga University. The objectives of the study were: 1.To identify the overall distribution of the physical scientists of the university, among the various disciplines. 2. To identify the types of information sought by the scientists. 3. To find out the various categories of information sources used by the scientists in order to get the required information. 4. To know whether the scientists have any formal training in information searching and 5. To see whether there was any correlation between the personal attributes of the scientists and their pattern of use of information sources and searching habits. Data required for the study were collected from the scholars using a structured questionnaire. The investigators found that nearly 90 per cent of the respondents seek information on the current trends in topics of their interest. All the respondents were used books, periodicals, theses and dissertations. CD versions of abstracts were used by fifty seven per cent of the respondents. Ninety five per cent of the respondents carry out information searches as their own and to search the theses and dissertations, scientists' preferred keyword index to the titles. Subject headings were used as the main access points while searching printed as well as CD versions of abstracting services. The study reveals that there was no correlation between the use of information sources and attributes of the scientists.

Bruce (1998)[63] investigated the user satisfaction with information seeking on the Internet. The principal objective of this study was to establish the reliability and validity of magnitude estimates of user satisfaction with information seeking on the Internet. Data were collected through an interview with thirty seven academics of five universities in the state of New South Wales: The University of Technology, Sydney; University of Sydney; University of New South Wales; Charles Stuart University; and the University of Newcastle. The major findings were: 1. Majority of academics used the Internet for information seeking at least once per month, and a large proportion used the Internet in this way everyday. 2. The main source of information searching knowledge was self-instruction with significant assistance from friends or colleagues. 3. There was no significant relationship between attending an Internet training session and an academic's satisfaction with information seeking on the Internet, and 4. There was no significant difference between the amount of satisfaction with information seeking derived by academics who regard themselves as frequent information searchers on the Internet and those who regard themselves as infrequent users. The data from the study indicates that Australian academic users generally have a high expectation of success and were satisfied with information seeking, regardless of how frequently they used the Internet or whether they have received any formal training.

Brown (1999)[64] assessed the information seeking behaviour of Astronomers, Chemists, Mathematicians and Physicists at the University of Oklahoma (OU). The study was intended to find out: the approaches and preferences for finding information; use of the OU library system; and use of indexing / abstracting tools available at OU. Data were collected through the questionnaire, which was e-mailed to all the Chemistry-Bio Chemistry (26), Mathematics (27), and Physics – Astronomy (27) faculty members at OU. Forty nine of the eighty persons queried, responded to the questionnaire. From the study it was found that majority of the scientists were used to scan current issues of journals to stay current in their fields; few scientists noted the WWW and the Internet as the primary source of current information. The indexing and abstracting tools used by chemistry-biochemistry faculty were chemical abstracts (print) and MEDLINE; mathematics faculty used ERIC-CDROM, ERIC via OCLC, current mathematical publications (print), MathSciNet (WWW) and mathematical reviews (print); and physics – astronomy faculty used physics abstracts (print), INSPEC (electronic via STM). Most of the scientists indicated the use of citations at the end of journal articles to find less recent information. Among the scientists only the chemists were making extensive use of document delivery service and table of contents altering service available at OU through Carl UnCover. The investigator pointed out that the scientists were embracing electronic bibliographic databases and would like to see the access to and the capabilities of these expanded. The investigator suggests that the primary goal of science libraries should be to obtain access to as many appropriate electronic bibliographic finding aids and databases possible.

Garg (2000)[65] conducted a study on information seeking patterns of users of engineering institutions in Rajasthan. The objectives of the study were: to determine the purpose and motives of information seeking; to find out degree of usefulness of various sources of information and study the use of different information channels; to discover the sources for professional and technical ideas of users; and to examine the nature of search for current information. A questionnaire was used for collecting the required data. A sample consisted of 200 faculty members were selected at random from seven Engineering institutions in Rajasthan. Analysis reveals that faculty members were motivated for seeking information by multiple motives namely general awareness, professional need and occupation, career development, state of art investigation etc. Majority of the faculty members uses both formal and informal sources of information. In the case of formal sources, journals were optimally utilized followed by books; where as face-to-face discussions occupy prime position in the case of informal sources. The most used electronic sources of information were computers followed by radio and television, e-mail, audio visual sources, Compact discs, online databases and multimedia, and the main sources for generating ideas were 'thinking' followed by 'reading' and 'conversation'.

Julien and Michels (2000)[66] examined the information seeking behaviour of individuals in daily life context. The study was intended to find out: 1.The information sources that participants considered ideal in daily life decision-making, 2. The criteria used by the people to select a source of help, and 3.The discrepancies exist between people's stated ideals and the sources actually used. Data were collected through interviews and personal diaries. In forty five of the seventy nine interviews (58 per cent), participants turned first to personal source of help with their questions. Of all 272 sources approached for help, 23 per cent were print sources, and print sources were used in forty three per cent of situations; twenty one per cent were electronic, out of this twelve per cent were faxes, voice mails and e-mails. Ease and speed of use were considered as the most important criteria for selecting particular ideal sources. Less important criteria included convenience (12 per cent), precision (11 per cent), recency (6 per cent) and simplicity (1 per cent). The investigators found that there was variation in information behaviour by gender. For male respondents, 65 per cent of their ideal sources were electronic in nature and for female respondents' choices for ideal sources included personal sources (51 per cent), print sources (29 per cent) and electronic sources (12 per cent).

Kuffalikar and Mahakulkar (2003)[67] analysed the information seeking behaviour of different categories of users using Bio Chemistry and Microbiology department libraries of Nagpur University. Objectives of the study were: to examine the purpose of the users visit to the departmental libraries; to ascertain the dependence of the users on other departmental libraries; to check the relative use of bibliographical sources and tools in the information search; identifying the presence of invisible college in the information seeking behaviour of the users; to ascertain the dependence of the users on informal modes of communication and their changing preferences. Questionnaire, interview and observation were employed for data collection. The purposes of users visit to the departmental libraries were different as per their academic ranks and categories. Users mostly depend on their departmental libraries but in some cases, occasionally they visit other libraries to satisfy their information needs and using the Internet frequently i.e. once or twice a week and spend 1-6 hours for browsing the net. There was a clear indication of "invisible college" and user dependence was more on informal modes of communication, than the formal. Internet surfing, attending conferences/ workshops/seminars/ refresher courses have widely helped the users in seeking current, updated information in their respective fields.

5. INFORMATION NEEDS AND USE STUDIES

Understanding the electronic information environment requires an awareness of the information system, the user needs and the technologies that are available to support user interaction with information. Attention to users of digital information systems and their need from an information retrieval perspective is very important. This section reviews the studies on information needs and use.

Sanjeev Kumar and Mishra (1993)[68] studied the use of National Institute of Fashion Technology Library. The study was intended to determine: the suitability of the library opening hours; frequency of library use by the members; users' information requirements; users information search/strategy; the most frequently used services; and the periodicals/ forecasting journals most frequently used. To carry out the survey, questionnaire method was used. The respondents have the opinion that library timing was very convenient and all the respondents were users of the library, 35.83 per cent visited the library daily. Issuing of books was the major reason (83.3 per cent) of library use followed by use of reference materials (70 per cent). Twenty per cent of the respondents stated that they used library to get audio/visual materials.

Vijaya Lakshmi and Kanakachary (1994)[69] studied the information need and use pattern in humanities. The investigators try to find out: the parameters and scope of the field of humanities by descriptive definition and study the growth of information in this field and attempts at bibliographic control in the West and in India; the infrastructure and facilities provided in libraries and institution for humanities in India and to identify specific requirements and problems in information dissemination and provision of resources; the information needs and use patterns of peoples interested in the field of humanities in order to organize information provision and access. Data were collected through two questionnaires. First was meant for the library users of humanities associated institutions/libraries/centers and second was meant for librarians in these institutions. From the analysis it is found that 80.52 per cent of the respondents were engaged in some form of research activity – 60.49 per cent were working towards research degree, 24.49 per cent were involved in research out of their own personal interest.

With regard to the nature of information most used, 60.46 per cent of the respondents indicated critical and analytical information, while 56.51 per cent indicated theoretical and historical. The most used library service was the borrowing of books (87.45 per cent) and the main problems faced by the respondents were inadequacy of library materials, lack of computer facilities and poor Xeroxing facilities. 72.94 per cent of the respondents indicated that they required information for their personal research activity, followed by updating of knowledge (53.92 per cent) and general awareness or reading (49.60 per cent). The investigators suggested that there should be resource sharing and inter linking or networking of humanities libraries to ensure effective and efficient access to information.

Markusova, Giljarevskij, and Cherny (1994)[70] conducted a study, which presents a sociological, and bibliometrical approach to the assessment of information use and output on research activity. The objectives of the study were: 1.To describe the types of scientific research in the former Soviet Union, to describe how information is acquired and used, and to describe the value of this information to the research process, 2. To identify significant differences among the fields of science with regard to: the source of information required by scientists; the satisfaction with information and library services; the sources of information critical for research projects; the kinds of information that are most difficult to get; the dissemination of research results and the impact of such activity on future work, and 3.To study significant differences in access to the published information among scientists working in different regions of Russia. Data were collected through questionnaire. Six thousand questionnaires were distributed to scientists and engineers participating in the working communities of the former Soviet Union, partly by mail and partly by direct distribution. Majority of the respondents pointed out that their research could not be done efficiently without the support of Western colleagues who were among the main sources of up to date information. The respondents faced problems in acquiring foreign journals and foreign books. The investigators pointed out that geographic location had a strong impact on access to the foreign journals, books, conference proceedings and database search. The respondents were pleased with the assistance of the librarians and information officers. All the respondents were using journals as sources of information followed by books (80 per cent). Ninety three per cent of the respondents listed foreign journals which contain information critical to the project. The results of the study confirm the poor state of Russian science in that the scientists have been cut from main flow of information and must relay on the generosity of foreign colleagues to obtain information.

Okocha (1995)[71] studied the socio-cultural factors that enhanced the use and the transfer of scientific information among Agricultural Scientists in South Eastern Nigeria. The study had three objectives: 1.To determine whether information behavior among scientists of the South Eastern ecological zone of Nigeria was influenced by social factors of attaining professional development, career prospects, job security, official status and peer acceptance. 2.To examine whether information behavior among scientists of the South Eastern ecological zone of Nigeria was influenced by cultural factors such as access to information technology, adequate and relevant information resources, scientists' previous information habits and their educational levels, and 3.To highlight implications of some of these factors for agricultural development. Data were collected through questionnaires and interviews. Questionnaires were distributed to a stratified random sample of three hundred scientists within South Eastern Nigeria. Out of which two hundred and forty five usable responses were analysed statistically. Study reveals that scientists were motivated in the use and transfer of scientific information more by social factors of self development (53.3 per cent) and job security (12.9 per cent) than by social factors of scientific problem solution (19.6 per cent) and intellectual contribution (12.6 per cent). The factors, which influenced the use of the respondents and transfer of scientific information, were: 1.Development in 'information technology', 2.'Relevant and adequate information sources', and 3. 'Previous information attitudes'. The Scientists also indicated preference for computerization of information services as serial management control and circulation control as areas of high priority.

Wilkins and Leckie (1997)[72] investigated the work related information needed and sought by professional and managerial staff of the University of Western Ontario. The investigators were intended to find out: the information seeking habits of the non faculty professional and managerial staff of The University of Western Ontario; to explore what role (if any) the campus library system played in meeting the information needs of this group; to test the critical incident technique as a methodology for gaining a more detailed understanding of the interrelationships between the nature of professional and administrative work within the university setting and the information needs that arise from such work. Questionnaire and follow up interview were used for collecting data. Of the 361 questionnaires distributed, forty-eight were returned. SPSS was used for data analysis. The analysis shows that most of the respondents (53 per cent) had worked for the university between ten and twenty years and the highest number of respondents (44 per cent) were involved in managerial and supervisory activities. Professional literature/ current developments in their fields were the type of information needed by the majority of respondents (82 per cent), followed by internal university information and regulations (71 per cent). Eighty five per cent of the respondents ranked reference books were the most important and CD-ROM databases were considered to be the least important. Majority of the respondents felt that coworkers were their most important source of information (74per cent) and 60 per cent of the respondents were using the library for research related to the job.

Nicholas and Martin (1997)[73] conducted a study on information needs of journalists. The study was intended to find out the characteristics of information need such as subject, nature, function, viewpoint, authority, quantity, quality and place of origin, and the obstacles that stand in the way of people meeting their information needs. For collecting data the author conducted fifty semi structured, one hour long taped information needs interviews with journalists from a number of national news papers: The Independent, The Sunday Times and The Guardian. From the analysis it was found that the chief characteristics of journalists information needs were: 1.The sheer size of their information appetites, 2. Requirements for authoritative and current information, and 3. The speed with which they need information. Journalists needed information for fact checking, current awareness, research and to obtain a context. The Internet, with its enormous geographical reach had impact on foreign correspondents of the newspapers and the trusty information package-the cutting was being increasingly replaced by printouts, downloaded profile files and book marked websites. The investigators pointed out that the lack of time; information overload, and lack of training were the major obstacles to meeting information needs. It was found that there were big changes taking place in journalists' information needs and information seeking behaviour and computerization was largely seen to be the agent of this change.

Crabtree and Crawford (1997)[74] assessed the library needs of health care personnel in a large regional hospital in Springfield. The major objectives of the study were to find out: 1.Use of library services and materials during recent three-year period, 2. Motivation in using the library, and 3. User's opinion regarding library personnel services and resources. Questionnaire method was used for data collection. A needs assessment questionnaire was distributed to a sample of 422 non-physician employees of St. John, out of which 286 were returned. The results of the study shows that literature searches and photocopying were identified as the most frequently used services. Lesser-used services included answering of reference questions, inter library loan, computer training and faxing. The materials consulted most frequently were traditional resources such as journals and books. Less used materials included CD-ROM searches, brochures, pamphlets, videos and microfiche. Investigators found that the motivation behind using the library was preparation of a talk, paper or proposal, job related issues, decision-making, self-instruction, teaching and managerial problems. Most liked aspects of the library included friendly, courteous, helpful librarians and professionalism of library staff, broad-based resources available and currency and quality of resources, accessibility of information and easy access to well organized resources, and least preferred aspects of library included insufficient hours of service, collection deficiencies and lack of more flexible library policies. Based on the survey operational changes occurred in library's computer system. Computerized resources, which include MEDLINE, CINAHL, CANCER LIT, Health STAR, Micromedex and Silver Platter's PDQ, were now available across St. John's wide area network via remote access.

Medical students information needs and resource selection was investigated by Cogdill. et al. (1997)[75]. The study was intended to find out: the information needed to manage the patient's problem; and the resources used to pursue each information need. Participants in this study were eighty-eight first-year medical students at the University of North Carolina at Chapel Hill. In the context of the training session, students were asked to record the information they needed to manage the patient and also the information resources they used for each of their information needs. Chi-square statistic was used to test the significant association among the data. The investigator pointed out that medical students needed information pertained to diagnosis, treatment and disease and most frequently identified resources were MEDLINE and textbooks. Results of the study suggest that librarians serving the information needs of medical students cannot overlook the importance of textbooks, increasingly available in both print and electronic formats.

Mendes and Meadows (1997)[76] studied the ways in which four groups of health professionals (consultants, junior medical staff, nurses and administrators) working in three hospitals in Brazil and UK, use libraries and information resources. Data were collected through questionnaire and interview method. The investigation was carried out in two stages. The first stage examined the role of the library and second looked at information activities that did not involve the library. The study reveals that the information activities of health professionals in Brazil and UK were followed a generally similar pattern. However, UK health professionals clearly have better access to publications than their Brazilian counterparts, due to the latter's problem of acquiring foreign publications, the language barrier, poor access to electronic information sources and greater difficulty in attending conferences. The investigators recommends that teaching hospitals in Brazil should make greater use of electronic communication and act as a focus for the information needs of non teaching hospitals.

Suriya and Abdul Raheem (1998)[77] analysed the development of Information and Communication Technology (ICT) infrastructure among four different groups of nations. The main objectives of the study were: 1.Identification of the nature of information technology parameters that were being adopted in the sample groups of nations. 2. Measuring the distribution of the individual ICT infrastructure across the sample groups. 3. Comparing the status of the overall ICT performance between the groups. 4. Assessing the adequacy of the available information technology units in the selected regions, and 5. Assessing the impact of the ICT factors on the economic (Gross National Product (GNP)) and the educational development of the nations. Study was based on the cross-section data (1995) representing the ICT infrastructure in fifty countries, which were representative of four different socio-economic backgrounds viz.: High Income (HIN); Upper Middle Income (UMIN); Lower Middle Income (LMIN); and Low Income (LIN) group of nations. The concentration of radios was found to be high in LIN followed by televisions (24.72 per cent), telephones (18.4 per cent), newspapers (13.22 per cent), computers (4.5 per cent), mobile phones (2.7 per cent), Internet (2.2 per cent) and fax machines (1.4 per cent). The analysis reveals that the ICT infrastructure becomes the driving force behind the economic development of the nations and the ICT gap between HIN and the other groups were getting widened. The investigator found that the relationship between ICT and the GNP was highly positive and the ICT variables affecting the educational performance of the nations are different. I.e. the penetration of telephones, Internet hosts and the computer networks in HIN; print and the television in UMIN; and the print in LMIN and LIN have determined the educational development of these nations.

Agada (1999)[78] describes the Information Use Environment (IUE) of African – American gatekeepers in Harambee, an inner city neighbourhood in Milwaukee, Wisconsin. The investigator studied the information needs of gatekeepers; the preferred information sources; and the perception and use of information sources. The data were collected through interview method. In depth one-on-one interviews were held with a purposive sample of twenty gatekeepers identified through community-based organizations between April and May 1997. Findings indicate that the types of information sought were most related to race relations, crime and family and the main problem in finding information was lack of awareness of appropriate information sources. Most preferred information sources among the gatekeepers were personal information sources and the least preferred information sources were, search computer files (Internet), monitor information on TV, and use of specialized resource directories. Reasons for choice of information sources were: 1.Familiarity and reliability of sources, 2.Awareness of sources, 3.Accessibility, and 4.Appropriateness to need. The study suggested that the IUE modal provides a useful structure with which to describe the information behaviours of a group.

Biradar and Sampath Kumar (2000)[79] analysed the use pattern of periodicals by teachers and research scholars of Kuvempu University. The investigators were intended to find out: the use pattern of periodicals by teachers and research scholars; importance of different sources of information; the personal attributes of users such as designation, qualification, sex, age, nature of work have any impact on the use of periodicals or not; the interested areas of teachers and research scholars, in magazines and newspapers; and respondents opinion about the availability of sources in parent organization. Questionnaire method was used to collect the data. The study reveals that Kannada newspapers (50 per cent), English newspapers (48 per cent) and Kannada magazines (36 per cent) were the most frequently used sources. Research (85.18 per cent), scientific (70.37 per cent), teaching (66.66 per cent), current affaires (62.96 per cent) were the major priority areas of science respondents. While priority areas for social science respondents were research (86.95 per cent), teaching (78.26 per cent) and current affaires (65.21 per cent). Kannada and English newspapers (51.21 per cent) were most frequently used by male respondents. In case of female respondents, primary periodicals, Kannada newspapers and Kannada magazines (44.44 per cent) were more frequently used. The investigator indicates that majority of the users do not use sources like online services (61 per cent), college libraries (56 per cent), special libraries (54 per cent) and CD-ROMs (46 per cent).

Use pattern of information sources among the postgraduate students in the Gulbarga University was studied by Tadasad and Metesheela (2001)[80]. Data were collected through questionnaire method. The investigators reported that books (65.68 per cent), newspapers (50 per cent), class notes (40.2 per cent) and popular magazines (39.71 per cent) were the most useful sources of information. Memoranda, diaries and letters, CD databases, trade catalogues, microforms and laboratory notes were never used by a majority of postgraduate students. The study reveals that personal attributes viz. gender, year of study, medium of instruction at under graduate and post graduate level, area of habitation, stay at hostels, marital status and frequency of visits to university library have no bearing on the use of specific sources of information.

Rowland and Rubbert (2001)[81] evaluated the needs and practices of part-time and distance-learning students in higher education in UK. The objectives of the study were: 1. To ascertain current practice and future prospects regarding the use of professional level information services by students who are located remotely from their institutions of higher education or who study on a part time basis, which restricts their access to constitutional information services, and 2. To assess the students' perception of future developments of information services in the higher education sector. Data were collected through telephone and face-to-face interviews, focus groups and questionnaire survey. Data analysis reveals that the university libraries considered in the study often do not cater for the specialized needs of part time and distance learners, which leads to an increasing use of the Internet and employer resources as a substitute for traditional information channels. Biggest barriers in using the university libraries for all students were time and geographical constraints. For using Internet majority of the students (53 per cent) spent less than ten hours per month. Nearly 48 per cent of the respondents found that there was high competition for books in university libraries. As a result the respondents wished for an electronic library that would send them material on request via e-mail. A majority (62 per cent) of mature students was members of professional associations, information services of which were valued highly as another important work and study- related information channel. Key demands made by students relating to information services were: 1.Special arrangements for library opening hours for part-time students, 2. Closer liaison between departmental and library staff to ensure the availability of information resources, 3. Better introductory sessions on the avaiiability of subject specific information services including electronic resources, 4. Easier access to academic resources via the Internet provided free of charge, and 5. Implimentation of a subject related gateway service for distance learning and part-time students.

Xie and Wolfram (2002)[82] studied the contributing factors for the organizational usability of state digital libraries. The study was intended to fund out: the type of users and reason for using a sate digital library; the contributing factors, which influence digital library; and mutual impact of physical and digital libraries. Data were collected through a library survey of 313 Wisconsin Libraries and a web based survey for end users. Data were analysed using SPSS. The results of the analysis shows that the highest percentage of daily usage came from libraries affiliated with educational environments and the factors that influence organizational usability were access, promotion and training, content and format usage, and design. Majority of the respondents were informed about the state digital library services through physical libraries, but they learned how to use the system on their own. Technology based promotion methods were most frequently reported, consisting of bookmarks (59 per cent) and web site links (50 per cent). The investigators found that the availability of digital library did not negatively impact the use of physical library resources for most digital library users. The study reveals that the influence of digital libraries and physical libraries on each other was significant. On one hand physical libraries emerge as the key players in the use and evaluation of state digital libraries. The study also recognizes that even though intended audiences of state digital libraries were quite diverse, the dependence on physical libraries limits the audience to library users. The investigators pointed out that it becomes essential to set up new channels to attract non library users who wish to access state digital libraries from home or the work place and bypass libraries as access locations and training centers.

Marchionini (2002)[83] describes how user interfaces for the Bureau of Labor Statistics (BLS) website evolved over a 5-year period along with the larger organizational interface and how this co-evolution has influenced the institution itself. The research objectives were: 1.To gain a better understanding of how non-specialists think about, access and use of statistical data, 2. To understand and document how federal statistical agencies, the Bureau of Labor Statistics in particular, can adopt and adapt technologies to better serve the needs of diverse constituencies, and 3. To design and test user interface tools that help citizens to understand what federal statistics are available, access the statistics that are most pertinent to their needs, and use these data to answer questions and make decisions. Data were collected through interviews with BLS staff and transactions log analysis. The investigation reveals that the work at BLS had changed due to Internet technology. There was a continued growth in usage since the introduction of the BLS website, but a decreasing acceleration in growth. Technological migration and consolidation toward Wintel platforms and software usage was strongly related to site structure. The investigator pointed out that most of the users were non-specialists, casual users who visit the site only occasionally and then for relatively short periods of time, and often access BLS from home. From the study it was evident that electronic dissemination of statistical information and user interfaces devoted to non-specialists not only leads to more usage by non-specialists but also begins to change the data provider itself.

Sridhar, Sampath Kumar and Anil Kumar (2003)[84] studied the usefulness of library collection and information use pattern by Sericulture scientists. The investigators were intended to know: the opinion about the collection of the library; present information use pattern of library resources and services; and the most preferred journals by the scientists and research scholars. The data required for the study were collected through questionnaire and interview. The analysis reveals that primary periodicals (44 per cent) and Kannada newspapers (30 per cent) were most frequently used sources. Majority of the respondents were satisfied with reference service (64 per cent) and newspaper clipping service (58 per cent). The services such as reprographic services, Internet services, CAS were not satisfactory. Indian Journal of Sericulture (68 per cent), SERIDOC Abstract Journal (60 per cent), and Indian Silk (48 per cent) were the first priority national journals of the respondents and the least used services were online and CD-ROM services. The study shows that Sericulture scientists not only depend upon their own institute library collection but also depend upon agriculture libraries and sericulture libraries.

The reading habits of public library users in two branches of public library of Mysore city was studied by Nikam and Rajashekara (2003)[85]. The major objectives of the study were: 1.To identify the demographic characteristics of the users of the public libraries covered, 2. To examine the working pattern of the public libraries under study, 3. To assess the reading habits of public library users, and 4. To examine the influence of electronic media on the reading habits of public library users. Data were collected through questionnaire method from 200 public library users. The investigators found that 71.5 per cent of the users visited the library for reading purpose, while 59.5 per cent visited for improving general knowledge, followed by 23.5 per cent for entertainment. One of the major factors that influenced reading habits was the socio economic background of the public library users. Twenty two per cent of the respondents have the opinion that electronic media was better than the printed media, and electronic media saves time.

Ikhizama and Oduwole (2003)[86] studied the use of information sources by Agriculture scientists in Nigerian Universities of Agriculture (UOA). The study was carried out to investigate the use of information sources, activities on which information was being sought, and the constraints faced by agricultural scientist in the three Nigerian Universities of Agriculture. Data were collected through questionnaire method. The results of the study were: 1.The most widely used information sources were professional journals, consulting with colleagues, abstracts and indexes, and CD-ROM. 2. Most of the respondents rely mostly on their institutions library collections for information, and 3. Major constraints to the use of information sources include gaps in publications in their institutions libraries and inadequate up-to-date reference sources.

Geetha (2004)[87] conducted a study to examine the information needs and information gathering behaviour of research scholars in the Pure Science departments of the University of Kerala. The objectives of the study include: 1.To find out the information needs of research scholars in Pure Science fields, in relation to their qualification, sex , category and discipline, 2. To examine the type of information sources required by the research scholars in Pure Science and to identify their approach to information contained in different information sources, 3. To identify the communication channels through which information is acquired by research scholars in Pure Science; and to examine the frequency of use of various sources of information, 4.To ascertain the opinion of the researchers in Pure Science regarding the adequacy of information sources and services in libraries, 5. To find out the problems faced by research scholars in Pure Science, in using the libraries and their response towards the existing systems, and under utilization if any, of the existing facilities, and. 6. To examine the awareness of electronic or computer based sources in libraries and approach followed in CD/Online search method. Data were collected through a questionnaire survey, which were distributed to 170 research scholars in the University of Kerala. The analysis reveals that the collection of reference sources, indexing and abstracting sources, as well as computer based information sources in the Kerala University library system was only partially adequate to meet research scholars needs. The most used Internet based service is e-mail (76.10 per cent) followed by online search (73.58 per cent). The researchers in Chemistry (82.14 per cent), Mathematics (45.45 per cent), and Statistics (50 per cent) used e-mail service most. Majority of the researchers in Biochemistry (89.28 per cent), Aquatic Biology (94.11 per cent) and Zoology (78.95 per cent) were using online search. It was found that the research scholars possess knowledge about the use of electronic or computer based sources available in the library and the respondents used subject approach while conducting CD/Online searches. Seventy one per cent of the research scholars in all the disciplines except Mathematics (36.36 per cent) and Physics (47.62 per cent) were using the university library for 1-5 hours of reading per week.

The reviews show that an innovative information workspace with new interaction approaches is desired for users to interact with electronic data in novel multiple complementary ways. The reviews of related studies revealed that majority of the studies were conducted abroad. In India there are only a few studies conducted in the area of information search pattern in the electronic environment. Taking into account the constant development in the provision of recent electronic systems, the lack of understanding the information search pattern possess an obstacle in the process interpreting the way in which the electronic information services are being delivered. So there is a need for alternative research methods and conceptual frameworks, which will provide to the information science community, the evidence to acquire a more in-depth understanding of the users of information services.

REFERENCES

1. Charles, Susan K. & Clark, Katharine E. (1990) Enhancing CD-ROM searches with online updates: An examination of end-user needs, strategies and problems. *College and Research Libraries*, 51(4), pp.321-328.
2. Jakobovits, Leon A. & Nahl-Jakobovits, Diane. (1990) Measuring information searching Competence. *College and Research Libraries,* 51(5), pp.448-461.
3. Marshall, Joanne Gard. (1990) Diffusion of innovation theory and end-user searching. *Library and Information Science Research*, 12(1), pp.55 – 69
4. Olepors, Niels. (1990) Users, collection use and online searching: Investigation in Danish public libraries. *International Journal of Information and Library Research,* 2(2), pp.63-76.
5. Marghlani, Mohammad Amin & Hafez, Abdulrashid A. (1993) Online

search service at the King Abdulaziz University Library, Jeddah, Saudi Arabia. *International Information and Library Review*, 25, pp.27-41.

6. Sprague, Mary W. (1994) Information searching pattern of university administrators and non-faculty professional staff members. *The Journal of Academic Librarianship,* 19(6), pp.378-383.

7. Siddiqui, Moid A. (1996) A statistical study of online searches in an academic library. *International Forum on Information and Documentation,* 21(2), pp.3-20.

8. Chaya Devi, V. (1997) Attitude of the end-users towards on-line information retrieval – A case study of NSDRC Library, Visakhapattanam. *Annals of Library Science and Documentation,* 44(1), pp.18 – 31

9. Ray, Kathelin L. & Lang, Mary S. (1997) Analyzing search styles of patrons and staff: A replicative study of two university libraries. *Library Trends,* 41(3), pp.219-235.

10. Wood, Fred B., Wallingford, Karen T., & Siegel, Elliot R. (1997) Transitioning to the Internet: Results of a National Library of Medicine user survey. *Bulletin of Medical Library Association*, 85(4), pp.331 – 339.

11. Adeniran, Olatunde R. (1999) Library software in use in Southern Africa: A comparative analysis of search engines, database fine-tuning and maintenance tools. *The Electronic Library,* 17(1), pp.27-36.

12. Voorbij, Henkj. (1999) Searching Scientific information on the internet: a Dutch academic user survey. *Journal of the American Society for Information Science,* 50(7), pp.598 – 615.

13. Jansen, Bernard J. (2000) The effect of query complexity on Web searching results. *Information Research* [Internet] 6(1). Available from: <*http://InformationR.net/ir/6-1/paper87.html*> [Accessed May 20th 2004].

14. Pajarillo, Edmund. (2002) The use and evaluation of search databases by professional nurses: A case study. *The Electronic Library*, 19(5), pp.296-306.

15. Debowski, Shelda. (2001) Wrong: go back an exploration of novice search behaviours while conducting an information search. *The Electronic Library*, 19(6), pp.371-382

16. Zhang, Xiangmin. (2001) Collaborative relevance judgment: a group consensus method for evaluating user search performance. *Journal of the American Society for Information Science,* 53(3), pp. 220-231.

17. Cothey, Vivian. (2002) A longitudinal study of World Wide Web users' information seeking behaviour. *Journal of the American Society for Information Science and Technology*, 53(2), pp.67-78.

18. Wolfram, Dietmar. & Xie, Hong (Iris). (2002) Traditional IR for web users: A context for general audience digital libraries, *Information Processing and Management*, 38, pp.627-648.

19. Lucas, Wendy. & Topi, Heikki. (2002) Form and function: The impact of query term and operator usage on web search results. *Journal of the American Society for Information Science and Technology*, 53(2), pp.95-108.

20. Spink, Amanda H., Ozmutlu, Cenk. & Ozmutlu, Seda. (2002) Multitasking information seeking and searching process. *Journal of the American Society for Information Science and Technology,* 53(8), pp.639-652.

21. Spink, Amanda., et al. (2002) Information seeking and mediated searching study. Part 3 successive searching. *Journal of the American Society for Information Science and Technology,* 53(9), pp.716-727.

22. Ford, Nigel., Miller, David. & Moss, Nichola. (2002) Web search strategies and retrieval effectiveness: An empirical study. *Journal of Documentation*, 58(2), pp.30-48.

23. Ally Sornam, S. & Dhandapani. (2004) *Ranking of search engines a study among Internet users*. IN: Information communication, library and community development. Ramesh Babu, B. & Gopalakrishnan, S., ed. New Delhi, BRP. pp. 629-634.

24. Wouters, Paul., Hellsten, Iina. & Leydesdorff, Loet. (2004) Internet time and reliability of search engine [Internet] Available from: <*http://firstmonday.org/issues/issue9_10/wouters/index.html*>[Accessed September 25th 2004]

25. Moyo, Lesley M. (1996) Training needs for Internet usage in a learning environment: University of Botswana case. *International Forum on Information and Documentation,* 21(4), pp.25-33.

26. Lazinger, Susan S., Bar-Ilan, Judit. & Peritz, Bluma C. (1997) Internet use by faculty members in various disciplines: a comparative case study. *Journal of the American Society for Information Science,* 48(6), pp.508 – 518.

27. Obst, Oliver. (1998) Use of Internet resources by German medical professionals. *Bulletin of Medical Library Association,* 86(4), pp.528-533.

28. Zhang, Yin. (1999) Scholarly use of Internet based electronic

resources: A survey report. *Library Trends,* 47(4), pp.746 – 770.

29. Savolainen, Reijo. (1999) The role of the Internet in information seeking putting the networked services in context. *Information Processing and Management*, 35, pp. 765 – 782.

30. Dalgleish, Andrew. & Hall, Robert. (2000) Uses and perceptions of the World Wide Web in an information-seeking environment. *Journal of Librarianship and Information Science*, 32 (3), pp. 104-114.

31. Grimes, Deborah. & Boening, Carl H. (2001) Worries with the web: A look at student use of web resources. *College and Research Libraries,* 62 (1), pp. 11-21.

32. Byerley, Suzanne L. & Chambers, Mary Beth. (2002) Accessibility and usability of web based library databases for non visual users. *Library Hi Tech*, 20(2), pp.169-178.

33. D'Elia, George, et al. (2002) The impact of the Internet on public library use: An analysis of the current consumer market for library and Internet services. *Journal of the American Society for Information Science and Technology*, 53(10), pp. 802-820.

34. Nicholas, David., Hunbington, Paul. & Williams, Peter. (2002) Evaluating metrics for comparing the use of websites: A case study of two consumer health websites. *Journal of Information Science,* 28(1), pp. 63-75.

35. Maheswarappa, B.S. & Ebnazar, C. Emmanual. (2003) Use of Internet resources and services in Gulbarga city: An exploratory study. *SRELS Journal of Information Management*, 40(4), pp. 404 – 420.

36. Kumbar, Mallinath. & Shirur, Shiddayya. (2003) Internet and its use in Sree Jayachamarajendra College of Engineering: A case study. *SRELS Journal of Information Management*, 40(2), pp. 169-176.

37. Vaughan, Liwen. & Thelwall, Mike. (2003) Scholarly use of the web: What are the key inducers of links to journal websites. *Journal of American Society for Information Science and Technology,* 54(1), pp. 29-38.

38. Winship, Ian R. (1986) The use of online information services in UK higher education libraries. *British Journal of Academic Librarianship*, 1(3), pp. 191-205.

39. Abels, Eleen G., Liebscher, Peter. & Denman, Daniel W. (1996) Factors that influence the use of electronic networks by science and engineering faculty at small institutions. Part I. Queries. *Journal*

of the American Society for Information Science, 47 (2), pp. 146–158.

40. Mc Murdo, G. & Meadows, A. J. (1996) Acceptance and use of computer mediated communication by information students. *Journal of Information Science,* 22 (5), pp. 335 – 348.
41. Philip, G. (1996) Use of leading-edge information systems by academic chemists in the UK: Part II constraints and the need for usability engineering. *Journal of Information Science,* 22 (2), pp. 93 – 106.
42. Liebscher, Peter., Abels, Eileen G. & Denman, Daniel W. (1997) Factors that influence the use of electronic networks by science and engineering faculty at small institutions. Part II preliminary use indicators. *Journal of American Society for Information Science,* 48 (6), pp. 496 – 507.
43. Tomney, Hilary. & Burton, Paul F. (1998) Electronic journals: a study of usage and attitudes among academics. *Journal of Information Science*, 24 (6), pp. 419 – 429.
44. Pullinger, David. (1999) Academics and the new information environment: the impact of local factors on use of electronic journals. *Journal of Information Science*, 25 (2), pp. 164 – 172.
45. Costa, Sely. & Meadows, Jack. (2000) The impact of computer usage on scholarly communication among social scientists. *Journal of Information Science,* 26 (2), pp. 255-262.
46. Monopoli, Maria. & Nicholas, David. (2000) A user –centered approach to the evaluation of subject based information gateways: Case study SOSIG. *Aslib Proceedings,* 52 (6), pp. 218-231.
47. Belecis, Deborah D., et al. (2001) The measurement of use of web based information resources: An early look at vendor supplied data. *College and Research Libraries*, 62 (4), pp. 434-453.
48. Brown, Christine D. (2001) The role of computer-mediated communication in the research process of music scholars: an exploratory investigation. *Information Research* [Internet] 6(2).Available from: <http://InformationR.net/ir/6-2/paper99.html > [Accessed on April 15th 2004].
49. Cooper, Michael D. (2001) Use patterns of web based catalogues. *Journal of the American Society for Information Science and Technology*, 52 (2), pp. 137-148.
50. Rogers, Sally A. (2001) Electronic journal usage at Ohio State University. *College and Research Libraries*, 62(1), pp. 25-33.
51. Monopoli, Maria & Nicholas, David. (2001) A user evaluation of

subject based information gateways: case study ADAM. *Aslib Proceedings,* 53, pp. 39 – 50.

52. Pettigrew, Karen E., Durrance, Joan C. & Unruh, Kenton T. (2002) Facilitating community information seeking using the Internet: Findings from three public libraries–community network systems. *Journal of the American Society for Information Science and Technology*, 53 (11), pp. 894-903.

53. Monopoli, Mariya., et al. (2002) A user oriented evaluation of digital libraries: Case study of the electronic journals service of the library and electronic journals service of the library and information service of the university of Patras, Greece. *Aslib Proceedings,* 54 (2), pp. 103-117.

54. Hewitson, Andrew. (2002) Use and awareness of electronic information services by academic staff at Leeds Metropolitan University: A qualitative study. *Journal of Librarianship and Information Science,* 34 (1), pp. 45-52.

55. Franklin, B. & Plum, T. (2004) Library usage patterns in the electronic information environment. *Information Research* [Internet] 9(4). Available from: <http://InformationR.net/ir/9-4/paper187.html > [Accessed on October 4th 2005].

56. Wiberley, Stephen E. & Jones, William G. (1989) Patterns of information seeking in the Humanities. *College and Research Libraries*, 50 (6), pp. 638-645.

57. Berger, Kenneth W. & Hines, Richard W. (1994) What does the user really want? The library user survey project at Duke University. *The Journal of Academic Librarianship*, 20 (5), pp. 306-309.

58. Hsieh-Yee, Ingrid. (1996) Students use of online catalogues and other information channels. *College and Research Libraries,* 57, pp. 161-175.

59. Curtis, Karen L., et al. (1997) Information seeking behavior of Health Sciences faculty: the impact of new information technologies. *Bulletin of Medical Library Association,* 85 (4), pp. 402 – 410.

60. Baldwin, Nancy Sadler. & Rice, Ronald E. (1997) Information seeking behavior of securities analysts: individual and institutional influences, information sources and channels, and outcomes. *Journal of the American Society for Information Science,* 48 (8), pp. 674 – 693.

61. Pelzer, Nancy L., Wise, William H. & Leysen, Joan M. (1998) Library use and information seeking behavior of Veterinary Medical students revised in the electronic environment. *Bulletin of Medical Library Association,* 86 (3), pp. 346 – 355.

62. Jange, Suresh. & B. S.Maheswarappa. (1998) Information seeking behaviour of Physical scientists: A case study with reference to Gulbarga University. *Kelpro Bulletin,* 2 (1), pp. 38-42.

63. Bruce, Harry. (1998) User satisfaction with information seeking on the Internet. *Journal of the American Society for Information Science*, 49 (6), pp. 541 – 545.

64. Brown, Cecelia M. (1999) Information seeking behavior of scientists in the electronic information age: Astronomers, Chemists, Mathematicians and Physicists. *Journal of the American Society for Information Science,* 50 (10), pp. 929 – 943.

65. Grag, B.S. (2000) Information seeking patterns of users of engineering institutions in Rajasthan. *Library Herald,* 37 (4), pp. 229 – 239.

66. Julien, Heidi. & Michels, David. (2000) Source selection among information seekers: Ideals and realities. *Canadian Journal of Information and Library Science,* 25 (1), pp. 2-17.

67. Kuffalikar, Chitra Rekha & Mahakulkar, Vaishali. (2003) A study of information seeking behaviour of the user in P.G. Departments of Biochemistry and microbiology, Nagpur University. *Indian Journal of Information Library & Society*, 16, pp. 185-196.

68. Sanjeev Kumar & Mishra, Sanjaya. (1993) Use of National Institute of Fashion Technology Library: A survey. *ILA Bulletin,* 283 (3), pp. 116-123.

69. VijayaLakshmi, B. & Kannakachary, M. (1994) Information needs and use patterns in Humanities: A survey and proposal for setting up a national documentation center for Humanities. *International Forum on Information and Documentation*, 19, pp. 37-41.

70. Markusova, V.A., Giljarevskij, R.S. & Cherny, A.T. (1994) Communication among Russian scientists and between them and world science. *International Forum on Information and Documentation,* 19, pp. 17-27.

71. Ockacha, Kingsley Ferewisky. (1995) Socio-cultural departments of the use and transfer of scientific information by agricultural scientists in South Eastern Nigeria. *Information and Library Review,* 27, pp. 301 – 316.

72. Wilkins, Janie L. Hassard. & Leckie, Gloria J. (1997) University professional and managerial staff: Information needs and seeking. *College and Research Libraries*, 58 (7), pp. 561-573.

73. Nicholas, David. & Martin, Helen. (1997) Assessing information needs: a case study of journalists. *Aslib Proceedings,* 49 (2), pp. 43 – 52.

74. Crabtree, Anna Beth. & Crawford, Julia H. (1997) Assessing and addressing the library needs of health care personnel in a large regional hospital. *Bulletin of Medical Library Association,* 85 (2), pp.167 – 175.

75. Cogdill, Keith W., et al. (1997) First year medical students information needs and resource selection: responses to a clinical scenario. *Bulletin of Medical Library Association,* 85 (1), pp.51 – 54.

76. Mendes, Helena. & Meadows, A. J. (1997) Personal information acquisition by health professionals in Brazilian and British hospitals: A comparative study. *Journal of Librarianship and Information Science,* 29 (4), pp. 189-193.

77. Suriya, M., & Abdul Raheem, A. (1998) Information and communication technology infrastructure and sustainable development in high middle and low-income countries. *International Forum on Information and Documentation,* 23 (2), pp. 3-10.

78. Agada, John. (1999) Inner city gatekeepers: an exploratory survey of their information use environment. *Journal of the American Society for Information Science,* 50 (1), pp.74 – 85.

79. Biradar, B. S. & Sampath Kumar, B. T. (2000) Periodical use pattern by teacher and research scholars of Kuvempu University; A case study. *SRELS Journal of Information Management*, 37 (4), pp. 301-314.

80. Tadasad, P. G. & Metesheela, D. (2001) Use pattern of information sources by post graduate students in a university environment: A case study of Gulbarga University, Gulbarga. *SRELS Journal of Information Management,* 38 (3), pp. 231-254.

81. Rowland, Fytton. & Rubbert, Iris. (2001) An evaluation of the information needs and practices of part-time and distance learning students in the context of educational and social change through life long learning. *Journal of Documentation*, 57 (6), pp. 741-762.

82. Xie, Hong (Iris). & Wolfram, Dictmar. (2002) State digital library usability: contributing organizational factors. *Journal of the American Society for Information Science and Technology*, 53 (13), pp. 1085-1097.

83. Marchionini, Gary. (2002) Co-evolution of user and organizational interfaces: A longitudinal case study of WWW dissemination of national statistics. *Journal of the American Society for Information Science and Technology*, 53 (14), pp. 1192-1209.

84. Sridhar, B.S., Sampath Kumar, B.T. & Anil Kumar. M. (2003) Information use pattern by sericulture scientists: A case study of

Karnataka state Sericulture Research and Development Institute Library, Bangalore. *SRELS Journal of Information Management,* 40 (3), pp. 255-265.

85. Nikam, Khaiser. & Rajashekara, N. (2003) Reading habits of public library users: A survey. *SRELS Journal of Information Management,* 40 (4), pp. 337-363.

86. Ikhizama, B. O. & Oduwole, A. A. (2003) Pattern of usage of information sources by scientist in Nigerian Universities of Agriculture (UOA). *Library Progress*, 23 (1), pp. 1-6.

87. Geetha, P. (2004) *Information needs and use pattern of pure scientists.* IN: New frontiers of knowledge in Information Science. Devarajan, G., ed. New Delhi, ESS ESS Publications. pp. 320-382.

4

Information Search Pattern in Electronic Environment

A Case study

THE MAIN AIM of this study is to examine the information search pattern of the science doctoral students in the electronic environment. In an electronic environment the studies, which focus on how researchers search information, the type of information needed, the services they used and their priorities in searching for information are highly relevant, because they provide a basis for reorganizing libraries and information centers and reshaping their information support activities. The information search pattern of the respondents may be different depending upon their personal attributes and environment. The other objectives of the study are:

1. To find out the type of electronic information resources used currently by the science doctoral students in the universities in India and to examine the place of access and the frequency of use of various electronic information resources.
2. To examine the frequency of use of Internet tools and resources, and to find out the average time spent per week for using these resources by the science doctoral students in the universities.

3. To identify the Internet facilities used for communication in the electronic environment by the science doctoral students in the universities.
4. To find out the frequency of use of various Internet search engines by the science doctoral students in the universities.
5. To investigate different search methods used by the science doctoral students in the universities in retrieving information from electronic information resources.
6. To examine the awareness of advanced search methods among the science doctoral students in the universities in the country.
7. To find out the purpose of conducting electronic information searches by the science doctoral students in the universities and to identify the difficulties faced by them in the online search.
8. To examine the science doctoral students overall ability in using the electronic information resources, and to find out the impact of electronic information resources on research.
9. To investigate whether the availability of electronic information resources influenced the use of printed documents among the science doctoral students in the universities.
10. To compare the use and search pattern of electronic information resources by the science doctoral students in the different universities in Kerala.
11. To make a comparative study of the use and search pattern of electronic information resources by the doctoral students in various science disciplines in the universities in the country.

The study attempts to find out the type of various electronic information sources used and the methods of searching information in the electronic information resources especially on the Internet by the science doctoral students in the universities. In India, universities are the nucleus of research activities in all major science disciplines. The population of the present study is the full time science doctoral students in the departments of the four universities in Kerala state in India, namely University of Kerala, University of Calicut, Cochin University of Science and Technology (CUSAT), Mahatma Gandhi University. The principal method used to collect the data was the questionnaire survey.

Table 4.1 shows the response rate of the science doctoral students per university. The table shows that 276 science doctoral students who are using the electronic information sources were responded to the survey and the response rate is 90.2 per cent. In University of Kerala, 88.9 per cent of the science doctoral students responded and in the University of Calicut, the response rate is 92 per cent. The response rate in Cochin University of Science and Technology, M. G. University and is 89.5 per cent and 96.9 per cent respectively.

TABLE 4.1 : Response Rate of the Science Doctoral Students

University	*Questionnaires Distributed*	*Questionnaires Returned*	
		Number	*Percentage*
University of Kerala	144	128	88.9
University of Calicut	50	46	92
Cochin University of Science and Technology	76	68	89.5
Mahatma Gandhi. University	32	31	96.9
Total	**302**	**273**	**90.2**

The discipline wise distribution of the science doctoral students is: 44.2 per cent from the Physical Sciences, 21.7 per cent from Biological Sciences,15.6 per cent from Bio Sciences, 9.4 per cent from Environmental Science and 7.6

per cent of respondents from Mathematical Science.

Information Technology, the combination of computing and data processing with communications and access to data or information, is one of the key technologies of the present, and has had a profound effect on every aspect of modern society, including research. The progress of a nation depends on its research work, which in turn depends on the available information. Research in any discipline is an intellectual activity involving analysis, testing and experimentation, consultation and reference of other research material, communications with peers and colleagues, preparation of papers and reports, and so on. Research will come to stand still if pertinent information as urgently required by the researcher is not collected, processed, organized, received and finally communicate to him. Researchers require an in information environment which provides in an integrated, and ideally uniform manner, the services necessary to meet all the research needs and which delivers the services through the single window of the computer screen on the researchers' s desk. The proper information environment must be created in order that the researchers concentrate his energy and time on actual research rather than futile haunting for materials and data. In order to serve the researcher efficiently and effectively it is necessary to ascertain their information search pattern and use of the various electronic information sources in the electronic environment.

In an electronic environment the studies which focus on how the researchers search information, on the type and sources of information needed, on the nature of information sought, and the services they use are highly relevant, because they provide a basis for reorganizing libraries and Information centers and reshaping their information support activities. In the developed countries, the importance of studying and identifying the information use and search pattern of doctoral students in the electronic environment is greatly emphasized and conducted a number of studies in this regard. Such studies however have not been done extensively in India and not much data is available regarding researchers information search pattern in the electronic environment. This study seeks to investigate how the doctoral students are searching information in the electronic information resources especially in those resources located on the Internet. In an era of continuous technological developments in conjunction with information overload, information search pattern studies continue to be a vital tool enabling information use and hence information delivery. The study will help librarians and other information managers in India and other developing countries to develop an Information and Communication Technology based library system where the doctoral students can access and search the latest electronic information sources. Many libraries are taking steps to switch over from their traditional roles into technology enabled service-centered roles; in this context the present study will be of great help to plan and develop a well automated Information and Communication Technology enabled library system.

1. GENERAL INFORMATION

General information about the science doctoral students, such as age, gender, qualification and stage of research work, etc are analyzed first.

1.1. Age wise Distribution

Table 4.2 depicts the age wise distribution of the science doctoral students. Analysis shows that majority (64.2 per cent) of them are within the age group of 25-30. About 28.6 per cent of them are below 25 years of age and a very few have 31-35 years of age.

TABLE 4.2 : Age wise distribution of the Science Doctoral Students

Age Range	*University of Kerala*	*University of Calicut*	*CUSAT*	*M. G. University*	*Grand Total*
< 25	33(25.8%)	10(21.7%)	24(35.3%)	11(35.5%)	78(28.6%)
25 – 30	86(67.2%)	31(67.4%)	42(61.8%)	16(51.6%)	175(64.2%)
31 – 35	6(4.7%)	3(6.5%)	1(1.5%)	3(9.7%)	13(4.7%)
41 – 45	1(0.8%)	_	1(1.5%)	_	2(0.7%)
> 45	2(1.6%)	2(4.3%)	_	1(3.2%)	5(1.8%)
Grand Total	**128(100%)**	**46(100%)**	**68(100%)**	**31(100%)**	**273(100%)**

It is also found that majority of the respondents in the Universities under study are below 25 years and only very few of them are above 30 years of age.

1.2. Gender wise distribution

Table 4.3 indicates the gender wise distributions of science doctoral students in the universities. The analysis revealed that females dominate in number in the universities under study compared to males.

TABLE 4.3 : Gender wise distributions of the Science Doctoral Students

Gender	*University of Kerala*	*University of Calicut*	*CUSAT*	*M. G. University*	*Grand Total*
Male	60(46.9%)	7(15.2%)	28(41.2%)	14(45.2%)	109(39.9%)
Female	68(53.1%)	39(84.8%)	40(58.8%)	17(54.8%)	164(60.1%)
Grand Total	**128(100%)**	**46(100%)**	**68(100%)**	**31(100%)**	**273(100%)**

The analysis reveals that majority (60.1 per cent) of the science doctoral students in the universities are female and nearly two fifth (39.9 per cent) of them are male. The majority of the science doctoral students in the University of Kerala (53.1 per cent), CUSAT (58.8 per cent), M. G. University (54.8 per cent), University of Calicut (84.8 per cent) and Kannur University (66.7 per cent) are female.

1.3. Qualification wise distribution

The qualifications of the science doctoral students are given in Table 4.4. It is seen that majority (65.8 per cent) of them have only post graduation and a few (34.4 per cent) of them possess M. Phil degree also.

TABLE 4.4 : Qualification wise distributions of the Science Doctoral Students

Quali-fication	*University of Kerala*	*University of Calicut*	*CUSAT*	*M. G. University*	*Grand Total*
M. Sc	60(46.9%)	39(84.8%)	55(80.9%)	24(77.4%)	178(65.6%)
M. Phil	68(53.1%)	7(15.2%)	13(19.1%)	7(22.6%)	95(34.4%)
Grand Total	**128(100%)**	**46(100%)**	**68(100%)**	**31(100%)**	**273(100%)**

As seen in the Table 4.4 majority of the science doctoral students in the University of Calicut (84.8 per cent), CUSAT (80.9 per cent) and M. G. University (77.4 per cent) possess only post graduation. On the other hand majority (53.1 per cent) of the science doctoral students in University of Kerala are M. Phil holders.

1.4. Stage of research work of Doctoral students

Table 4.5 gives the stage of research work wise distribution of the science doctoral students in the universities under study. Analysis shows that nearly 36.2 per cent of the science doctoral students are in the beginning stage of their research work and about 34.1 per cent of them are in the analysis stage of research work. A very few number of the scholars are in the data collection and report writing stage of the research.

TABLE 4.5 : Stages of research work of the Science Doctoral students

Stage of Research Work	*University of Kerala*	*University of Calicut*	*CUSAT*	*M. G. University*	*Grand Total*
M. Sc	60(46.9%)	39(84.8%)	55(80.9%)	24(77.4%)	178(65.6%)
Beginning	41(32%)	19(41.3%)	26(38.2%)	13(41.9%)	99(36.2%)
Data Collection	31(24.2%)	7(15.2%)	4(5.9%)	3(9.7%)	45(16.3%)
Analysis	41(32%)	14(30.4%)	30(44.1%)	7(22.6%)	92(34.1%)
Report Writing	15(11.7%)	6(13%)	8(11.8%)	8(25.8%)	37(13.4%)
Grand Total	**128(100%)**	**46(100%)**	**68(100%)**	**31(100%)**	**273(100%)**

It is seen that nearly 32 per cent of the science doctoral students in University of Kerala are in the beginning stage while 32 per cent of them are engaged in analysis stage of the research. In University of Calicut, a good number (41.3 per cent) of the scholars are in the beginning stage and few (30.4 per cent) of them are in the analysis stage of research work. A good number (44.1 per cent) of the science doctoral students in CUSAT are in the analysis stage of the research work and about 38.2 per cent of them are in the beginning stage. In M. G. University, 41.9 per cent of the scholars are in the beginning stage of research work.

1.5. Experience in using electronic information resources

Table 4.6 shows the details of experience in using various electronic information resources related to their research of the science doctoral students. The analysis shows that a good number (41.7 per cent) of the science doctoral students have up to one year experience and a considerable (34.1 per cent) of them had more than 2.5 years experience in using electronic information resources. A few (24.3 per cent) of them indicated that they have 1 to 2.5 years experience in using electronic information resources.

TABLE 4.6 : Experience in using electronic information resources

Experience	*University of Kerala*	*University of Calicut*	*CUSAT*	*M. G. University*	*Grand Total*
Up to 1 year	51(39.8%)	22(47.8%)	30(44.1%)	11(35.5%)	114(41.7%)
1 -2.5 years	30(23.4%)	17(37%)	13(19.1%)	7(22.6%)	67(24.3%)
More than 2.5 years	47(36.7%)	7(15.2%)	25(36.8%)	13(41.9%)	92(34.1%)
Grand Total	**128(100%)**	**46(100%)**	**68(100%)**	**31(100%)**	**273(100%)**

It is found that a good number of science doctoral students in University of Kerala (39.8 per cent), University of Calicut (47.8 per cent) and CUSAT (44.1 per cent) have up to 1-year experience in using electronic information resources. A good number (41.9 per cent) of the science doctoral students in M. G. University indicated more than 2.5 years experience in using the electronic information resources.

2. PLACES OF ACCESSING ELECTRONIC INFORMATION RESOURCES

Table 4.7 gives the place of accessing various electronic information resources by the science doctoral students in the universities in Kerala related to their research work. Analysis shows that majority (69.9 per cent) of the respondents is accessing Internet resources from their departments and about 61.6 per cent of them are accessing it from the university libraries. Majority of the science doctoral students are accessing electronic journals and nearly 52.5 per cent of them are accessing it from the university libraries. A good number (46 per cent) of them are accessing electronic journals from the departments. Majority of the scholars are accessing network based services and a good number (47.1 per cent) of them are accessing it from the university libraries. Majority of the scholars are accessing CD/DVD databases, and a few number (38.4 per cent) of them are accessing it from the departments. Majority of them are not accessing audio/video recordings related to their research.

TABLE 4.7 : Place of accessing electronic information resources

Electronic Information Resources	*Not Accessed*	*Home*	*Departments*	*University Library*
Audio/Video Recordings	179(64.9%)	48(17.4%)	56(20.3%)	23(8.3%)
CD/DVD Databases	104(37.6%)	62(22.5%)	106(38.4%)	75(27.2%)
Electronic Journals	70(25.4%)	20(7.2%)	127(46%)	145(52.5%)
Network Based Services	85(30.8%)	15(5.4%)	127(46%)	130(47.1%)
Internet Resources	8(2.9%)	39(14.1%)	193(69.9%)	170(61.6%)

It is found that most of the science doctoral students are accessing Internet resources related to their research. Majority of them are accessing electronic journals, network based services and CD/DVD databases. Where as majority of them are not accessing audio/video recordings related to their research. Majority of the science doctoral students indicated that they are accessing Internet resources from both the departments and university libraries. Majority of the scholars are accessing electronic journals from the university libraries and a good number (46 per cent) of them are accessing it from the departments. A good number of them are accessing network-based services from the university libraries and a few them are accessing CD/DVD databases from the departments.

2.1. Places of accessing electronic information resources according to University

To find out the type of electronic information resources used by the science doctoral students and the places of access to these sources in the universities under study, the responses are analyzed university wise and presented in Tables 4.8 to 4.11. Table 4.8 shows the places of access to the electronic information resources by the science doctoral students in the University of Kerala.

TABLE 4.8 : Places of accessing of electronic information resources in University of Kerala

Electronic Information Resources	*No Access*	*Home*	*Department*	*University Library*
Audio/Video Recordings	73(57%)	33(25.8%)	26(20.3%)	15(11.7%)
CD/DVD Databases	52(40.6%)	30(23.4%)	44(34.4%)	28(21.9%)
Electronic Journals	34(26.6%)	11(8.6%)	64(50%)	66(51.6%)
Network Based Services	43(33.6%)	10(7.8%)	57(44.5%)	55(43%)
Internet Resources	5(3.9%)	21(16.4%)	84(65.6%)	86(67.2%)

Analysis shows that most of the science doctoral students in the University of Kerala are accessing Internet resources related to their research. Majority of them are accessing electronic journals, network based services and CD/DVD databases. About 57 per cent of the scholars are not accessing audio/video recordings related to their research. In University of Kerala, nearly 67.2 per cent of the science doctoral students are accessing Internet resources from the university library and 65.6 per cent of them are accessing it from the departments. About 51.6 per cent of the scholars indicated that they are accessing electronic journals from the university library and 50 per cent of them are accessing it from the departments. A good number of them are accessing network-based services from both the departments (44.5 per cent) and the university library (43 per cent). A few numbers (34.4 per cent) of them are accessing CD/DVD databases from the departments.

It is found that the most of the science doctoral students in the University of Kerala are accessing Internet resources related to their research. Majority of them are accessing electronic journals, network based services and CD/DVD databases. Majority of the scholars are not accessing audio/video recordings related to their research. Majority of them are accessing Internet resources and electronic journals from both the university library and departments. A good number of them are accessing network-based services and a few respondents are accessing CD/DVD databases from the departments.

Table 4.9 indicates the places where the science doctoral students in University of Calicut are accessing the electronic information resources related to their research. Analysis revealed that in University of Calicut, a large majority of the science doctoral students are accessing Internet resources related to their research. Majority of them are not accessing audio/video recordings (69.6%), CD/DVD databases (54.3%), electronic journals (54.3%) and network-based services (52.2%) related to the research work. In University of Calicut, majority (50 per cent) of the science doctoral students are accessing Internet resources from the departments and a few number (37 per cent) of them are accessing it from the university library. Few of them are accessing network based services (28.3 per cent) and electronic journals (26.1 per cent) from the university library. A few number (26.1 per cent) of them indicated that they are accessing CD/DVD databases from the departments.

TABLE 4.9 : Places of Accessing Electronic Information Resources in University of Calicut

Electronic Information Resources	*No Access*	*Home*	*Department*	*University Library*
Audio/Video Recordings	32(69.6%)	4(8.7%)	9(19.6%)	–
CD/DVD Databases	25(54.3%)	12(26.1%)	12(26.1%)	3(6.5%)
Electronic Journals	25(54.3%)	2(4.3%)	6(13%)	12(26.1%)
Network Based Services	24(52.2%)	2(4.3%)	7(15.2%)	13(28.3%)
Internet Resources	3(6.5%)	2(4.3%)	23(50%)	17(37%)

It is revealed that in University of Calicut, large majority of the science doctoral students are accessing Internet resources. Majority of them are accessing it from the departments. Majority of them are not accessing audio/video recordings, CD/DVD databases, electronic journals and network based services related to the research work. A few number of them are accessing network based services and electronic journals from the university library. A few number of the scholars are accessing CD/DVD databases from the departments.

Table 4.10 shows the place of getting access to the electronic information resources by the science doctoral students in CUSAT. All the scholars in CUSAT are accessing Internet resources. A large majority of them are accessing electronic journals (86.8 per cent) and network based services

(85.3 per cent) and majority of them are accessing CD/DVD databases (75 per cent) related to their research work. Nearly 66.2 per cent of the respondents have no access to audio/ video recordings. In CUSAT, large majority (89.7 per cent) of the science doctoral students are accessing Internet resources from the departments and about 58.8 per cent of them are accessing it from the university library. About 72.1 per cent of the doctoral students are accessing electronic journals and network based services from the departments. Majority (61.8 per cent) of them are accessing CD/DVD databases from the departments and few (32.4 per cent) of them are accessing it from the university library.

TABLE 4.10 : Places of Accessing Electronic Information Resources in CUSAT

Electronic Information Resources	*No Access*	*Home*	*Department*	*University Library*
Audio/Video Recordings	45(66.2%)	9(13.2%)	17(25%)	6(8.8%)
CD/DVD Databases	17(25%)	16(23.5%)	42(61.8%)	22(32.4%)
Electronic Journals	9(13.2%)	1(1.5%)	49(72.1%)	39(57.4%)
Network Based Services	10(14.7%)	1(1.5%)	49(72.1%)	42(61.8%)
Internet Resources	–	8(11.8%)	61(89.7%)	40(58.8%)

It is found that in CUSAT, all the science doctoral students are accessing Internet resources. Large majority of them are accessing electronic journals and network-based services related to their research. Majority (75 per cent) of them are accessing CD/DVD databases. Where as majority of them have no access to audio/video recordings. It is also found that large majority of the science doctoral students are accessing Internet resources and majority of them are accessing network-based services, electronic journals and CD/DVD databases from the departments.

The places where the science doctoral students in M. G. University are accessing electronic information resources related to their research are analysed and summarised in Table 4.11. Analysis shows that in M. G. University, all the respondents are using Internet resources. Large majority (93.5 per cent) of them are accessing electronic journals related to their research. Majority of the doctoral students are using CD/DVD databases (67.7 per cent) and network based services (80.6 per cent). A large majority (87.1 per cent) of them are not accessing audio/video recordings related to their research.

TABLE 4.11 : Places of accessing Electronic Information Resources in M.G. University

Electronic Information Resources	*No Access*	*Home*	*Department*	*University Library*
Audio/Video Recordings	27(87.1%)	1(3.2%)	3(9.7%)	2(6.5%)
CD/DVD Databases	10(32.3)	3(9.7%)	6(19.4%)	21(67.7%)
Electronic Journals	2(6.5%)	4(12.9%)	6(19.4%)	27(87.1%)
Network Based Services	6(19.4%)	2(6.5%)	13(41.9%)	20(64.5%)
Internet Resources	_	6(19.4%)	23(74.2%)	26(83.9%)

In M. G. University, majority (83.9 per cent) of the doctoral students are accessing Internet resources from the university library and about 74.2 per cent of them are accessing it from the departments. Large majority (87.1 per cent) of them are accessing electronic journals from the university library. About 67.7 per cent of the respondents are accessing CD/DVD databases from the university library and few (19.4 per cent) of them are accessing it from the departments. Nearly 64.5 per cent of them are accessing network-based services from the university library. It is found that in M. G. University, all the respondents are using Internet resources. Large majority of them are accessing electronic journals related to their research. Majority of them are using CD/DVD databases and network based services. Where as a large majority of the scholars are not accessing audio/video recordings. Large majority of them are accessing electronic journals and majority of them are accessing Internet resources, CD/DVD databases, and network based services from the university library.

2.2. Places of Accessing Electronic Information Resources according to Discipline

The places of getting access to electronic information resources by the doctoral students in various science disciplines are presented in Tables 4.12 to 4.18.

The Table 4.12 gives the place of accessing electronic information resources by the doctoral students in Bio Sciences. Analysis shows that all the doctoral students in Bio Sciences are accessing Internet resources. Large majority (86 per cent) of them are accessing it from the departments. About 74.4 per cent of the doctoral students are accessing Internet resources from the university libraries. Large majority (93 per cent) of them are accessing electronic journals and 83.7 per cent of them are accessing it from the departments. Nearly 72.1 per cent of them are using electronic journals from the university libraries. About 79.1 per cent of the doctoral students are using network based services and 65.1 per cent of them are accessing it from the departments. Majority (69.8 per cent) of the scholars are using CD/DVD databases and 55.8 per cent of them are accessing it from the departments. Majority of the scholars are accessing audio/video recordings and a good number (44.2 per cent) of them are accessing it from the departments.

TABLE 4.12 : Places of accessing Electronic Information Resources by the Doctoral Students in Bio Sciences

Electronic Information Resources	*No Access*	*Home*	*Department*	*University Library*
Audio/Video Recordings	21(48.8%)	14(32.6%)	19(44.2%)	5(11.6%)
CD/DVD Databases	13(30.2%)	12(27.9%)	24(55.8%)	11(25.6%)
Electronic Journals	3(7%)	7(16.3%)	36(83.7%)	31(72.1%)
Network Based Services	9(20.9%)	4(9.3%)	28(65.1%)	22(51.2%)
Internet Resources	_	9(20.9%)	37(86%)	32(74.4%)

It is found that in Bio Sciences, all the respondents are using Internet resources. Large majority (93 per cent) of them are using electronic journals related to their research. Majority of the doctoral students are using network-based services, CD/DVD databases and audio/video recordings in relation to their research work. It is also found that large majority (86 per cent) of the doctoral students are accessing Internet resources and majority of them are accessing electronic journals, network based services and CD/DVD databases from the departments. A good number of them are also accessing audio/video recordings from the departments.

The place of accessing electronic information resources by the doctoral students in Biological Sciences is given in Table 4.13. Analysis reveled that most of the doctoral students in Biological Sciences are using Internet resources and about 73.3 per cent of them are accessing it from the departments. About 51.7 per cent of them indicated that they are accessing

Internet resources from the university libraries. Majority (58.3 per cent) of them are accessing network-based services and a few number (38.3 per cent) of them are accessing it from the university libraries, while 36.7 per cent of them are accessing it from the departments. Nearly 55 per cent of the doctoral students are using electronic journals and few (35 per cent) of them are accessing it from the university libraries. A good number (48.3 per cent) of them are using CD/DVD databases and few of them are accessing it from the departments. Majority of them are not using audio/video recordings and a few of them are accessing it from the departments.

TABLE 4.13 : Places of accessing Electronic Information Resources by the Doctoral Students in Biological Sciences

Electronic Information Resources	*No Access*	*Home*	*Department*	*University Library*
Audio/Video Recordings	37(61.7%)	8(13.3%)	14(23.3%)	4(6.7%)
CD/DVD Databases	31(51.7%)	12(20%)	20(33.3%)	6(10%)
Electronic Journals	27(45%)	5(8.3%)	16(26.7%)	21(35%)
Network Based Services	25(41.7%)	4(6.7%)	22(36.7%)	23(38.3%)
Internet Resources	1(1.7%)	8(13.3%)	44(73.3%)	31(51.7%)

It is found that most of the doctoral students in Biological Sciences are using Internet resources. Majority of them are accessing electronic journals and network-based services related to their research. Majority of the scholars are not using CD/DVD databases and audio/video recordings. Majority of them are accessing Internet resources from the departments.

A few numbers of them are accessing electronic journals and network based services from the university libraries. A few numbers of the doctoral students are using CD/DVD databases and audio/video recordings from the departments.

Table 4.14 gives the place of accessing electronic information resources by the doctoral students in Computer Science. Analysis shows that all the respondents in Computer Science are accessing Internet resources, network based services, electronic journals and CD/DVD databases related to their research. All the doctoral students are accessing electronic journals and CD/DVD databases from the departments. Majority of them are accessing Internet resources, network based services and audio/video recordings from the departments.

TABLE 4.14 : Places of accessing Electronic Information Resources by the Doctoral Students in Computer Science

Electronic Information Resources	*No Access*	*Home*	*Department*	*University Library*
Audio/Videoo Recordings	1(25%)	_	3(75%)	_
CD/DVD Databases	_	1(25%)	4(100%)	_
Electronic Journals	_	_	4(100%)	1(25%)
Network Based Services	_	_	3(75%)	2(50%)
Internet Resources	_	1(25%)	3(75%)	_

It is revealed that all the doctoral students in Computer Science are accessing Internet resources, network based services, electronic journals and CD/DVD databases related to their research. All the doctoral students are accessing electronic journals and CD/DVD databases from the departments. Majority of them are accessing Internet resources, network based services and audio/video recordings from the departments.

The place of accessing electronic information resources by the doctoral students in Environmental Science is given in Table 4.15. Analysis shows that most of the doctoral students in the Environmental Science are accessing Internet resources. Majority (80.8 per cent) of them are accessing it from the university libraries. Nearly 61.5 per cent of them are accessing electronic journals and network-based services related to research. Majority of them are using electronic journals (53.8 per cent) and network based services (57.7 per cent) from the university libraries. About 76.9 per cent of the doctoral students are accessing CD/DVD databases and a few numbers (30.8 per cent) of them is using it from the university libraries. A few numbers of the scholars are accessing audio/video recordings and few (30.8 per cent) of them are using it from home.

TABLE 4.15 : Places of accessing Electronic Information Resources by the Doctoral Students in Environmental Science

Electronic Information Resources	*No Access*	*Home*	*Department*	*University Library*
Audio/Video Recordings	16(61.5%)	8(30.8%)	1(3.8%)	5(19.2%)
CD/DVD Databases	6(23.1%)	8(30.8%)	6(23.1%)	8(30.8%)
Electronic Journals	10(38.5%)	–	5(19.2%)	14(53.8%)
Network Based Services	10(38.5%)	2(7.7%)	5(19.2%)	15(57.7%)
Internet Resources	1(3.8%)	1(3.8%)	5(19.2%)	21(80.8%)

It is revealed that most (96.2 per cent) of the doctoral students in the Environmental Science are accessing Internet resources. Majority of them are accessing CD/DVD databases, electronic journals and network-based services related to their research. Majority of the doctoral students are not accessing audio/video recordings. It is also revealed that majority of them are accessing Internet resources, electronic journals and network based services from the university libraries. Few of them are using CD/DVD databases from the university libraries.

Table 4.16 shows the place of accessing electronic information resources by the doctoral students in Mathematical Science. Analysis revealed that most of the doctoral students in Mathematical Science are accessing Internet resources. Large majority (85.8 per cent) of them are using it from the departments. Nearly 52.4 per cent of the respondents are accessing electronic journals and a good number (42.9 per cent) of them are accessing it from the departments. A good number of the doctoral students are accessing network-based services and few (38.1 per cent) of them are using it from the university libraries. Large majority (85.7 per cent) of them are not accessing audio/video recordings and majority (71.4 per cent) of them are not accessing CD/DVD databases.

It is found that most of the respondents in Mathematical Science are accessing Internet resources. Majority (52.4 per cent) of them are accessing electronic journals related to their research. Large majority of the doctoral students are not accessing audio/video recordings. Majority of them are not accessing CD/DVD databases and network-based services related to research. Large majority of them are using Internet resources and a good number of them are accessing electronic journals from the departments. A few numbers of them are accessing network-based services from the university libraries.

TABLE 4.16 :Places of accessing Electronic Information Resources by the Doctoral Students in Mathematical Science

Electronic Information Resources	*No Access*	*Home*	*Department*	*University Library*
Audio/Video Recordings	18(85.7%)	–	3(14.3%)	2(9.5%)
CD/DVD Databases	15(71.4%)	2(9.5%)	3(14.3%)	3(14.3%)
Electronic Journals	10(47.6%)	–	9(42.9%)	6(28.6%)
Network Based Services	11(52.4%)	–	6(28.6%)	8(38.1%)
Internet Resources	1(4.8%)	1(4.8%)	18(85.8%)	12(57.1%)

Table 4.17 gives the places of accessing electronic information resources by the doctoral students in Physical Sciences. Analysis indicates that most (95.9 per cent) of the doctoral students in Physical Sciences are accessing Internet resources. Majority (70.5 per cent) of them are using it from the departments. Nearly 60.7 per cent of the doctoral students are using Internet resources from the university libraries. About 83.6 per cent of the scholars are accessing electronic journals and majority (59 per cent) of them are using it from the university libraries. Majority (75.4 per cent) of the doctoral students are accessing network-based services and about 51.6 per cent of them are using it from the departments. Nearly 68 per cent of the scholars are accessing CD/DVD databases and good number of them is accessing it from the departments. Majority (70.5 per cent) of them are not accessing audio/video recordings and very few of them are accessing it from home.

TABLE 4.17 : Places of accessing Electronic Information Resources by the Doctoral Students in Physical Sciences

Electronic Information Resources	*No Access*	*Home*	*Department*	*University Library*
Audio/Video Recordings	86(70.5%)	18(14.8%)	16(13.1%)	7(5.7%)
CD/DVD Databases	39(32%)	27(22.1%)	49(40.2%)	47(38.5%)
Electronic Journals	20(16.4%)	8(6.6%)	57(46.7%)	72(59%)
Network Based Services	30(24.6%)	5(4.1%)	63(51.6%)	60(49.2)
Internet Resources	5(4.1%)	19(15.6%)	86(70.5%)	74(60.7%)

It is revealed that most (95.9 per cent) of the doctoral students in Physical Sciences are accessing Internet resources. Majority of them are using electronic journals, network based services and CD/DVD databases related to their research. Where as majority of the doctoral students are not accessing audio/video recordings. Majority of them are accessing Internet resources and network- based services from the departments. Majority of the doctoral students are accessing electronic journals from the university libraries. A good number of them are accessing CD/DVD databases from the departments.

3. FREQUENCY OF ACCESSING ELECTRONIC INFORMATION RESOURCES

The responses of the science doctoral students regarding the frequency of accessing various electronic information resources related to their research work are summarised in Table 4.18. Analysis shows that most frequently accessed electronic information resources by the science doctoral students are Internet resources. Majority (59.4 per cent) of the respondents are using Internet resources once in a day and nearly 30 per cent them are using it once in a week. Next most used electronic information source is electronic journals; about 33 per cent of the science doctoral students are accessing electronic journals once in a week and 22.5 per cent of them are accessing it once in a day. Nearly 69 per cent of them are using network-based services. About 22.5 per cent of the respondents are using it daily and 30.4 per cent of them are using it once in a week. Majority of them are using CD/DVD databases and 10.5 per cent of them are using it once in a day. A few numbers of them are rarely using audio/video recordings.

TABLE 4.18 : Frequency of accessing Electronic Information Resources

Electronic Information Resources	*Rarely*	*Once in a Month*	*Once in a Week*	*Once in a Day*
Audio/Video Recordings	50(18.1%)	8(2.9%)	20(7.2%)	19(6.9%)
CD/DVD Databases	51(18.5%)	52(18.8%)	40(14.5%)	29(10.5%)
Electronic Journals	9(3.3%)	44(15.9%)	91(33%)	62(22.5%)
Network Based Services	8(2.9%)	26(9.4%)	84(30.4%)	73(26.4%)
Internet Resources	8(2.9%)	19(6.9%)	77(27.9%)	164(59.4%)

It is found that most frequently accessed electronic information resources by the science doctoral students are Internet resources. Majority (59.4 per cent) of them are using it once in a day. Next most used electronic information resource is electronic journals and few of them are accessing it once in a day. Few of the scholars are using network-based services once in a day. Majority of them are using CD/DVD databases and very few of them are using it once in a day. A few of them are rarely using audio/video recordings.

3.1. Relation between Frequency of Use of Electronic Information Resources and Personal Attributes

ANOVA test was used to verify the relation between the use of electronic information resources and the personal attributes of science doctoral students such as age, sex and experience in using the electronic information resources and the results are given in Tables 4.19 to 4.24.

The Table 4.19 shows the mean and standard deviations on the use of electronic information resources for science doctoral students based on gender.

TABLE 4.19 : Mean and SD of the Science Doctoral Students on the Use of Electronic Information Resources based on Gender

Groups	*N*	*Mean*	*Standard Deviation*	*Minimum*	*Maximum*
Male	110	55.5560	20.95095	7.50	106.75
Female	166	48.2498	20.63619	2.50	103.00
Total	**276**	**51.1617**	**21.03174**	**2.50**	**106.75**

Table 4.20 shows the analysis of variance of the use of electronic information resources based on the gender of the science doctoral students. The analysis of variance test indicates that the F value is 8.193 and the significance value is .005, which is less than 0.05. Hence, it is clear that there is significant difference in the use of electronic information resources between male and female. Analysis shows that that the mean score 55.56 of male is significantly higher than the mean score 48.25 of females.

TABLE 4.20 : ANOVA Test of the Use of Electronic Information Resources for Science Doctoral Students Based on Gender

Source of Variance	*Sum of Squares*	*d. f*	*Mean Square*	*F*	*Sig.*
Between Groups	3531.573	1	3531.573	8.193	.005
Within Groups	118110.336	274	431.060		
Total	**121641.909**	**275**			

The ANOVA test establishes that there is significant difference in the use of electronic information resources between male and female science doctoral students. It is also found that male doctoral students are using electronic information resources more than female doctoral students.

Table 4.21 shows the mean and standard deviations on the use of electronic information resources for science doctoral students based on age.

TABLE 4.21 : Mean and SD of the Science Doctoral Students on the Use of Electronic information resources Based on Age

Groups	*N*	*Mean*	*Standard Deviation*	*Mini-mum*	*Maxi-mum*
Below 25 Years	79	47.2213	21.78159	2.50	106.75
25 – 30 Years	177	52.6519	20.98531	7.00	103.00
31 – 35 Years	13	55.6923	16.36885	26.00	80.00
41 – 45 Years	2	65.0000	4.24264	62.00	68.00
Above 45 Years	5	43.3500	18.16900	16.75	67.00
Total	**276**	**51.1617**	**21.03174**	**2.50**	**106.75**

The analysis of variance of the use of electronic information resources based on the age of the science doctoral students is given in Table 4.22. The analysis of variance test indicates that the F value is 1.465 and the significance value is 0.213 which is higher than 0.05. Hence it is clear that there is no significant difference in the use of electronic information resources between the science doctoral students in different age groups

TABLE 4.22 : ANOVA Test of the Use of Electronic Information Resources for Science Doctoral Students Based on Age

Source of Variance	*Sum of Squares*	*d. f*	*Mean Square*	*F*	*Sig.*
Between Groups	2574.615	4	643.654	1.465	.213
Within Groups	119067.293	271	439.363		
Total	**121641.909**	**275**			

The ANOVA test established that there is no significant difference in the use of electronic information resources among the science doctoral students in different age groups.

The mean and standard deviations on the use of electronic information resources for science doctoral students based on the experience in using the electronic information resources are given in Table 4.23.

TABLE 4.23 : Mean and SD of the Science Doctoral Students on the Use of Electronic Information Resources based on the Experience of Using

Groups	*N*	*Mean*	*Standard Deviation*	*Mini-mum*	*Maxi-mum*
Up to one Year	115	41.5272	20.15753	7.00	106.75
1-2.5 years	67	50.8060	18.63077	2.50	94.00
More than 2.5 years	94	63.2021	17.38284	24.00	103.00
Total	**276**	**51.1617**	**21.03174**	**2.50**	**106.75**

Table 4.24 shows the analysis of variance of the use of electronic information resources based on the experience of the science doctoral students in using electronic information

resources. The analysis of variance test shows that the F value is 34.094 and the significance value is .000, which is less than 0.05. Hence it is clear that there is a significant difference in the use of electronic information resources between the science doctoral students based on their experience in using the electronic information resources.

TABLE 4.24 : ANOVA Test of the Use of Electronic Information Resources for Science Doctoral Students Based on the Experience

Source of Variance	*Sum of Squares*	*d. f*	*Mean Square*	*F*	*Sig.*
Between Groups	24310.588	2	12155.294	34.094	.000
Within Groups	97331.320	273	356.525		
Total	**121641.909**	**275**			

It is established that the use of electronic information resources is different among the science doctoral students based on their experience in using the electronic information resources.

3.2. Frequency of Accessing Electronic Information Resources according to University

The frequency of accessing the electronic information resources by the science doctoral students in the universities studied is further analysed.

Table 4.25 summarises the frequency of accessing various electronic information resources by the science doctoral students in University of Kerala. The most frequently used electronic information resources by the science doctoral students in the University of Kerala are Internet resources. A good number (48.4 per cent) of them are using it once in a day. About 35.9 per cent of them indicated that they are using Internet resources once in a week. Majority of the scholars are accessing electronic journals and 21.9 per cent of them are using it once in a day. About 31.3 per cent of them are accessing electronic journals once in a week. Nearly 32 per cent of the science doctoral students are accessing network-based services once in a week and 25 per cent of them are accessing it once in a day. Majority of the respondents are accessing CD/DVD databases but few of them accessing it daily. About 18.8 per cent of them are rarely accessing audio/video recordings

TABLE 4.25 : Frequency of accessing Electronic Information Resources in University of Kerala

Electronic Information Resources	*Rarely*	*Once in a Month*	*Once in a Week*	*Once in a Day*
Audio/Video Recordings	24(18.8%)	5(3.9%)	12(9.4%)	14(10.9%)
CD/DVD Databases	23(18%)	20(15.6%)	18(14.1%)	15(11.7%)
Electronic Journals	6(4.7%)	20(15.6%)	40(31.3%)	28(21.9%)
Network Based Services	2(1.6%)	10(7.8%)	41(32%)	32(25%)
Internet Resources	3(2.3%)	12(9.4%)	46(35.9%)	62(48.4%)

It is revealed that the most used electronic information resources by the science doctoral students in the University of Kerala are Internet resources. A good number (48.4 per cent) of them are using it once in a day. Majority of the respondents are accessing electronic journals and few of them are using it once in a day. A few numbers of the scholars are accessing network-based services once in a week and very few them are accessing CD/DVD databases daily. A very few number of the science doctoral students are rarely accessing audio/video recordings.

The science doctoral students' frequency of accessing various electronic information resources in University of Calicut is analysed and summarised in Table 4.26. Analysis revealed that in University of Calicut, the most frequently accessed information sources are Internet resources. About 30.4 per cent of the science doctoral students are using it once in a day and 41.3 per cent of them are using it once in a week. A few number of them are accessing network based services (21.7 per cent) and electronic journals (19.6 per cent) once in a week. About 21.7 per cent of the scholars are accessing CD/DVD databases rarely and very few of them are accessing it once in a month.

TABLE 4.26 : Frequency of accessing Electronic Information Resources in University of Calicut

Electronic Information Resources	*Rarely*	*Once in a Month*	*Once in a Week*	*Once in a Day*
Audio/Video Recordings	7(15.2%)	1(2.2%)	3(6.5%)	3(6.5%)
CD/DVD Databases	10(21.7%)	6(13.1%)	3(6.5%)	2(4.3%)
Electronic Journals	3(6.5%)	7(15.2%)	9(19.6%)	2(4.3%)
Network Based Services	1(2.2%)	6(13.1%)	10(21.7%)	5(10.9%)
Internet Resources	5(10.9%)	5(10.9%)	19(41.3%)	14(30.4%)

It is found that in University of Calicut also the most frequently accessed information sources are Internet resources. A good number (41.3 per cent) of the science doctoral students are using it once in a week and few of them are using it once in a day. A few number of the scholars are accessing network based services and electronic journals once in a week. A very few number of them are accessing CD/DVD databases and audio/video recordings rarely.

Table 4.27 shows the frequency of accessing various electronic information resources by the science doctoral students in CUSAT. Analysis shows that all the science doctoral students in CUSAT are accessing Internet resources.

Majority (80.9 per cent) of them are accessing it once in a day. Next most used electronic information resource is electronic journals and a good number (41.2 per cent) of the science doctoral students are accessing it once in a day. About 32.8 per cent of them are using electronic journals once in a week. Large majority of the scholars are accessing network-based services and a good number (41.2 per cent) of them are accessing it once in a day. Nearly 31 per cent of them are accessing network-based services once in a week. About 14.7 per cent of the respondents indicated that they are using CD/DVD databases once in a day and 22.1 per cent of them are accessing it once in a week. Few of them are accessing audio/video recordings rarely.

TABLE 4.27 : Frequency of accessing Electronic Information Resources in CUSAT

Electronic Information Resources	*Rarely*	*Once in a Month*	*Once in a Week*	*Once in a Day*
Audio/Video Recordings	15(22.1%)	2(2.9%)	5(7.4%)	1(1.5%)
CD/DVD Databases	13(19.1%)	13(19.1%)	15(22.1%)	10(14.7%)
Electronic Journals	_	8(11.8%)	23(33.8%)	28(41.2%)
Network Based Services	1(1.5%)	6(8.8%)	21(30.9%)	30(44.1%)
Internet Resources	_	2(2.9%)	11(16.2%)	55(80.9%)

It is revealed that most frequently used electronic information resources by the doctoral students in CUSAT are Internet resources. Majority (80.9 per cent) of them are accessing it once in a day. Next most used electronic information resource is electronic journals. A good number of the science doctoral students are using electronic journals and network based services once in a day. A very few of them are using CD/DVD databases once in a week. Very few number of them are accessing audio/video recordings rarely.

Table 4.28 shows the frequency of accessing electronic information resources by the science doctoral students in M. G. University. The most frequently used electronic information resources by the science doctoral students in the M. G. University are Internet resources. Most of them are using it once in a day. Next most used electronic information resource is electronic journals and majority (58.1 per cent) of the respondents are accessing it once in a week. Nearly 38.7 per cent of them are using network-based services once in a week while 16.1 per cent of them are accessing it once in a day. A good number (41.9 per cent) of the science doctoral students are accessing CD/DVD databases once in a month. Large majority of them are not accessing audio/video recordings and 9.7 per cent of them are accessing it rarely.

TABLE 4.28 : Frequency of accessing Electronic Information Resources in M. G. University

Electronic Information Resources	*Rarely*	*Once in a Month*	*Once in a Week*	*Once in a Day*
Audio/Video Recordings	3(9.7%)	_	_	1(3.2%)
CD/DVD Databases	4(12.9%)	13(41.9%)	3(9.7%)	1(3.2%)
Electronic Journals	_	8(25.8%)	18(58.1%)	3(9.7%)
Network Based Services	4(12.9%)	4(12.9%)	12(38.7%)	5(16.1%)
Internet Resources	_	_	1(3.2%)	30(96.8%)

It is reveled that the most frequently used electronic information resources by the science doctoral students in the M. G. University are Internet resources. Most (96.8 per cent) of them are using it once in a day. Next most frequently used electronic information resource is electronic journals and majority (58.1 per cent) of the doctoral students are accessing it once in a week. A few numbers of them are using network-based services once in a week. A good number (41.9 per cent) of the scholars are accessing CD/DVD databases once in a month. Very few number of them are accessing audio/video recordings rarely.

3.3. Relation between the Frequency of Use of Electronic Information Resources and the University

Table 4.29 shows the mean and standard deviations on the use of electronic information resources for science doctoral students based on their university.

TABLE 4.29 : Mean and Standard Deviation of the Science Doctoral Students on the Use of Electronic Information Resources based on the University

Groups	*N*	*Mean*	*Standard Deviation*	*Minimum*	*Maximum*
University of Kerala	128	51.6680	21.31989	7.50	106.75
University of Calicut	46	35.2717	18.53082	2.50	79.00
CUSAT	68	59.0191	18.91703	11.00	94.00
M. G. University	31	54.4945	14.75941	22.50	92.00
Total	**273**	**51.1617**	**21.03174**	**2.50**	**106.75**

Table 4.30 shows the analysis of variance of the use of electronic information resources based on the university of the science doctoral students.

TABLE 4.30 : ANOVA Test of the Use of Electronic Information Resources by the Science Doctoral Students based on University

Source of Variance	*Sum of Squares*	*d. f*	*Mean Square*	*F*	*Sig.*
Between Groups	16460.948	4	4115.237	10.603	.000
Within Groups	105180.961	271	388.122		
Total	**121641.909**	**275**			

The analysis of variance test indicates that the F value is 10.603 and the significance value is .000, which is less than 0.05. Hence, it is clear that there is a significant difference in the use of electronic information resources between the science doctoral students in different universities. The ANOVA test establishes that there is significant difference in the use of electronic information resources between the science doctoral students in different universities.

3.4.. Frequency of Accessing Electronic Information Resources according to Discipline

The frequency of accessing electronic information resources by the doctoral students in various science disciplines is given in Tables 4.31 to 4.36.

The Table 4.31 shows the frequency of accessing various electronic information resources by the science doctoral students in Bio Sciences. Analysis revealed that the most used electronic information resources by the doctoral students in Bio Sciences are Internet resources. Majority (65.1 per cent) of them are using it once in a day. The second most used electronic information resources are electronic journals, majority (55.8 per cent) of the doctoral students are using it once in a week and few (30.2 per cent) of them are using it once in a day. A good number (46.5 per cent) of them are using network-based services once in a week and few of them are accessing it once in a day. Nearly 23.3 per cent of them are using CD/DVD databases once in a week and about 20.9 per cent of them are accessing it once in a month. A very few number (16.3 per cent) of them are using audio/ video recordings once in a week. It is found that the most used electronic information resources by the doctoral students in Bio Sciences are Internet resources. Majority (65.1 per cent) of them are using it once in a day. The second most used electronic information resources are electronic journals and majority (55.8 per cent) of the doctoral students are using it once in a week. A good number of them are using network-based services once in a week and few of them are accessing it once in a day. A few number of the scholars are using CD/DVD databases once in a week and a very few number of them are using audio/video recordings rarely.

TABLE 4.31 : Frequency of accessing Electronic information resources by the Doctoral Students in Bio Sciences

Electronic Information Resources	*Rarely*	*Once in a Month*	*Once in a Week*	*Once in a Day*
Audio/Video Recordings	8(18.6%)	3(7%)	7(16.3%)	4(9.3%)
CD/DVD Databases	6(14%)	9(20.9%)	10(23.3%)	5(11.6%)
Electronic Journals	_	3(7%)	24(55.8%)	13(30.2%)
Network Based Services	_	2(4.7%)	20(46.5%)	12(27.9%)
Internet Resources	_	1(2.3%)	14(32.6%)	28(65.1%)

Table 4.32 gives the frequency of accessing various electronic information resources by the science doctoral students in Biological Sciences. From the analysis, it is found that the most used electronic information resources by the doctoral students in Biological Sciences are Internet resources. A good number (43.3 per cent) of them are using it once in a day. Nearly 36.7 per cent of them are using Internet resources once in a week. The second most used electronic information resources are network based services and few number (25 per cent) of the scholars are using it once in a week. About 21.7 per cent of them are using network based services once in a day. Majority of the doctoral students are using electronic journals and few (20 per cent) of them are accessing it once in a month. Nearly 11.7 per cent of them are accessing electronic journals once in a day. A few number (16.7 per cent) of the respondents are using CD/DVD databases once in a week and few (18.3 per cent) of them are using audio/video recordings rarely.

TABLE 4.32 : Frequency of accessing Electronic Information Resources by the Doctoral Students in Biological Sciences

Electronic Information Resources	*Rarely*	*Once in a Month*	*Once in a Week*	*Once in a Day*
Audio/Video Recordings	11(18.3%)	2(3.3%)	5(8.3%)	5(8.3%)
CD/DVD Databases	9(15%)	6(10%)	10(16.7%)	4(6.7%)
Electronic Journals	4(6.7%)	12(20%)	10(16.7%)	7(11.7%)
Network Based Services	2(3.3%)	5(8.3%)	15(25%)	13(21.7%)
Internet Resources	2(3.3%)	9(15%)	22(36.7%)	26(43.3%)

It is revealed that the most used electronic information resources by the doctoral students in Biological Sciences are Internet resources. A good number (43.3 per cent) of them are using it once in a day. The second most used electronic information resources are network-based services and little number of the doctoral students is using it once in a day. A very few of them are using electronic journals once in a day. A very few number of the doctoral students are using CD/DVD databases once in a week and very few them are using audio/video recordings rarely.

The frequency of accessing electronic information resources by the Computer Science doctoral students is given in Table 4.33. The analysis shows that all the respondents in Computer Science are using Internet resources and network based services once in a day. Nearly 75 per cent of them are using CD/DVD databases once in a day. Half of the doctoral students are using electronic journals and audio/video recordings once in a day. It is revealed that all the respondents in the Computer Science are using Internet resources and network based services once in a day. Majority of the doctoral students are using CD/DVD databases once in a day. About half of them are using electronic journals and audio/video recordings once in a day.

TABLE 4.33 : Frequency of accessing Electronic Information Resources by the Doctoral Students in Computer Science

Electronic Information Resources	*Once in a Month*	*Once in a Week*	*Once in a Day*
Audio/Video Recordings	1(25%)	_	2(50%)
CD/DVD Databases	_	1(25%)	3(75%)
Electronic Journals	1(25%)	1(25%)	2(50%)
Network Based Services	_	_	4(100%)
Internet Resources	_	_	4(100%)

The doctoral students in Environmental Science were requested to indicate their frequency of use of various electronic information resources and the responses are given in Table 4.34. Analysis shows that most used electronic information resources in Environmental Science are Internet resources. Nearly 38.5 per cent of the doctoral students are using Internet resources once in a day and 34.6 per cent of them are using it once in a week. Majority of the respondents are using CD/DVD databases and few (30.8 per cent) of them are accessing it one in a month. A few numbers (34.6 per cent) of them are using network-based services once in a week and about 15.4 per cent of them are using it once in a day. Nearly 26.9 per cent of the scholars are using electronic journals once in a week and a very few (11.5 per cent) of them are using it once in a day. A few number (23.1 per cent) of the doctoral students are using audio/video recordings rarely.

TABLE 4.34 : Frequency of accessing Electronic Information Resources by the Doctoral Students in Environmental Science

Electronic Information Resources	*Rarely*	*Once in a Month*	*Once in a Week*	*Once in a Day*
Audio/Video Recordings	6(23.1%)	1(3.8%)	1(3.8%)	2(7.7%)
CD/DVD Databases	8(30.8%)	8(30.8%)	3(11.5%)	1(3.8%)
Electronic Journals	2(7.7%)	4(15.4%)	7(26.9%)	3(11.5%)
Network Based Services	–	3(11.5%)	9(34.6%)	4(15.4%)
Internet Resources	2(7.7%)	4(15.4%)	9(34.6%)	10(38.5%)

It is found that most of the studied used electronic information resources in Environmental Science are Internet resources. A few numbers of the doctoral students are using Internet resources once in a day. Some (34.6 per cent) of the respondents are using network-based services once in a week and very few of them are using it once in a day. A few numbers of them are using electronic journals once in a week and very few of them are using it once in a day. Some (34.6 per cent) of them are using CD/DVD databases once in a month. A very few of them are using audio/video recordings rarely.

Table 4.35 shows the frequency of accessing electronic information resources by the doctoral students in Mathematical Science. Analysis reveals that the most used electronic information resources by the doctoral students in Mathematical Science are Internet resources. A good number (42.9 per cent) of them are using it once in a week while 38.1 per cent of them are using it once in a day. The second most used electronic information resources are electronic journals and few number (23.8 per cent) of them are using it once in a month, about 19 per cent of them are using it once in a week. Nearly 23.8 per cent of the doctoral students are using network-based services once in a month and 19 per cent of them are using it once in a day. A very few number of the doctoral students are using CD/DVD databases and audio/ video recordings rarely.

TABLE 4.35 : Frequency of accessing Electronic Information Resources by the Doctoral Students in Mathematical Science

Electronic Information Resources	*Rarely*	*Once in a Month*	*Once in a Week*	*Once in a Day*
Audio/Video Recordings	3(14.3%)	_	_	_
CD/DVD Databases	3(14.3%)	2(9.5%)	_	1(4.8%)
Electronic Journals	_	5(23.8%)	4(19%)	2(9.5%)
Network Based Services	_	5(23.8%)	1(4.8%)	4(19%)
Internet Resources	2(9.5%)	1(4.8%)	9(42.9%)	8(38.1%)

It is found that the most used electronic information resources by the doctoral students in Mathematical Science are Internet resources. A good number (42.9 per cent) of them are using it once in a week, and few of them are using it once in a day. The second most used electronic information resources are electronic journals and few of them are using it once in a month. A few number of the doctoral students are using network based services once in a month and very few of them are using it once in a day. A very few number of them are using CD/DVD databases and audio/video recordings rarely.

The doctoral students in Physical Sciences were requested to indicate their frequency of use of various electronic information resources and the responses are given in Table 4.36. The analysis shows that the most used electronic information resources by the doctoral students in Physical Sciences are Internet resources. Majority (72.1 per cent) of them are using it once in a day. The second most used electronic information resources are electronic journals, about 36.9 per cent of the scholars are using it once in a week and 28.7 per cent of them are using it once in a day. Nearly 32 per cent of the doctoral students are using network based services once in a week while 29.5 per cent of them are using it once in a day. Majority of the scholars are using CD/DVD databases and very few (12.3 per cent) of them are using it once in a day. Nearly 18 per cent of them are rarely using audio/video recordings.

TABLE 4.36 : Frequency of Accessing Electronic Information Resources by the Doctoral Students in Physical Sciences

Electronic Information Resources	*Rarely*	*Once in a Month*	*Once in a Week*	*Once in a Day*
Audio/Video Recordings	22(18%)	1(0.8%)	7(5.7%)	6(4.9%)
CD/DVD Databases	25(20.5%)	27(22.1%)	16(13.1%)	15(12.3%)
Electronic Journals	3(2.5%)	19(15.6%)	45(36.9%)	35(28.7%)
Network Based Services	6(4.9%)	11(9%)	39(32%)	36(29.5%)
Internet Resources	2(1.6%)	4(3.3%)	23(18.9%)	88(72.1%)

It is revealed that the most used electronic information resources by the doctoral students in Physical Sciences are Internet resources. Majority (72.1 per cent) of them are using it once in a day. The second most used electronic information resources are electronic journals and few of them are using it once in a day. A few number of the doctoral students are using network based services once in a week and few of them are using it once in a day. A very few number of the scholars are using CD/DVD databases once in a day and very few of them are rarely using audio/video recordings.

3.5. Relation between the Frequency of Use of Electronic Information Resources and Discipline of the Doctoral Students

Table 4.37 shows the mean and standard deviations on the use of electronic information resources for doctoral students based on their discipline.

TABLE 4.37 : Mean and S. Ds of the Science Doctoral Students on the Use of Electronic Information Resources according to Discipline

Groups	*N*	*Mean*	*Standard Deviation*	*Minimum*	*Maximum*
Bio Sciences	41	60.5872	17.78893	13.00	92.00
Biological Sciences	60	46.2208	22.09734	7.00	103.00
Computer Science	3	86.4375	18.64401	62.00	106.75
Environmental Science	26	44.0769	17.72382	12.50	85.00
Mathematical Science	21	32.9048	17.83001	8.25	68.00
Physical Sciences	122	53.7654	19.26189	2.50	101.00
Total	**273**	**51.1617**	**21.03174**	**2.50**	**106.75**

Table 4.38 shows the analysis of variance of the use of electronic information resources based on the discipline of the doctoral students.

TABLE 4.38 : ANOVA Test of the Use of Electronic Information Resources for Science Doctoral Students according to Discipline

Source of Variance	*Sum of Squares*	*d. f*	*Mean Square*	*F*	*Sig.*
Between Groups	19394.119	5	3878.824	10.243	.000
Within Groups	102247.789	270	378.696		
Total	**121641.909**	**275**			

The analysis of variance test indicates that the F value is 10.243 and the significance value is .000, which is less than 0.05. Hence, it is clear that there is a significant difference in the use of electronic information resources between the science doctoral students in different disciplines. The ANOVA test establishes that there is significant difference in the use of electronic information resources by the science doctoral students in different disciplines.

4. THE WAYS OF IDENTIFYING ELECTRONIC INFORMATION RESOURCES FOR RESEARCH

The responses of the science doctoral students regarding the ways they used for identifying the electronic information resources for research according to the university and the discipline are further analysed.

4.1 Ways of Identifying Electronic Information Resources for Research according to University

Table 4.39 indicates how the science doctoral students in the five universities in Kerala are identifying the electronic information resources for their research work. Analysis shows that for identifying the electronic information resources, nearly large majority (84.1 per cent) of the science doctoral students are using Internet search engines. A good number of them are using seminars and conferences (47.5 per cent), bibliographical citations in printed documents (47.1 per cent) and citations in electronic sources (45.7 per cent) for identifying electronic information resources. A few number (21 per cent) of them are subscribing mailing list or news groups for finding electronic information resources.

Majority of the science doctoral students in University of Kerala are using Internet search engines (82.8 per cent) and bibliographical citations in printed sources (51.6 per cent) for identifying electronic information resources for research. A good number of them are using personal communication (49.2 per cent), seminars and conferences (46.9 per cent) and citations in e-sources (41.4 per cent) for identifying electronic information resources. In University of Calicut, nearly large majority (84.8 per cent) of the doctoral students are using Internet search engines. A good number (43.5 per cent) of them are using personal communication for identifying electronic information resources for research. In

CUSAT also large majority (86.8 per cent) of the science doctoral students are using Internet search engines. Majority of them are using personal communication (73.5 per cent), citations in e-sources (60.3 per cent) and seminars and conferences (57.4 per cent) for identifying electronic information resources for research. The most used way for identifying electronic information resources in M. G. University is Internet search engines. Majority of them are using seminars and conferences (61.3 per cent), citations in e-sources (64.5 per cent) and bibliographical citations in printed sources (58.1 per cent). All the science doctoral students in the Kannur University are using Internet search engine for identifying the electronic information resources for research.

TABLE 4.39 : Ways of Identifying Electronic Information Resources according to University

Identifying Electronic Information Resources	*Kerala*	*Calicut*	*CUSAT*	*M. G.*	*Grand Total*
Through personal communication	63 (49.20%)	20 (43.50%)	50 (73.50%)	14 (45.20%)	147 (53.30%)
Seminars and conferences	60 (46.90%)	12 (26.10%)	39 (57.40%)	19 (61.30%)	130 (47.50%)
Citations in e- sources	53 (41.40%)	10 (21.70%)	41 (60.30%)	20 (64.50%)	124 (45.70%)
Bibliographical citations in printed sources	66 (51.60%)	16 (34.80%)	29 (42.60%)	18 (58.10%)	129 (47.10%)
Use Internet search engines	106 (82.80%)	39 (84.80%)	59 (86.80%)	25 (80.60%)	229 (84.10%)
Subscribe to mailing list or news groups	24 (18.80%)	8 (17.40%)	20 (29.40%)	5 (16.10%)	58 (21%)

It is revealed that for identifying the electronic

information resources, nearly large majority (84.1 per cent) of the science doctoral students are using Internet search engines. It is also found that majority of the science doctoral students in University of Kerala, University of Calicut and M. G. University are using Internet search engines for finding electronic information resources for research. A large majority of the science doctoral students in CUSAT are also using Internet search engines for identifying electronic information resources for research.

4.2. Ways of Identifying Electronic Information Resources for Research according to Discipline

Table 4.40 indicates how the doctoral students in various science disciplines are identifying the electronic information resources for their research. Analysis shows that a large majority (90.7 per cent) of the doctoral students in Bio Sciences are using Internet search engines for identifying electronic information resources for research. Nearly 69.8 per cent of them are using seminars and conferences, and citations in e-sources for finding the electronic information resources for research. Majority (83.3 per cent) of the doctoral students in Biological Sciences are using Internet search engines and a good number (40 per cent) of them are using citations in printed sources for finding electronic information resources for research. All the doctoral students in Computer Science are using Internet search engines for finding the electronic information resources. About 75 per cent of them are using seminars and conferences, and citations in e-sources for finding the electronic information resources for research. In Environmental Science, large majority (92.3 per cent) of the doctoral students are using Internet search engines and majority of them are using personal communication (79.9 per cent), citations in printed sources (61.5 per cent), and seminars and conferences (53.8 per cent) for finding the electronic information resources for research. Majority of the doctoral students in Mathematical

Science are using Internet search engines (81 per cent), personal communication (61.9 per cent), and seminars and conferences (52.4 per cent) for finding the electronic information resources for research. In Physical Sciences also majority (80.3 per cent) of the doctoral students are using Internet search engines for finding the electronic information resources for research. Nearly 57.4 per cent of them are also using personal communication and 50 per cent of them are using citations in e-sources for identifying the electronic information resources.

TABLE 4.40 : Ways of Identifying Electronic Information Resources for Research according to Discipline

Discipline	*Through personal comm-unication*	*Seminars and confer-ences*	*Citations in e-sources*	*Citations in printed sources*	*Use Internet search engines*	*Mailing list or news groups*
Bio Sciences	19 (44.20%)	21 (48.80%)	30 (69.80%)	30 (69.80%)	39 (90.70%)	13 (30.20%)
Biological Sciences	23 (38.30%)	23 (38.30%)	15 (25%)	24 (40%)	50 (83.30%)	8 (13.30%)
Computer Science	2 (50%)	3 (75%)	3 (75%)	2 (50%)	4 (100%)	1 (25%)
Environmental Science	20 (76.90%)	14 (53.80%)	11 (42.30%)	16 (61.50%)	24 (92.30%)	8 (30.80%)
Mathematical Science	13 (61.90%)	11 (52.40%)	6 (28.60%)	6 (28.60%)	17 (81%)	–
Physical Sciences	70 (57.40%)	59 (48.40%)	61 (50%)	52 (42.60%)	98 (80.30%)	28 (23%)
Grand Total	**147 (53.30%)**	**131 (47.50%)**	**126 (45.70%)**	**130 (47.10%)**	**232 (84.10%)**	**58 (21%)**

It is found that all the respondents in Computer Science and a large majority of the doctoral students in Bio Sciences and Environmental Science are using Internet search engines for finding the electronic information resources for research. Majority of the doctoral students in Biological Sciences, Mathematical Science and Physical Sciences are also using Internet search engines for identifying the electronic information resources for research.

5. METHODS OF LEARNING INTERNET

The responses of the science doctoral students regarding the methods of learning Internet are further analysed.

5.1. Methods of Learning Internet According to University

Table 4.41 describes how the science doctoral students in the universities in Kerala have learned to use the Internet. Majority of the science doctoral students are learned to use the Internet through self-learning (58.3 per cent) and by the assistance from friends and teachers (54.3 per cent). For learning Internet a very few number of them are used the online instruction, literature (computer magazines etc) and the instruction from the library staff.

TABLE 4.41 : Methods of Learning Internet According to University

Method of learning Internet	*Kerala*	*Calicut*	*CUSAT*	*M. G.*	*Grand Total*
By a course	17 (13.3%)	7 (15.2%)	5 (7.4%)	4 (12.9%)	33 (12.3%)
Instruction by library staff	12 (9.4%)	1 (2.2%)	10 (14.7%)	–	23 (8.3%)
Friends,	72 (56.3%)	26 (56.5%)	33 (48.5%)	19 (61.3%)	150 (54.3%)
Self learning	67 (52.3%)	19 (41.3%)	53 (77.9%)	21 (67.7%)	160 (58.3%)
From literature	10 (7.8%)	6 (13.0%)	16 (23.5%)	4 (12.9%)	36 (13%)
On line instruction	16 (12.5%)	4 (8.7%)	19 (27.9%)	6 (19.4%)	45 (16.7%)

Analysis shows that majority of the science doctoral students in University of Kerala have learned to use the Internet with the assistance of friends and teachers (56.3 per cent) and self-learning method (52.3 per cent). In University of Calicut also majority (56.5 per cent) of the doctoral students are learned Internet with the assistance of friends and teachers. A good number (41.3 per cent) of them have learned it through self-learning method. Majority (77.9 per cent) of the science doctoral students in CUSAT learned to use the Internet through self-learning. A good number (48.5 per cent) of them learned it with the assistance of friends and teachers. In M. G. University, majority of the scholars are learned Internet through self-learning (67.7 per cent) and assistance of friends and teachers (61.3 per cent).

It is revealed that majority of the science doctoral students have learned to use the Internet through self-learning method and by the assistance from friends and teachers. It is also found that majority of the science doctoral students in CUSAT and M. G. University have learned the Internet through self-learning method. Majority of the respondents in University of Kerala and University of Calicut have learned the Internet with the assistance from friends and teachers.

5.2. Methods of Learning Internet According to Discipline

Table 4.42 describes how the doctoral students in various science disciplines have learned to use various Internet tools and services. Analysis shows that majority (58.1 per cent) of the doctoral students in Bio Sciences have learned to use Internet with the assistance of friends and teachers. About 55.8 per cent of them learned to use the Internet by self-learning method. Majority of the doctoral students in Biological Sciences have learned the Internet by self-learning method and a good number of them are learned to use Internet with the assistance of friends and teachers. Nearly 75 per cent of the respondents in Computer science have learned to use the Internet with the help of friends and teachers. In the

Environmental science majority (57.7 per cent) of the scholars have learned the Internet by self-learning method. Majority (61.9 per cent) of the doctoral students in Mathematical Science have learned to use Internet with the assistance of friends and teachers and about 52.4 per cent of them learned to use the Internet by self-learning method. Nearly 64.8 per cent of the doctoral students in Physical Sciences are learned the Internet by self-learning method. About 53.3 per cent of them are learned to use Internet with the assistance of friends and teachers.

TABLE 4.42 : Methods of Learning Internet According to Discipline

Discipline	*Methods of learning Internet*					
	By a course	*Instruction by library staff*	*Friends, teachers assistance*	*Self learning*	*From Literature*	*On line instruction*
Bio Sciences	4 (9.30%)	2 (4.70%)	25 (58.10%)	24 (55.80%)	2 (4.70%)	6 (14%)
Biological Sciences	11 (18.30%)	2 (3.30%)	29 (48.30%)	30 (50%)	5 (8.30%)	6 (10%)
Computer Science	2 (50%)	1 (25%)	3 (75%)	2 (50%)	1 (25%)	2 (50%)
Environmental Science	5 (19.20%)	3 (11.50%)	11 (42.30%)	15 (57.70%)	7 (26.90%)	5 (19.20%)
Mathematical Science	1 (4.80%)	4 (19%)	13 (61.90%)	11 (52.40%)	1 (4.80%)	–
Physical Sciences	11 (9%)	11 (9%)	65 (53.30%)	79 (64.8	20 (16.40%)	26 (21.30%)
Grand Total	**34 (12.30%)**	**23 (8.30%)**	**150 (54.30%)**	**161 (58.30%)**	**36 (13%)**	**46 (16.70%)**

Although a variety of methods are used to learn the Internet, majority of the doctoral students in Bio Sciences, Computer Science and Mathematical Science are used the assistance of friends and teachers and majority of the doctoral students in Biological Sciences, Environmental Science and Physical sciences are used self-learning method for learning the Internet.

6. FREQUENCY OF USE OF INTERNET TOOLS AND RESOURCES

The science doctoral students' frequency of use of various Internet tools and resources is given in Table 4.43. Analysis shows that the most frequently used Internet tool is e-mail. Most of the science doctoral students are using e-mail and a good number (48.9 per cent) of them are using it once in a day. The second most frequently used Internet service is online search and about 48.6 per cent of the respondents are using it once in a day. Nearly 70.3 per cent of them are using external catalogue / databases and few (23.2 per cent) of them are using it once in a week. Majority of them are using document delivery services (54 per cent), electronic journals (83.3 per cent), WWW resources (78.3 per cent) and down loading services (73.6 per cent) related to their research. A few numbers of them are using electronic journals (24.6 per cent), WWW resources (30.1 per cent) and down loading services (13 per cent) once in a day. Nearly 37.7 per cent of the respondents are using electronic journals once in a week. Majority of them are using the discussion list, news groups and few of them are using it rarely.

It is found that the most frequently used Internet tool is e-mail. Nearly most (94.6 per cent) of the science doctoral students are using e-mail and a good number (48.9 per cent) of them are using it once in a day. The second most frequently used Internet service is online search and a good number (48.6 per cent) of the respondents are using it once in a day. Majority of them are using electronic journals, WWW resources, down loading services, external catalogue/ databases, discussion list, news groups and document delivery services related to their research. A few numbers of them are using electronic journals and WWW resources once in a day.

TABLE 4.43 : Frequency of Use of Internet Tools and Resources by the Science Doctoral Students

Internet Tools/ Resources	*Never*	*Rarely*	*Once in a Month*	*Once in a Week*	*Once in a Day*
E – mail	15(5.4%)	25(9.1%)	23(8.3%)	78(28.3%)	135(48.9%)
Discussion list, News groups	124(44.9%)	63(22.8%)	25(9.1%)	41(14.9%)	23(8.3%)
External catalogue / Databases	82(29.7%)	71(25.7%)	38(13.8%)	64(23.2%)	21(7.6%)
Document delivery services	127(46%)	69(25%)	26(9.4%)	37(13.4%)	17(6.2%)
Electronic journals	46(16.7%)	22(8%)	36(13%)	104(37.7%)	68(24.6%)
WWW resources	60(21.7%)	23(8.3%)	35(12.7%)	75(27.2%)	83(30.1%)
Down loading services	73(26.4%)	50(18.1%)	43(15.6%)	74(26.8%)	36(13%)
Online search	17(6.2%)	1(0.4%)	22(8%)	102(36.8%)	134(48.6%)

6.1. Frequency of Use of Internet Tools and Resources according to University

The science doctoral students' frequency of use of Internet tools and resources in the five universities in Kerala are given in Tables 4.44 to 4.47. Table 4.44 gives the frequency of use of various Internet tools and resources by the science doctoral students in University of Kerala.

Analysis revealed that the most used Internet tool by the science doctoral students in University of Kerala is e-mail. Nearly 94.5 per cent of them are using e-mail and few (33.6 per cent) of them are using it once in a day. The second most used Internet service is online search and a good number (48.4 per cent) of the doctoral students are using it once in a day while 41.4 per cent of them are using it once in a week. Nearly 79.7 per cent of the respondents are using electronic journals and a good number (44.5 per cent) of them are using it once in a week. Majority (68.7 per cent) of the science doctoral students are using external catalogue/ databases and few (22.7 per cent) of them are using it once in a week. Nearly 76.6 per cent of the scholars are using WWW resources and about 34.4 per cent of them are using it once in a week. Majority (69.5 per cent) of the scholars are using down loading services and 25 per cent of them are using it once in a week. Majority of them are not using document delivery services related to their research.

TABLE 4.44 : Frequency of Use of Internet Tools and Resources by the Science Doctoral Students in University of Kerala

Internet Tools/ Resources	*Never*	*Rarely*	*Once in a Month*	*Once in a Week*	*Once in a Day*
E – mail	7(5.5%)	13(10.2%)	14(10.9%)	51(39.8%)	43(33.6%)
Discussion list, News groups	54(42.2%)	25(19.5%)	21(16.4%)	18(14.1%)	10(7.8%)
External catalogue / Dsatabases	40(31.3%)	24(18.8%)	21(16.4%)	29(22.7%)	14(10.9%)
Document delivery services	67(52.3%)	22(17.2%)	10(7.8%)	22(17.2%)	7(5.5%)
Electronic journals	26(20.3%)	_	16(12.5%)	57(44.5%)	29(22.7%)
WWW resources	30(23.4%)	7(5.5%)	15(11.7%)	44(34.4%)	32(25%)
Down loading services	39(30.5%)	22(17.2%)	17(13.3%)	32(25%)	18(14.1%)
Online search	8(6.2%)	_	5(3.9%)	53(41.4%)	62(48.4%)

It is revealed that the most used Internet tool by the science doctoral students in University of Kerala is e-mail. Large majority (94.5 per cent) of them are using e-mail and few of them are using it once in a day. The second most used Internet service is online search and a good number of the doctoral students are using it once in a day. Majority of the respondents are using electronic journals and a good number of them are using it once in a week. Majority of the doctoral students are using external catalogue/ databases and few of them are using it once in a week. Majority of them are using WWW resources and down loading services where as few of them are using it once in a week. Majority of them are not using document delivery services related to their research.

Table 4.45 shows the frequency of use of various Internet tools and resources by the science doctoral students in the University of Calicut. Analysis revealed that in University of Calicut also the most used Internet tool is e-mail. A large majority (87 per cent) of the science doctoral student are using e-mail and few (32.6 per cent) of them are using it once in a day. The second most used Internet service is online search and about 30.4 per cent of them are using it once in a day. Nearly 67.4 per cent of the science doctoral students are using WWW resources and few (24 per cent) of them are using it once in a week. Majority (60.9 per cent) of the scholars are using electronic journals and few (23.9 per cent) of them are using it once in a week. Majority (58.7 per cent) of the scholars are using external catalogue/ databases while few (34.8 per cent) of them are using it rarely. Nearly 52.2 per cent of the science doctoral students are using down loading services and 19.6 per cent of them are using it once in a week. Majority of them are not using document delivery services (63 per cent) and discussion list, news groups (58.7 per cent) related to their research.

TABLE 4.45 : **Frequency of Use of Internet Tools and Resources by the Science Doctoral Students in University of Calicut**

Internet Tools/ Resources	*Never*	*Rarely*	*Once in a Month*	*Once in a Week*	*Once in a Day*
E – mail	6(13%)	5(10.9%)	6(13%)	14(30.4%)	15(32.6%)
Discussion list, News groups	27(58.7%)	14(30.4%)	2(4.3%)	1(2.2%)	2(4.3%)
External catalogue / Databases	19(41.3%)	16(34.8%)	6(13%)	4(8.7%)	1(2.2%)
Document delivery services	29(63%)	12(26.1%)	2(4.3%)	2(4.3%)	1(2.2%)
Electronic journals	19(41.3%)	6(13%)	7(15.2%)	11(23.9%)	3(6.5%)
WWW resources	15(32.6%)	8(17.4%)	6(13%)	11(24%)	6(13%)
Down loading services	22(47.8%)	7(15.2%)	7(15.2%)	9(19.6%)	1(2.1%)
Online search	7(15.2%)	_	10(21.7%)	15(32.6%)	14(30.4%)

It is revealed that in University of Calicut also the most used Internet tool is e-mail. Large majority (87 per cent) of the science doctoral students are using e-mail and few of them are using it once in a day. The second most used Internet service is online search and few numbers of them are using it once in a day. Majority of the scholars are using WWW resources and electronic journals and few of them are using it once in a week. Majority of the scholars are using external catalogue/ databases while few of them are using it rarely. Majority of the science doctoral students are using down loading services and few of them are using it once in a week. Majority of them are not using document delivery services and discussion list, news groups related to their research.

The frequency of use of Internet tools and resources by the science doctoral students in CUSAT is analysed and summarised in Table 4.46.

TABLE 4.46 : Frequency of Use of Internet Tools and Resources by the Science Doctoral Students in CUSAT

Internet Tools/ Resources	*Never*	*Rarely*	*Once in a Month*	*Once in a Week*	*Once in a Day*
E – mail	–	3(4.4%)	3(4.4%)	12(17.6%)	50(73.5%)
Discussion list, News groups	26(38.2%)	20(29.4%)	2(2.9%)	10(14.7%)	10(14.7%)
External catalogue / Databases	18(26.5%)	22(32.4%)	3(4.4%)	19(27.9%)	6(8.8%)
Document delivery services	21(30.9%)	18(26.5%)	13(19.1%)	7(10.3%)	9(13.2%)
Electronic journals	–	13(19.1%)	8(11.8%)	15(22.1%)	32(47.1%)
WWW resources	9(13.2%)	1(1.5%)	9(13.2%)	12(17.6%)	37(54.4%)
Down loading services	11(16.2%)	13(19.1%)	12(17.6%)	17(25%)	15(22.1%)
Online search	2(2.9%)	–	2(2.9%)	24(35.3%)	40(58.8%)

The analysis shows that all the science doctoral students in CUSAT are using both e-mail and electronic journals related to their research. Nearly 73.5 per cent of them are using e-mail once in a day. A good number (47.1 per cent) of them are using the electronic journals once in a day. Most of the scholars are using online search and majority (58.8 per cent) of them are using it once in a day. Nearly

86.8 per cent of the scholars are using WWW resources and 54.4 per cent of them are using it once in a day. Majority (83.8 per cent) of the doctoral students are using down loading services and few of them are using it once in a week. Nearly 73.5 per cent of them are using external catalogue/ databases and few of them are using it rarely. Majority of them are using discussion list, newsgroups and document delivery services, and few of them are using it rarely.

It is revealed that most of the science doctoral students in CUSAT are using both e-mail and electronic journals related to their research. Majority (73.5 per cent) of them are using e-mail and a good number (47.1 per cent) of them are using the electronic journals once in a day. Most of the respondents are using online search and majority of them are using it once in a day. Large majority of the science doctoral students are using WWW resources and majority of them are using it once in a day. Majority of the doctoral students are using down loading services and few of them are using it once in a week. Majority of them are using discussion list, newsgroups and document delivery services, and few of them are using it rarely.

Table 4.47 gives the frequency of use of various Internet tools and resources in M. G. University. Analysis reveals that the most used Internet service by the science doctoral students in M. G. University is online search. All the respondents are using online search and a good number (48.4 per cent) of them are using it once in a day. Most of the science doctoral students are using electronic journals and down loading services. About 64.5 per cent of them are using electronic journals once in a week while a good number (45.1 per cent) of them are using down loading services once in a week. Nearly 93.5 per cent of the scholars are using e-mail and majority (80.6 per cent) of them are using it once in a day. Majority (83.9 per cent) of the scholars are using external catalogue/ databases and few (32.3 per cent) of them are using it once in a week. Nearly 80.6 per cent of the doctoral students are using WWW resources and about 25.8 per cent of them are using it once in a day. Majority (74.2 per cent) of the science doctoral students are using document delivery services and majority of them are using it rarely. A good number (48.4 per cent) of them are using discussion list, newsgroups and few of them are using it once in a week.

TABLE 4.47 : Frequency of Use of Internet Tools and Resources by the Science Doctoral Students in M. G. University

Internet Tools/ Resources	*Never*	*Rarely*	*Once in a Month*	*Once in a Week*	*Once in a Day*
E – mail	2(6.5%)	3(9.7%)	_	1(3.2%)	25(80.6%)
Discussion list, News groups	16(51.6%)	3(9.7%)	_	11(35.5%)	1(3.2%)
External catalogue / Databases	5(16.1%)	8(25.8%)	8(25.8%)	10(32.3%)	_
Document delivery services	8(25.8%)	17(54.8%)	1(3.2%)	5(16.1%)	_
Electronic journals	1(3.2%)	3(9.7%)	4(12.9%)	20(64.5%)	3(9.7%)
WWW resources	6(19.4%)	5(16.1%)	5(16.1%)	7(22.6%)	8(25.8%)
Down loading services	1(3.2%)	8(25.8%)	6(19.4%)	14(45.1%)	2(6.5%)
Online search	_	1(3.2%)	5(16.1%)	10(32.3%)	15(48.4%)

It is found that the most used Internet service by the science doctoral students in M. G. University is online search. All the respondents are using online search and a good number (48.4 per cent) of them are using it once in a day. Most of the science doctoral students are using electronic journals and majority of them are using it once in a week. Most of them are using down loading services and a good number of them are using it once in a week. Large majority of the doctoral students are using e-mail and majority of them are using it once in a day. Majority of the scholars are using external catalogue/ databases and few of them are using it once in a week. Majority of them are using WWW resources and few of them are using it once in a day. Majority of the science doctoral students are using document delivery services and majority of them are using it rarely. A good number of them are using discussion list, newsgroups and few of them are using it once in a week.

Relation between the Use of Internet Tools and Resources and the University of the Science Doctoral Students

Table 4.48 shows the mean and standard deviations on the use of Internet tools and resources for science doctoral students based on their university.

TABLE 4.48 : Mean and S. Ds of the Science Doctoral Students on the Use of Internet Tools and Resources according to University

Groups	*N*	*Mean*	*Standard Deviation*	*Minimum*	*Maximum*
University of Kerala	128	23.0391	7.50265	2.00	40.00
University of Calicut	46	17.8696	6.68534	7.00	38.00
CUSAT	68	26.7353	6.61210	12.00	40.00
M. G. University	31	24.8065	5.39394	17.00	35.00
Total	**273**	**23.3152**	**7.46034**	**2.00**	**40.00**

Table 4.49 shows the analysis of variance of the use of Internet tools and resources based on the university of the science doctoral students.

TABLE 4.49 : **ANOVA Test of the Use of Internet Tools and Resources for Science Doctoral Students Based on University**

Source of Variance	*Sum of Squares*	*d. f*	*Mean Square*	*F*	*Sig.*
Between Groups	2254.813	4	563.703	11.705	.000
Within Groups	13050.763	271	48.158		
Total	**15305.576**	**275**			

The analysis of variance test indicates that the F value is 11.705 and the significance value is .000, which is less than 0.05. Hence, it is clear that there is a significant difference in the use of Internet tools and resources by the science doctoral students in different universities. The ANOVA test establishes that there is significant difference in the use of electronic information resources between science doctoral students based on their universities.

6.2. Frequency of Use of Internet Tools and Resources according to Discipline

The use of Internet tools and resources by the doctoral students in various science disciplines are given in Tables 4.50 to 4.55.

Table 4.50 shows the frequency of use of various Internet tools and resources by the doctoral students in Bio Sciences. Analysis shows that most frequently used Internet services in Bio Sciences are electronic journals and online search. Nearly 97.7 per cent of the doctoral students are using electronic journals and online search related to research. Majority (60.5 per cent) of the doctoral students are conducting online search and a good number (44.2 per cent) of them are using electronic journals once in a day. About 48.8 per cent of them are using electronic journals (48.8 per cent) once in a week. The second most used Internet tool is e-mail and majority (55.8 per cent) of the doctoral students are using it once in a day. Large majority (88.4 per cent) of the scholars are using external catalogue/ databases and a good number (46.5 per cent) of them are using it once in a week. Nearly 81.4 per cent of the doctoral students are using WWW resources and few (37.2 per cent) of them are using it once in a day. Majority of the doctoral students are using discussion list, newsgroups and a few number (32.6 per cent) of them are using it rarely. Nearly 51.2 per cent of the scholars are using document delivery services and 18.6 per cent of them are using it once in a week.

TABLE 5.50 : Frequency of Use of Internet Tools and Resources by the Doctoral Students in Bio Sciences

Internet Tools/ Resources	*Never*	*Rarely*	*Once in a Month*	*Once in a Week*	*Once in a Day*
E – mail	2(4.7%)	3(7%)	4(9.3%)	10(23.3%)	24(55.8%)
Discussion list, News groups	14(32.6%)	14(32.6%)	6(14%)	8(18.6%)	1(2.3%)
External catalogue / Databases	5(11.6%)	8(18.6%)	5(11.6%)	20(46.5%)	5(11.6%)
Document delivery services	21(48.8%)	7(16.3%)	4(9.3%)	8(18.6%)	3(7%)
Electronic journals	1(2.3%)	–	2(4.7%)	21(48.8%)	19(44.2%)
WWW resources	8(18.6%)	1(2.3%)	3(7%)	15(34.9%)	16(37.2%)
Down loading services	9(20.9%)	10(23.3%)	5(11.6%)	15(34.9%)	4(9.3%)
Online search	1(2.3%)	–	–	16(37.2%)	26(60.5%)

It is found that most frequently used Internet services in Bio Sciences are electronic journals and online search. Majority (60.5 per cent) of doctoral students are conducting online search and a good number (44.2 per cent) of them are using electronic journals once in a day. The second most used Internet tool is e-mail and majority of the doctoral students are using it once in a day. Large majority of the respondents are using external catalogue/ databases and a good number of them are using it once in a week. Majority of the doctoral students are using WWW resources and few of them are using it once in a day. Majority of the scholars are using discussion list, newsgroups and a few number of them are using it rarely. Majority of the doctoral students are using document delivery services and very few of them are using it once in a week.

Table 4.51 gives the frequency of use of various Internet tools and resources by the doctoraj students in Biological Sciences.

Analysis reveals that most used Internet tool by the doctoral students in Biological Sciences is e-mail. Large majority (93.3 per cent) of the doctoral students are using e-mail and few (36.7 per cent) of them are using it once in a day. The second most used Internet service is online search, a large majority of the doctoral students are using online search and about 43.3 per cent of them are using it once in a day. Nearly 86.7 per cent of the respondents are using WWW resources and few (25 per cent) of them are accessing it once in a day. Majority (75 per cent) of the scholars are using electronic journals and few number (31.7 per cent) of them are using it once in a week. Majority of the doctoral students are using external catalogue/ databases and down loading services and few of them are using it once in a day. A good number (46.7 per cent) of the respondents are using discussion list, newsgroups and document delivery services. A very few of them are using it once in a day.

TABLE 4.51 : Frequency of Use of Internet Tools and Resources by the Doctoral Students in Biological Sciences

Internet Tools/ Resources	*Never*	*Rarely*	*Once in a Month*	*Once in a Week*	*Once in a Day*
E – mail	4(6.7%)	4(6.7%)	9(15%)	21(35%)	22(36.7%)
Discussion list, News groups	32(53.3%)	9(15%)	7(11.7%)	6(10%)	6(10%)
External catalogue / Databases	21(35%)	12(20%)	11(18.3%)	8(13.3%)	8(13.3%)
Document delivery services	33(55%)	10(16.7%)	6(10%)	8(13.3%)	3(5%)
Electronic journals	15(25%)	8(13.3%)	11(18.3%)	19(31.7%)	7(11.7%)
WWW resources	8(13.3%)	8(13.3%)	12(20%)	17(28.3%)	15(25%)
Down loading services	22(36.7%)	9(15%)	7(11.7%)	15(25%)	7(11.7%)
Online search	5(8.3%)	1(1.7%)	11(18.3%)	17(28.3%)	26(43.3%)

It is found that most used Internet tool by the doctoral students in Biological Sciences is e-mail. Large majority of the doctoral students are using e-mail and a few number of them are using it once in a day. The second most used Internet service is online search, a large majority of the scholars are using online search and a good number of them are using it once in a day. Large majority of the doctoral students are using WWW resources and few of them are accessing it once in a day. Majority of the scholars are using electronic journals and few of them are using it once in a week. Majority of them are using external catalogue/ databases and down loading services and very few number of them are using it once in a day. A good number of the doctoral students are using discussion list, newsgroups and document delivery services and a very few of them are using it once in a day.

The frequency of use of Internet tools and resources by the doctoral students in Computer Science are given in Table 4.52. Analysis shows that all the respondents in the Computer Science are using e-mail, external catalogue/ databases, electronic journals, WWW resources, down loading services and online search. All the doctoral students are using e-mail and online search once in a day. Majority of them are using electronic journals (75 per cent), WWW resources (50 per cent) and document delivery services (50 per cent) once in a day. Nearly 50 per cent of them are using discussion list, newsgroups and external catalogue/ databases once in a week.

TABLE 4.52 : Frequency of Use of Internet Tools and Resources by the Doctoral Students in Computer Science

Internet Tools/ Resources	*Never*	*Rarely*	*Once in a Month*	*Once in a Week*	*Once in a Day*
E – mail	_	_	_	_	4(100%)
Discussion list, News groups	1(25%)	_	_	2(50%)	1(25%)
External catalogue / Databases	_	1(25%)	_	2(50%)	1(25%)
Document delivery services	1(25%)	_	_	1(25%)	2(50%)
Electronic journals	_	_	1(25%)	_	3(75%)
WWW resources	_	_	_	2(50%)	2(50%)
Down loading services	_	1(25%)	1(25%)	1(25%)	1(25%)
Online search	_	_	_	_	4(100%)

It is revealed that in Computer Science all the respondents are using e-mail, external catalogue/databases, electronic journals, WWW resources, down loading services and online search related to the research. All of them are using e-mail and online search once in a day. Majority of them are using electronic journals, WWW resources and document delivery services once in a day. Nearly half of the doctoral students are using discussion list, newsgroups and external catalogue/ databases once in a week.

Table 4.53 gives the frequency of use of various Internet tools and resources by the doctoral students in Environmental Science. Analysis reveals that most used Internet tool by the doctoral students in Environmental Science is e-mail. Most (96.2 per cent) of the doctoral students are using e-mail and good number (46.2 per cent) of them are using it once in a week. The second most used Internet service is online search, a large majority of the respondents are using online search and about 38.5 per cent of them are using it once in a day. Majority (84.6 per cent) of the doctoral students are using electronic journals and about 34.6 per cent of them are using it once in a week. Nearly 73.1 per cent of the scholars are using down loading services and 30.8 per cent of them are using it once in a month. Majority of the doctoral students are using WWW resources and 38.5 per cent of them are using it once in a week. Majority of the respondents are using discussion list, newsgroups and external catalogue/ databases, and about 30.8 per cent of them are using it rarely.

It is found that most used Internet tool by the doctoral students in Environmental Science is e-mail. Most (96.2 per cent) of the doctoral students are using e-mail and a good number (46.2 per cent) of them are using it once in a week. The second most used Internet service is online search, a large majority of the doctoral students are using online search and few of them are using it once in a day. Majority of them are using electronic journals and WWW resources, and few of them are using it once in a week. Majority of the scholars are using down loading services and few of them are using it once in a month. Majority of the respondents are using discussion list, newsgroups and external catalogue/ databases, and few number of them are using it rarely.

TABLE 4.53 : Frequency of Use of Internet Tools and Resources by the Doctoral Students in Environmental Science

Internet Tools/ Resources	*Never*	*Rarely*	*Once in a Month*	*Once in a Week*	*Once in a Day*
E – mail	1(3.8%)	4(15.4%)	4(15.4%)	12(46.2%)	5(19.2%)
Discussion list, Newsgroups	11(42.3%)	8(30.8%)	4(15.4%)	2(7.7%)	1(3.8%)
External catalogue/ Databases	10(38.5%)	8(30.8%)	4(15.4%)	3(11.5%)	1(3.8%)
Document delivery services	17(65.4%)	7(26.9%)	1(3.8%)	1(3.8%)	–
Electronic journals	4(15.4%)	1(3.8%)	10(38.5%)	9(34.6%)	2(7.7%)
WWW resources	8(30.8%)	4(15.4%)	3(11.5%)	10(38. 5%)	1(3.8%)
Down loading services	7(26.9%)	3(11.5%)	8(30.8%)	7(26.9%)	1(3.8%)
Online search	2(7.7%)	–	3(11.5%)	11(42.3%)	10(38.5%)

Table 4.54 presents the frequency of use of various Internet tools and resources by the doctoral students in Mathematical Science.

Analysis shows that most used Internet tool by the doctoral students in Mathematical Science is e-mail. Most (95.2 per cent) of the doctoral students are using e-mail and a few number (33.3 per cent) of them are using it once in a week. The second most used Internet service is online search, a large majority of the respondents are using online search and about 38.1 per cent of them are using it once in a day. Nearly 61.9 per cent of the doctoral students are using WWW resources and few of them are using it once in a day. Majority of them are using electronic journals (52.4 per cent) and down loading services (57.1 per cent) and very few of them are using it once in a day. Majority of the respondents are not using discussion list, newsgroups, external catalogue/ databases and document delivery services and very few of them are using it rarely.

TABLE 4.54 : Frequency of Use of Internet Tools and Resources by the Doctoral Students in Mathematical Science

Internet Tools/ Resources	*Never*	*Rarely*	*Once in a Month*	*Once in a Week*	*Once in a Day*
E – mail	1(4.8%)	7(33.3%)	3(14.3%)	7(33.3%)	3(14.3%)
Discussion list, News groups	15(71.4%)	2(9.5%)	1(4.8%)	3(14.3%)	_
External catalogue / Databases	15(71.4%)	6(28.6%)	_	_	_
Document delivery services	14(66.7%)	2(9.5%)	3(14.3%)	2(9.5%)	_
Electronic journals	10(47.6%)	6(28.6%)	2(9.5%)	2(9.5%)	1(4.8%)
WWW resources	8(38.1%)	3(14.3%)	4(19%)	2(9.5%)	4(19%)
Down loading services	9(42.9%)	4(19%)	3(14.3%)	4(19%)	1(4.8%)
Online search	2(9.5%)	_	4(19%)	7(33.3%)	8(38.1%)

It is revealed that most used Internet tool by the doctoral students in Mathematical Science is e-mail. Most (95.2 per cent) of the doctoral students are using e-mail and a few number of them are using it once in a week. The second most used Internet service is online search, a large majority of the scholars are using online search and a few number of them are using it once in a day. Majority of the scholars are using WWW resources, electronic journals and down loading services and very few of them are using it once in a day. Majority of them are not using discussion list, newsgroups, external catalogue/ databases and document delivery services, and a few number of them are using it rarely.

Table 4.55 shows the frequency of use of various Internet tools and resources by the doctoral students in Physical Sciences. Analysis reveals that most used Internet tools by the doctoral students in Physical Sciences are e-mail and online search. Large majority (94.3 per cent) of the doctoral students are using e-mail and majority (63.1 per cent) of them are using it once in a day. Nearly 94.3 per cent of them are using online search and good number (49.2 per cent) of them are using it once in a day. Large majority (86.9 per cent) of the scholars are using electronic journals and about 43.4 per cent of them are using it once in a week. Nearly 78.7 per cent of the doctoral students are using down loading services and few of them are using it once in a day. Majority of the scholars are using WWW resources and 36.9 per cent of them are using it once in a day. Majority of the respondents are using external catalogue/ databases and about 25.4 per cent of them are using it once in a week. Majority of the respondents are using discussion list, newsgroups (58.2 per cent) and document delivery services (66.4 per cent) and few of them are using it rarely.

It is revealed that most used Internet tools by the doctoral students in Physical Sciences are e-mail and online search. Majority of the doctoral students are using e-mail and good number of them are using online search once in a day. Large majority of the doctoral students are using electronic journals and a good number of them are using it once in a week. Majority of the respondents are using down loading services and few of them are using it once in a day. Majority of the doctoral students are using WWW resources and few of them are using it once in a day. Majority of the respondents are using external catalogue/databases and few of them are using it once in a week. Majority of the respondents are using discussion list, newsgroups and document delivery services, and few of them are using it rarely.

TABLE 4.55 : Frequency of Use of Internet Tools and Resources by the Doctoral Students in Physical Sciences

Internet Tools/ Resources	*Never*	*Rarely*	*Once in a Month*	*Once in a Week*	*Once in a Day*
E – mail	7(5.7%)	7(5.7%)	3(2.5%)	28(23%)	77(63.1%)
Discussion list, News groups	51(41.8%)	30(24.6%)	7(5.7%)	20(16.4%)	14(11.5%)
External catalogue / Databases	31(25.4%)	36(29.5%)	18(14.8%)	31(25.4%)	6(4.9%)
Document delivery services	41(33.6%)	43(35.2%)	12(9.8%)	17(13.9%)	9(7.4%)
Electronic journals	16(13.1%)	7(5.7%)	10(8.2%)	53(43.4%)	36(29.5%)
WWW resources	28(23%)	7(5.7%)	13(10.7%)	29(23.8%)	45(36.9%)
Down loading services	26(21.3%)	23(18.9%)	19(15.6%)	32(26.2%)	22(18%)
Online search	7(5.7%)	_	4(3.3%)	51(41.8%)	60(49.2%)

6.3. Relation between the Use of Internet Tools and Resources and the Discipline of the Doctoral Students

Table 4.56 shows the mean and standard deviations on the

use of Internet tools and resources for doctoral students based on their disciplines.

TABLE 4.56 : Mean and S. Ds of the Science Doctoral Students on the Use of Internet Tools and Resources Based on Discipline

Groups	*N*	*Mean*	*Standard Deviation*	*Minimum*	*Maximum*
Bio Sciences	41	26.3488	6.06270	8.00	37.00
Biological Sciences	60	21.5167	8.12506	9.00	38.00
Computer Science	3	33.5000	5.32291	27.00	40.00
Environmental Science	26	19.7692	5.62358	6.00	29.00
Mathematical Science	21	16.5238	5.29735	2.00	26.00
Physical Sciences	122	24.7213	6.97607	7.00	40.00
Total	**273**	**23.3152**	**7.46034**	**2.00**	**40.00**

Table 4.57 provides the details of variance of the use of Internet tools and resources based on the discipline of the doctoral students.

TABLE 4.57 : ANOVA Test of the Use of Internet Tools and Resources for Science Doctoral Students Based on Discipline

Source of Variance	*Sum of Squares*	*d. f*	*Mean Square*	*F*	*Sig.*
Between Groups	2541.447	5	508.289	10.752	.000
Within Groups	12764.129	270	47.275		
Total	**15305.576**	**275**			

The analysis of variance test indicates that the F value is 10.752 and the significance value is .000, which is less than 0.05. Therefore, it is clear that there is a significant difference in the use of Internet tools and resources by the doctoral students in different science disciplines. The ANOVA test establishes that there is significant difference in the use of Internet tools and resources by the science doctoral students in different disciplines.

7. TIME SPENT FOR USING INTERNET TOOLS AND RESOURCES

Table 4.58 shows the average time spent per week for using various Internet tools and resources related to their research by the science doctoral students in the Universities in Kerala.

TABLE 4.58 : Time Spent for Using Internet Tools and Resources by the Science Doctoral Students

Internet Tools/ Resources	*< 30 Minutes*	*Up to 1 Hour*	*1 - 2 Hours*	*2 – 5 Hours*	*> 5 Hours*
E – mail	60(21.7%)	64(23.2%)	61(22.1%)	47(17%)	29(10.5%)
Discussion list, News groups	57(20.7%)	41(14.9%)	31(11.2%)	15(5.4%)	8(2.9%)
External catalogue / Databases	66(23.9%)	48(17.4%)	37(13.4%)	28(10.1%)	15(5.4%)
Document delivery services	55(19.9%)	38(13.8%)	28(10.1%)	18(6.5%)	10(3.6%)
Electronic journals	18(6.5%)	22(8%)	77(27.9%)	62(22.5%)	51 (18.5%)
WWW resources	28(10.1%)	34(12.3%)	60(21.7%)	50(18.1%)	44 (15.9%)
Down loading services	40(14.5%)	51(18.5%)	54(19.6%)	27(9.8%)	31(11.2%)
Online search	1(0.4%)	23(8.3%)	90(32.6%)	105(38%)	40 (14.5%)

Analysis shows that about 23.2 per cent of the science doctoral students are using e-mail for up to 1 hour per week and 22.1 per cent of them are using e-mail for 1-2 hours. A few (10.5 per cent) of the scholars are using e-mail for more than 5 hours. Nearly 38 per cent them are using online search for 2-5 hours while 32.6 per cent of them are using it or 1-2 hours per week. A few number (27.9 per cent) of the respondents are using electronic journals for 1-2 hours and 18.5 per cent of them are using it for more than 5 hours. About 21.7 per cent of the doctoral students are using WWW resources for 1-2 hours and 18.1 per cent of them are using it for 2-5 hours. A few number of the science doctoral students are using discussion list, news groups (20.7 per cent), external catalogue/ databases (23.9 per cent) and document delivery services (19.9 per cent) for less than 30 minutes.

It is found that a few number of the science doctoral students are using e-mail for up to 1 hour per week and few of them are using it for 1-2 hours. Nearly 38 per cent of the doctoral students are using online search for 2-5 hours per week while 32.6 per cent of them are using it or 1-2 hours. A few number of the science doctoral students are using electronic journals (27.9 per cent) and WWW resources (21.7 per cent) for 1-2 hours. A few number of them are using discussion list, news groups (20.7 per cent), external catalogue/ databases (23.9 per cent) and document delivery services (19.9 per cent) for less than 30 minutes. A very few number of them are using down loading services for 1-2 hours per week.

7.1. Time Spent for Using Internet Tools and Resources according to Universities

The average time spent per week for using Internet tools and resources by the science doctoral students in the five universities in Kerala are presented in Tables 4.59 to 4.62.

Table 4.59 depicts the average time spent per week by the science doctoral students in University of Kerala for using various Internet tools and resources related to their research. Analysis shows that in University of Kerala, a good number (46.1 per cent) of the science doctoral students are using online search for 2-5 hours per week and 29.7 per cent of them are using it for 1-2 hours. Nearly 24.2 per cent of the respondents are using e-mail for 1-2 hours and 23.4 per cent of them are using it for less than 30 minutes. Nearly 32 per cent of the science doctoral students are using electronic journals for 1-2 hours and 18.8 per cent of them are using it for more than 5 hours. About 18 per cent of the scholars are using discussion list and newsgroups for less than 30 minutes while 14.8 per cent of them are using it for 1-2 hours. The percentage of the scholars using external catalogue for up to 1 hour and for less than 30 minutes are 19.5 per cent and 14.8 per cent respectively. Nearly 21.9 per cent of the doctoral students are using WWW resources for more than 5 hours

TABLE 4.59 : Time Spent for Using Internet Tools and Resources by the Science Doctoral Students in University of Kerala

Internet Tools/ Resources	*< 30 Minutes*	*Up to 1 Hour*	*1 - 2 Hours*	*2 – 5 Hours*	*> 5 Hours*
E – mail	30(23.4%)	31(24.2%)	31(24.2%)	14(10.9%)	15(11.7%)
Discussion list, News groups	23(18%)	15(11.7%)	19(14.8%)	9(7%)	8(6.3%)
External catalogue/ Databases	19(14.8%)	25(19.5%)	16(12.5%)	17(13.3%)	11(8.6%)
Document delivery services	12(9.4%)	20(15.6%)	12(9.4%)	12(9.4%)	5(3.9%)
Electronic journals	4(3.1%)	8(6.3%)	41(32%)	25(19.5%)	24(18.8%)
WWW resources	4(3.1%)	20(15.6%)	28(21.9%)	18(14.1%)	28(21.9%)
Down loading services	15(11.7%)	22(17.2%)	20(15.6%)	11(8.6%)	21(16.4%)
Online search	_	7(5.5%)	38(29.7%)	59(46.1%)	16(12.5%)

and 21.9 per cent of them are using it for 1-2 hours. A very few number of them are using document delivery services (15.6 per cent) and down loading services (17.2 per cent) for up to 1 hour.

It is revealed that in University of Kerala, a good number of the science doctoral students are using online search for 2-5 hours per week and few of them are using it for 1-2 hours. A few number of them are using e-mail for 1-2 hours and few of them are using it for less than 30 minutes. A few number of the doctoral students are using electronic journals for 1-2 hours and very few of them are using it for more than 5 hours per week. A very few number of them are using discussion list, newsgroups for less than 30 minutes. A few number of the scholars are using WWW resources for more than 5 hours. A very few number of them are using document delivery services and down loading services for up to 1 hour. The average time spent per week by the science doctoral students in University of Calicut for using various Internet tools and resources are given in Table 4.60.

Analysis shows that in University of Calicut, nearly 28.3 per cent of the science doctoral students are using the e-mail up to 1 hour and about 26.1 per cent of them are using it for 1-2 hours per week. Nearly 37 per cent of the respondents are using online search for 1-2 hours per week and 26.1 per cent of them are using it for 2-5 hours. A few numbers (26.1 per cent) of the scholars are using electronic journals for 1-2 hours and 15.2 per cent of them are using it for 2-5 hours. WWW resources are using for 1- 2 hours by 19.6 per cent of the scholars and very few of them are using it for less than 30 minutes. Nearly 21.7 per cent of the scholars are using down loading services up to 1 hour and 17.4 per cent of them are using it for 1-2 hours. Few of them are using discussion list, newsgroups, external catalogue/ databases and document delivery services for less than 30 minutes.

TABLE 4.60 : Time Spent for Using Internet Tools and Resources by the Science Doctoral Students in University of Calicut

Internet Tools/ Resources	*< 30 Minutes*	*Up to 1 Hour*	*1 - 2 Hours*	*2 – 5 Hours*	*> 5 Hours*
E – mail	9(19.6%)	13(28.3%)	12(26.1%)	4(8.7%)	2(4.3%)
Discussion list, News groups	11(23.9%)	6(13%)	2(4.3%)	_	_
External catalogue/ Databases	15(32.6%)	5(10.9%)	6(13%)	1(2.2%)	_
Document delivery services	9(19.6%)	4(8.8%)	3(6.5%)	1(2.2%)	_
Electronic journals	7(15.2%)	_	12(26.1%)	7(15.2%)	2(4.3%)
WWW resources	9(19.6%)	7(15.2%)	9(19.6%)	5(10.9%)	1(2.2%)
Down loading services	6(13%)	10(21.7%)	8(17.4%)	_	_
Online search	_	4(8.7%)	17 (37%)	12(26.1%)	6(13%)

It is found that in University of Calicut, few number of the science doctoral students are using the e-mail up to 1 hour per week and few of them are using it for 1-2 hours. Nearly 37 per cent of the respondents are using online search for 1-2 hours and few of them are using it for 2-5 hours per week. A few number of the science doctoral students are using electronic journals for 1-2 hours and very few of them are using it for 2-5 hours. A very few number of the scholars are using WWW resources for 1- 2 hours and very few of them are using it for less than 30 minutes. Few number of the respondents are using down loading services up to 1 hour. Few of them are using discussion list, newsgroups, external catalogue/ databases and document delivery services for less than 30 minutes.

Table 4.61 gives the average time spent per week by the science doctoral students in CUSAT for using various Internet tools and resources related to their research. Analysis shows that in CUSAT, nearly a good number (39.7 per cent) of the science doctoral students are using online search for 2-5 hours per week and 36.8 per cent of them are using it for 1-2 hours. Nearly 30.9 per cent of the respondents are using electronic journals for 2-5 hours and 25 per cent of them are using it for more than 5 hours. About 25 per cent of the respondents are using e-mail for 2-5 hours and 22.1 per cent of them are using it for 1-2 hours. About 25 per cent of the science doctoral students are using discussion list and newsgroups for less than 30 minutes while 23.5 per cent of them are using it for up to 1 hour. The percentage of the scholars using external catalogue for less than 30 minutes and 1-2 hours are 26.5 per cent and 17.6 per cent respectively. Nearly 29.4 per cent of the science doctoral students are using WWW resources for 2-5 hours and 26.5 per cent of them are using it for 1-2 hours. Nearly a good number (39.7 per cent) of them are using document delivery services for less than 30 minutes and very few (13.2 per cent) of them are using it up to 1 hour. Nearly 23.5 per cent of them are using down loading services for 2-5 hours per week.

It is found that in CUSAT, a good number (39.7 per cent) of the science doctoral students are using online search for 2-5 hours and few of them are using it for 1-2 hours per week. A few numbers (30.9 per cent) of the scholars are using electronic journals for 2-5 hours and few of them are using it for more than 5 hours. A few numbers (25 per cent) of the scholars are using e-mail for 2-5 hours and few (22.1 per cent) of them are using it for 1-2 hours. Nearly a good number of them are using discussion list and newsgroups for less than 30 minutes while few of them are using it for up to 1 hour. A few number (29.4 per cent) of the science doctoral students are using WWW resources for 2-5 hours and few of them are using it for 1-2 hours. A few numbers of the respondents are using document delivery services for less than 30 minutes and very few of them are using it up to 1 hour. A few number of them using down loading services for up to 2-5 hours.

TABLE 4.61 :Time Spent for Using Internet Tools and Resources by the Science Doctoral Students in CUSAT

Internet Tools/ Resources	*< 30 Minutes*	*Up to 1 Hour*	*1 - 2 Hours*	*2 – 5 Hours*	*> 5 Hours*
E – mail	13(19.1%)	15(22.1%)	15(22.1%)	17(25%)	8(11.8%)
Discussion list, News groups	17(25%)	16(23.5%)	3(4.4%)	6(8.8%)	–
External catalogue/ Databases	18(26.5%)	11(16.2%)	12(17.6%)	5(7.4%)	4(5.9%)
Document delivery services	27(39.7%)	9(13.2%)	6(8.8%)	3(4.5%)	2(2.9%)
Electronic journals	5(7.4%)	11(16.2%)	14(20.6%)	21(30.9%)	17(25%)
WWW resources	8(11.8%)	4(5.9%)	18(26.5%)	20(29.4%)	9(13.2%)
Down loading services	3(4.4%)	15(22.1%)	16(23.5%)	16(23.5%)	7(10.3%)
Online search	–	2(2.9%)	25(36.8%)	27(39.7%)	12(17.5%)

Table 4.62 indicates the average time spent per week by the science doctoral students in M. G. University for using various Internet tools and resources. Analysis revealed that 35.5 per cent of the science doctoral students are spending 2-5 hours per week for using e-mail while 19.4 per cent of them are spending less than 30 minutes for using it. Nearly

32.3 per cent of the repondents are using electronic journals for 1-2 hours and 25.8 per cent of them are using it for 2-5 hours. About 32.3 per cent of the respondents are using online search up to 1 hour and 32.3 per cent of them are using it for 1-2 hours. A few numbers (19.4 per cent) of the doctoral students are using WWW resources for more than 5 hours and few of them are using it for 2-5 hours. A good number (48.4 per cent) of the respondents are using down loading services for less than 30 minutes and few (29 per cent)of them are using it for 1-2 hours. Nearly 41.9 per cent of the science doctoral students are using external catalogue/ databases for less than 30 minutes and 22.6 per cent of them

TABLE 4.62 : Time Spent for Using Internet Tools and Resources by the Science Doctoral Students in M. G. University

Internet Tools/ Resources	*< 30 Minutes*	*Up to 1 Hour*	*1 - 2 Hours*	*2 – 5 Hours*	*> 5 Hours*
E – mail	6(19.4%)	5(16.1%)	3(9.7%)	11(35.5%)	4(12.9%)
Discussion list, News groups	5(16.1%)	4(12.9%)	6(19.4%)	_	_
External catalogue/ Databases	13(41.9%)	7(22.6%)	2(6.5%)	4(12.9%)	_
Document delivery services	6(19.4%)	5(16.1%)	7(22.6%)	2(6.5%)	3(9.7%)
Electronic journals	2(6.5%)	3(9.7%)	10(32.3%)	8(25.8%)	7(22.6%)
WWW resources	5(16.1%)	3(9.7%)	5(16.1%)	6(19.4%)	6(19.4%)
Down loading services	15(48.4%)	4(12.9%)	9(29%)	_	2(6.5%)
Online search	1(3.1%)	10(32.3%)	10(32.3%)	6(19.4%)	4(12.9%)

are using it for 1-2 hours. About 22.6 per cent of the respondents are using document delivery services for 1-2 hours per week.

It is found that in M. G. University, a few number of the science doctoral students are spending 2-5 hours per week for using e-mail while few of them are spending less than 30 minutes for using it. A few number (32.3 per cent) of the scholars are using electronic journals for 1-2 hours and few of them are using it for 2-5 hours per week. A few number of them are using online search for 1-2 hours per week. A few number of the respondents are using WWW resources for more than 5 hours and few of them are using it for 2-5 hours. A good number (48.4 per cent) of the science doctoral students are using down loading services for less than 30 minutes and few of them are using it for 1-2 hours. A few number of the science doctoral students are using external catalogue/ databases for less than 30 minutes and few of them are using it for 1-2 hours. A few numbers of the scholars are using document delivery services for 1-2 hours per week.

7.2. Relation between the Time Spent for Using Internet Tools and Resources and the University of the Science Doctoral Students

Table 4.63 shows the mean and standard deviations on the time spent for using Internet tools and resources for science doctoral students based on their universities.

Table 4.64 shows the analysis of variance of the time spent for using Internet tools and resources based on the university of the science doctoral students.

TABLE 4.63 : Mean and S. Ds of the Science Doctoral Students on the Time Spent for Using Internet Tools and Resources according to University

Groups	*N*	*Mean*	*Standard Deviation*	*Minimum*	*Maximum*
University of Kerala	128	41.4766	14.62387	10.00	81.00
University of Calicut	46	45.4348	17.53682	11.00	80.00
CUSAT	68	35.6176	14.14955	13.00	79.00
M. G. University	31	33.5484	10.80691	18.00	61.00
Total	**273**	**39.7283**	**15.05319**	**10.00**	**81.00**

TABLE 4.64 : ANOVA Test of the Time Spent for Using Internet Tools and Resources for Science Doctoral Students Based on University

Source of Variance	*Sum of Squares*	*d. f*	*Mean Square*	*F*	*Sig.*
Between Groups	4298.983	4	1074.746	5.020	.001
Within Groups	58015.637	271	214.080		
Total	**62314.620**	**275**			

The analysis of variance test indicates that the F value is 5.020 and the significance value is .001, which is less than 0.05. Hence, it is clear that there is significant difference in the time spent for using Internet tools and resources among the science doctoral students in different universities. The ANOVA test establishes that there is significant difference in the time spent for using Internet tools and resources among the science doctoral students in different universities.

7.3. Time Spent for Using Internet Tools and Resources according to Discipline

The average time spent per week for using Internet tools and resources by the doctoral students in various science disciplines are given in Tables 4.65 to 4.70. Table 4.65 depicts the average time spent per week by the doctoral students in Bio Sciences for using various Internet tools and resources.

TABLE 4.65 : Time Spent for Using Internet Tools and Resources by the Doctoral Students in Bio Sciences

Internet Tools/ Resources	*< 30 Minutes*	*Up to 1 Hour*	*1 - 2 Hours*	*2 – 5 Hours*	*> 5 Hours*
E – mail	12(27.8%)	11(25.6%)	10(23.3%)	6(14%)	2(4.7%)
Discussion list, News groups	12(27.8%)	7(16.3%)	7(16.3%)	2(4.7%)	1(2.3%)
External catalogue/ Databases	8(18.6%)	6(14%)	16(37.2%)	4(9.3%)	4(9.3%)
Document delivery services	5(11.6%)	7(16.3%)	8(18.6%)	2(4.7%)	–
Electronic journals	2(4.7%)	3(7%)	11(25.6%)	16(37.2%)	10(23.3%)
WWW resources	3(7%)	5(11.6%)	10(23.3%)	9(20.9%)	8(18.6%)
Down loading services	5(11.6%)	11(25.6%)	9(20.9%)	4(9.3%)	5(11.6%)
Online search	–	–	20(46.5%)	21(48.8%)	1(2.3%)

Analysis shows that in Bio Sciences, 27.8 per cent of the doctoral students are using e-mail for less than 30 minutes and 23.3 per cent of them are using e-mail for 1 to 2 hours per week. Nearly 48.8 per cent of the doctoral students indicated 2-5 hours use of online search and 46.5 per cent of them are using it for 1 to 2 hours. A few number (37.2 per cent) of them are using electronic journals for 2 to 5 hours per week. Nearly 25.6 per cent of the respondents are using electronic journals for 1 to 2 hours and 23.3 per cent of them are using it for more than 5 hours. About 23.3 per cent of the doctoral students are using WWW resources for 1 to 2 hours and 20.9 per cent of them are using it for 2 to 5 hours. A few number (25.6 per cent) of the scholars are using down loading services up to 1 hour and 1 to 2 hours use is mentioned by 20.9 per cent of the respondents. Discussions lists, newsgroups are used for less than 30 minutes by 27.8 per cent of the doctoral students and 16.3 per cent of them are using it for 1 to 2 hours. Nearly 37.2 per cent of the scholars indicated that they are spending 1 to 2 hours for external catalogue/databases and 20.9 per cent of them are spending less than 30 minutes for using it. Document delivery services are using for 1 to 2 hours by 18.6 per cent of the doctoral students and 16.3 per cent of them are using it up to 1 hour.

It is found that in Bio Sciences, 27.8 per cent of the doctoral students are using e-mail for less than 30 minutes and 25.6 per cent of them are using it up to 1 hour per week. A good number of the doctoral students indicated 2-5 hours use of online search and 46.5 per cent of them are using it for 1 to 2 hours. A few number (37.2 per cent) of the scholars are using electronic journals for 2 to 5 hours and very few of them are using it for 1 to 2 hours. About 23.3 per cent of them are using WWW resources for 1 to 2 hours and 20.9 per cent of them are using it for 2 to 5 hours. A few number (25.6 per cent) of them are using down loading services up to 1 hour and 1 to 2 hour use is mentioned by 20.9 per cent of the respondents. About 27.8 per cent of the doctoral students are using discussions lists, newsgroups for less than 30 minutes. A few number of them indicated that they are spending 1 to 2 hours per week for external catalogue/ databases. A very few them are using document delivery services for 1 to 2 hours per week.

Table 4.66 shows the average time spent per week by the doctoral students in Biological Sciences for using various Internet tools and resources. Analysis shows that in Biological

Sciences, 25 per cent of the doctoral students are using e-mail for 1-2 hours, 23.3 per cent of the respondents are using it up to 1 hour and 21.7 per cent of them are using e-mail for less than 30 minutes per week. Nearly 36.7 per cent of the doctoral students indicated 2-5 hours use of online search and 25 per cent of them are using it for more than 5 hours. A few number (26.7 per cent) of the scholars are using electronic journals for 1 to 2 hours, and very few (15 per cent) of them are using it for 2-5 hours. About 21.7 per cent of the doctoral students are using WWW resources for 1 to 2 hours and 18.3 per cent of them are using it for more than 5 hours. A very few number (18.3 per cent) of them are using down loading services up to 1 hour and 1 to 2 hour use is mentioned by 11.7 per cent of the respondents. A very few number of the scholars are using discussions lists, newsgroups for up to 1 hour per week. Nearly 21.7 per cent of the doctoral students indicated that they are spending less than 30 minutes for external catalogue/databases and 16.7 per cent of them are spending up to 1 hour for using it. Nearly 16.7 per cent of the scholars are using document delivery services for less than 30 minutes by and 13.3 per cent of them are using it for 2 to 5 hours per week.

It is revealed that in Biological Sciences, 25 per cent of the doctoral students are using e-mail for 1-2 hours per week and 23.3 per cent of them are using it up to 1 hour. A few number (36.7 per cent) of the respondents indicated 2-5 hours use of online search and very few of them are using it for more than 5 hours. A few number (26.7 per cent) of the doctoral students are using electronic journals for 1 to 2 hours, and very few (15 per cent) of them are using it for 2-5 hours. About 21.7 per cent of the scholars are using WWW resources for 1 to 2 hours and very few of them are using it for more than 5 hours. A very few number of them are using down loading services and discussions lists, newsgroups for up to 1 hour. Nearly 21.7 per cent of the doctoral students indicated that they are spending less than 30 minutes for external catalogue/databases and 16.7 per cent of them are spending up to 1 hour for using it. A very few of them are using document delivery services for less than 30 minutes.

TABLE 4.66 : Time Spent for Using Internet Tools and Resources by the Doctoral Students in Biological Sciences

Internet Tools/ Resources	*< 30 Minutes*	*Up to 1 Hour*	*1 - 2 Hours*	*2 – 5 Hours*	*> 5 Hours*
E – mail	13(21.7%)	14(23.3%)	15(25%)	7(11.7%)	7(11.7%)
Discussion list, News groups	8(13.3%)	8(13.3%)	5(8.3%)	2(3.3%)	5(8.3%)
External catalogue/ Databases	13(21.7%)	10(16.7%)	8(13.3%)	5(8.3%)	3(5%)
Document delivery services	10(16.7%)	6(10%)	3(5%)	8(13.3%)	–
Electronic journals	7(11.7%)	7(11.7%)	16(26.7%)	9(15%)	6(10%)
WWW resources	9(15%)	11(18.3%)	13(21.7%)	8(13.3%)	11(18.3%)
Down loading services	9(15%)	11(18.3%)	7(11.7%)	4(6.7%)	7(11.7%)
Online search	–	4(6.7%)	14(23.3%)	22(36.7%)	15(25%)

The average time spent per week for using Internet tools and resources by the doctoral students in Computer Science is given in Table 4.67.

TABLE 4.67 : Time Spent for Using Internet Tools and Resources by the Doctoral Students in Computer Science

Internet Tools/ Resources	*< 30 Minutes*	*Up to 1 Hour*	*1 - 2 Hours*	*2 – 5 Hours*	*> 5 Hours*
E – mail	_	1(25%)	1(25%)	1(25%)	1(25%)
Discussion list, News groups	_	_	1(25%)	1(25%)	1(25%)
External catalogue/ Databases	1(25%)	_	_	2(50%)	1(25%)
Document delivery services	_	1(25%)	_	1(25%)	1(25%)
Electronic journals	_	_	_	_	4(100%)
WWW resources	_	_	_	1(25%)	3(75%)
Down loading services	_	_	1(25%)	1(25%)	2(50%)
Online search	_	_	_	_	4(100%)

Analysis shows that all the respondents in Computer Science are using electronic journals and online search for more than 5 hours per week. Majority of the doctoral students are using WWW resources (75 per cent) and down loading services (50 per cent) for more than 5 hours per week. One doctoral student is using e-mail, discussion list, newsgroups and document delivery services for more than 5 hours. Nearly 50 per cent of them are using external catalogue/ databases for 2-5 hours and one of them is using it for more than 5 hours.

It is revealed that all the respondents in Computer Science are using electronic journals and online search for more than 5 hours per week. Majority of the doctoral students are using WWW resources and down loading services for more than 5 hours. One doctoral student is using e-mail, discussion list, newsgroups and document delivery services for more than 5 hours. Nearly half of them are using external catalogue/ databases for 2-5 hours per week.

Table 4.68 gives the average time spent per week by the doctoral students in Environmental Science for using various Internet tools and resources. Analysis shows that in Environmental Science, 30.8 per cent of the doctoral students are using e-mail for 1-2 hours and 23.1 per cent of them are using it for 2-5 hours per week. Nearly 38.5 per cent of the scholars indicated 1-2 hours use of online search and 30.8 per cent of them are using it for 2-5 hours. A few numbers (30.8 per cent) of the doctoral students are using electronic journals for 2 -5 hours, and very few (19.6 per cent) of them are using it for 1-2 hours. About 38.5 per cent of the scholars are using WWW resources for 1 to 2 hours and 15.4 per cent of them are using it for 2- 5 hours. A few number (34.6 per cent) of the doctoral students are using down loading services for 1-2 hours and up to 1 hour use is mentioned by 23.1 per cent of the respondents. About 23.1 per cent of the scholars are using discussions lists, newsgroups for 1-2 hours per week and 23.1 per cent of them are using it for less than 30 minutes. Nearly 26.9 per cent of them indicated that they are spending less than 30 minutes for external catalogue/ databases. A very few number of them are using document delivery services for up to 1 hour.

It is found that in Environmental Science, a few number of the doctoral students are using e-mail for 1-2 hours per week and very few of them are using it for 2-5 hours. A few number of the scholars are using electronic journals and online search for 2-5 hours, and very few of them are using it for 1-2 hours. A few number of the scholars are using WWW resources for 1 to 2 hours and very few of them are using it for 2- 5 hours per week. A few number (34.6 per cent) of the doctoral students are using down loading services for 1-2 hours and very few of them are using it up to 1 hour. A very few number of them are using discussions lists, newsgroups for 1-2 hours per week. Nearly 26.9 per cent of them indicated that they are spending less than 30 minutes for external catalogue/databases. A very few number of them are using document delivery services for up to 1 hour.

TABLE 4.68 : Time Spent for Using Internet Tools and Resources by the Doctoral Students in Environmental Science

Internet Tools/ Resources	*< 30 Minutes*	*Up to 1 Hour*	*1 - 2 Hours*	*2 – 5 Hours*	*> 5 Hours*
E – mail	5(19.2%)	5(19.2%)	8(30.8%)	6(23.1%)	1(3.8%)
Discussion list, News groups	6(23.1%)	2(7.7%)	6(23.1%)	1(3.8%)	–
External catalogue/ Databases	7(26.9%)	3(11.5%)	2(7.7%)	3(11.5%)	1(3.8%)
Document delivery services	2(7.7%)	4(15.4%)	–	2(7.7%)	1(3.8%)
Electronic journals	–	3(11.5%)	11(19.6%)	8(30.0%)	–
WWW resources	1(3.8%)	2(7.7%)	10(38.5%)	4(15.4%)	1(3.8%)
Down loading services	2(7.7%)	6(23.1%)	9(34.6%)	1(3.8%)	1(3.8%)
Online search	–	4(15.4%)	10(38.5%)	8(30.8%)	2(7.7%)

Table 4.69 describes the average time spent per week for using the Internet tools and resources by the doctoral students in Mathematical Science.

TABLE 4.69 : Time Spent for Using Internet Tools and Resources by the Doctoral Students in Mathematical Science

Internet Tools/ Resources	*< 30 Minutes*	*Up to 1 Hour*	*1 - 2 Hours*	*2 – 5 Hours*	*> 5 Hours*
E – mail	9(42.9%	5(23.8%)	3(14.3%)	2(9.5%)	1(4.8%)
Discussion list, News groups	3(14.3%)	1(4.8%)	2(9.5%)	–	–
External catalogue/ Databases	4(19%)	–	1(4.8%)	1(4.8%)	–
Document delivery services	5(23.8%)	2(9.5%)	–	–	–
Electronic journals	2(9.5%)	2(9.5%)	2(9.5%)	2(9.5%)	3(14.3%)
WWW resources	3(14.3%)	2(9.5%)	4(19%)	1(4.8%)	3(14.3%)
Down loading services	4(19%)	3(14.3%)	2(9.5%)	3(14.3%)	–
Online search	–	4(19%)	1(4.8%)	7(33.3%)	7(33.3%)

Analysis shows that a good number (42.9 per cent) of the doctoral students in Mathematical Science are spending less than 30 minutes for using e-mail and a few (23.8 per cent) of them are using it for up to 1 hour per week. A few number (33.3 per cent) of the scholars are using online search for more than 5 hours and few (33.3 per cent) of them are using it for 2-5 hours per week. A very few (14.3 per cent) of the doctoral students are using electronic journals and WWW resources for more than 5 hours. Nearly 14.3 per cent of them are using down loading services for 2-5 hours per week. A very few number of the doctoral students are using discussion list, newsgroups (14.3 per cent), external catalogue/ databases (19 per cent) and document delivery services (23.8 per cent) for less than 30 minutes.

It is found that a good number of the doctoral students in Mathematical Science are spending less than 30 minutes for using e-mail and a few of them are using it for up to 1 hour per week. A few number of the scholars are using online search for more than 5 hours and few of them are using it for 2-5 hours per week. A very few number of the doctoral students are using electronic journals and WWW resources for more than 5 hours. A very few of them are using down loading services for 2-5 hours. A very few number of them are using discussion list, newsgroups, external catalogue/ databases and document delivery services for less than 30 minutes.

The average time spent per week for using Internet tools and resources by the doctoral students in Physical Sciences are given in Table 5.70. Analysis reveals that in Physical Sciences, 23 per cent of the doctoral students are using e-mail for up to 1 hour, 20.5 per cent of the respondents are using it 2-5 hours and 19.7 per cent of them are using e-mail for 1-2 hours per week. Nearly 38.5 per cent of the scholars indicated 2-5 hours use of online search and 36.9 per cent of them are using it for 1-2 hours. A few number (30.3 per cent) of the doctoral students are using electronic journals for 1 to 2 hours, and very few (22.6 per cent) of them are using it for more than 5 hours. About 22.1 per cent of the scholars are using WWW resources for 2-5 hours and 18.9 per cent of them are using it for 1-2 hours. A very few number (21.3 per cent) of the doctoral students are using down loading services for 1-2 hours and up to 1 hour use is mentioned by 16.4 per cent of the respondents. A few number of the scholars are using discussions lists, newsgroups for less than 30 minutes and 18.9 per cent of them are using it for up to 1 hour. Nearly 27 per cent of the doctoral students indicated that they are spending less than 30 minutes for external catalogue/databases and 23.8 per cent of them are spending up to 1 hour for using it. A few number of them are using document delivery services for less than 30 minutes per week.

TABLE 4.70 : Time Spent for Using Internet Tools and Resources by the Doctoral Students in Physical Sciences

Internet Tools/ Resources	*< 30 Minutes*	*Up to 1 Hour*	*1 - 2 Hours*	*2 – 5 Hours*	*> 5 Hours*
E – mail	21(17.2%)	28(23%)	24(19.7%)	25(20.5%)	17(13.9%)
Discussion list, News groups	28(23%)	23(18.9%)	10(8.2%)	9(7.4%)	1(0.8%)
External catalogue/ Databases	33(27%)	29(23.8%)	10(8.2%)	13(10.7%)	6(4.9%)
Document delivery services	33(27%)	18(14.8%)	17(13.9%)	5(4.1%)	8(6.6%)
Electronic journals	7(5.7%)	7(5.7%)	37(30.3%)	27(22.1%)	28(22.6%)
WWW resources	12(9.8%)	14(11.5%)	23(18.9%)	27(22.1%)	18(14.8%)
Down loading services	20(16.4%)	20(16.4%)	26(21.3%)	14(11.5%)	16(13.1%)
Online search	1(0.8%)	11(9%)	45(36.9%)	47(38.5%)	11(9%)

It is revealed that in Physical Sciences, few number of the doctoral students are using e-mail for up to 1 hour and few of them are using it 2-5 hours per week. A few number (38.5 per cent) of the scholars indicated 2-5 hours use of online search and 36.9 per cent of them are using it for 1-2 hours. A few number of the scholars are using electronic journals for 1 to 2 hours and very few of them are using it for more than 5 hours. A very few of the doctoral students are using WWW resources for 2-5 hours and 18.9 per cent of them are using it for 1-2 hours. A very few number of the scholars are using down loading services for 1-2 hours and up to 1 hour use is mentioned by 16.4 per cent of the respondents. A very few number of them are using discussions lists, newsgroups for less than 30 minutes. Nearly 27 per cent of the respondents are spending less than 30 minutes for external catalogue/databases and few of them are spending up to 1 hour for using it. A very few number of them are using document delivery services for less than 30 minutes per week.

7.5. Relation between the Time Spent for Using Internet Tools and Resources and the Discipline of the Doctoral Students

Table 4.71 shows the mean and standard deviations on time spent for using Internet tools and resources for doctoral students based on their discipline.

TABLE 4.71 : Mean and S. Ds of the Science Doctoral Students on the Time Spent for Using Internet according to Discipline

Groups	*N*	*Mean*	*Standard Deviation*	*Minimum*	*Maximum*
Bio Sciences	43	34.6744	11.30049	17.00	62.00
Biological Sciences	60	42.7000	16.57270	10.00	80.00
Computer Science	4	39.7500	9.46485	32.00	53.00
Environmental Science	26	42.1538	14.82617	20.00	70.00
Mathematical Science	21	51.0000	14.79189	13.00	79.00
Physical Sciences	122	37.5902	14.54531	17.00	81.00
Total	**276**	**39.7283**	**15.05319**	**10.00**	**81.00**

Table 5.72 shows the analysis of variance of the time spent for using Internet tools and resources based on the discipline of the doctoral students.

TABLE 4.72 : **ANOVA Test of the Time Spent for Using Internet by the Science Doctoral Students according to Discipline**

Source of Variance	*Sum of Squares*	*d. f*	*Mean Square*	*F*	*Sig.*
Between Groups	5006.935	5	1001.387	4.718	.000
Within Groups	57307.685	270	212.251		
Total	**62314.620**	**275**			

The analysis of variance test indicates that the F value is 4.718 and the significance value is .000, which is less than 0.05. Therefore, it is clear that there is significant difference in the time spent for using Internet tools and resources between the science doctoral students in different disciplines. The ANOVA test establishes that there is significant difference in the time spent for using Internet tools and resources between the science doctoral students in different disciplines.

8. INTERNET FACILITIES USED FOR COMMUNICATION

The Internet facilities used by the science doctoral students for communication is analysed university wise and discipline wise and represented in Tables 4.73 and 4.74.

8.1. Internet Facilities Used for Communication according to University

The science doctoral students in the universities in Kerala were requested to state the Internet facilities used for communication and the responses are given in Table 4.73.

Analysis shows that in the electronic environment a large majority (89.8 per cent) of the science doctoral students are using e-mail for communication. A very few number of them are using Internet chat and net phone for communication. Table 4.76 shows that large majority of the science doctoral students in University of Kerala (94.5 per cent) and CUSAT (91.2 per cent) are using e-mail for communication. Majority of the respondents in University of Calicut (82.6 per cent), and M. G. University (80.6 per cent) are also using e-mail for communication. A few number of the science doctoral students in M. G. University, CUSAT and University of Calicut are using Internet chat for communication.

TABLE 4.73 : Internet Facilities Used for Communication According to University

University Name	*Internet facility used for communication*			
	E-mail	*Chat*	*Net phone*	*None*
University of Kerala	121(94.5%)	_	_	7(5.5%)
University of Calicut	38(82.6%)	2(4.3%)	_	6(13.0%)
CUSAT	62(91.2%)	4(5.9%)	2(2.9%)	_
M. G. University	25(80.6%)	3(9.7%)	1(3.2%)	2(6.5%)
Grand Total	**246(89.8%)**	**9(3.3%)**	**3(1.5%)**	**15(5.4%)**

It is found that a large majority (89.8 per cent) of the science doctoral students are using e-mail for communication. It is also found that a large majority of the science doctoral students in University of Kerala and CUSAT are using e-mail for communication. Majority of the scholars in University of Calicut, and M. G. University are also using e-mail for communication.

8.2. Internet Facilities Used for Communication according to Discipline

Table 4.74 shows the Internet facilities used for communication by the doctoral students in various science disciplines.

Analysis revealed that a large majority of the doctoral students in Bio Sciences (88.4 per cent), Biological Sciences (90 per cent) and Physical Sciences (87.7 per cent) are using e-mail for communication. All the respondents in Computer Science and most of the doctoral students in Environmental

Science and Mathematical Science are using e-mail for communication. A very few number of them are using Internet chat and net phone for communication.

TABLE 4.74 : Internet Facilities Used for Communication According to Discipline

Discipline	*Internet facility used for communication*			
	E-mail	*Chat*	*Net phone*	*None*
Bio Sciences	36(88.4%)	1(2.3%)	2(4.7%)	2(4.7%)
Biological Sciences	54(90%)	2(3.3%)	–	4(6.7%)
Computer Science	3(100%)	–	–	–
Environmental Science	25(96.2%)	–	–	1(3.8%)
Mathematical Science	20(95.2%)	–	–	1(4.8%)
Physical Sciences	107(87.7%)	6(4.9%)	2(1.6%)	7(5.7%)
Grand Total	**245(89.8%)**	**9(3.3%)**	**4(1.5%)**	**15(5.4%)**

It is found that all the doctoral students in Computer Science and most of the scholars in Environmental Science and Mathematical Science are using e-mail for communication. A large majority of the doctoral students in Bio Sciences, Biological Sciences and Physical Sciences are using e-mail for communication.

9. FREQUENCY OF USE OF INTERNET SEARCH ENGINES

The science doctoral students were shown a list of search engines and were requested to indicate the frequency of using them. The result of the analysis is given in Table 4.75. Analysis shows that the most frequently used Internet search engine by the science doctoral students is Google. A large majority (86.2 per cent) of them are using it often. The second most used Internet search engine is Yahoo and majority (68.8 per cent) of the scholars are using it often. A few numbers (22.1 per cent) of them are using it sometimes. A large majority of the science doctoral students are not using the search engines WebCrawler (94.2 per cent), HotBot (93.5 per cent),

MetaEureka (93.1 per cent), WWW worm (92.4 per cent), Infoseek (91.7 per cent), WWW Virtual Library (84.8 per cent), Excite (84.4 per cent) and Lycos (80.4 per cent). Majority (68.8 per cent) of the science doctoral students are not using the search engine AltaVista while 27.5 per cent of them are using it sometimes.

TABLE 4.75 : Frequency of Use of Internet Search Engines

Search Engines	*Never*	*Sometimes*	*Often*
AltaVista	190(68.8%)	76(27.5%)	10(3.6%)
Excite	233(84.4%)	34(12.3%)	9(3.3%)
Yahoo	25(9%)	61(22.1%)	190(68.8%)
Google	18(6.5%)	20(7.2%)	238(86.2%)
Lycos	222(80.4%)	33(12.0%)	21(7.6%)
WebCrawler	260(94.2%)	11(4.0%)	5(1.8%)
WWW worm	255(92.4%)	9(3.3%)	12(4.3%)
WWW Virtual Library	234(84.8%)	26(9.4%)	16(5.8%)
HotBot	258(93.5%)	13(4.7%)	5(1.8%)
Infoseek	253(91.7%)	17(6.2%)	6(2.2%)
MetaEureka	257(93.1%)	13(4.7%)	6(2.2%)

It is found that the most frequently used Internet search engine by the science doctoral students in the universities in Kerala is Google. A large majority (86.2 per cent) of them are using it often. The second most used Internet search engine is Yahoo and majority of the scholars are using it often. Majority of the science doctoral students are not using the search engine AltaVista while few of them are using it sometimes. A large majority of them are not using the search engines WebCrawler, HotBot, MetaEureka, WWW worm, Infoseek, WWW Virtual Library, Excite and Lycos.

9.1. Frequency of Use of Internet Search Engines according to the University

The frequency of use of Internet search engines by the

science doctoral students in the five Universities in Kerala are analysed and given in the Tables 4.76 to 4.79.

Table 4.76 shows the frequency of use of various Internet search engines by the science doctoral students in the University of Kerala.

TABLE 4.76 : Frequency of Use of Internet Search Engines by the Science Doctoral Students in University of Kerala

Search Engines	*Never*	*Sometimes*	*Often*
AltaVista	99(77.4%)	26(20.3%)	3(2.3%)
Excite	118(90.2%)	7(5.5%)	3(2.3%)
Yahoo	16(12.5%)	21(16.4%)	91(71.1%)
Google	8(6.3%)	7(5.5%)	113(88.3%)
Lycos	110(85.9%)	13(10.2%)	5(3.9%)
WebCrawler	123(96.1%)	3(2.3%)	2(1.6%)
WWW worm	114(89%)	6(4.7%)	8(6.3%)
WWW Virtual Library	100(78.1%)	16(12.5%)	12(9.4%)
HotBot	120(93.8%)	3(2.3%)	5(3.9%)
Infoseek	120(93.8%)	8(6.3%)	–
MetaEureka	116(90.6%)	7(5.5%)	5(3.9%)

Analysis shows that the most frequently used Internet search engine in the University of Kerala is Google. A large majority (88.3 per cent) of the science doctoral students are using it regularly. The second most frequently used Internet search engine is Yahoo, about 77.1 per cent of the scholars are using it often. A few number (16.4 per cent) of them are using the search engine Yahoo sometimes. Majority of the doctoral students are not using the search engine AltaVista while a few number (20.3 per cent) of them are using it sometimes. A large majority of them are not using the search engines HotBot (93.8 per cent), Infoseek (93.7 per cent), MetaEureka (90.6 per cent), Excite (90.2 per cent), WWW worm (89 per cent), Lycos (85.9 per cent) and WWW Virtual

Library (78.1 per cent). Most (96.1 per cent) of them are not using the search engine WebCrawler. It is revealed that the most frequently used Internet search engine in the University of Kerala is Google. A large majority (88.3 per cent) of the science doctoral students are using it regularly. The second most frequently used Internet search engine is Yahoo and majority of the scholars are using it often. Majority of them are not using the search engine AltaVista while a few number of them are using it sometimes. A large majority of the scholars are not using the search engines HotBot, Infoseek, MetaEureka, Excite, WWW worm, Lycos and WWW Virtual Library. Most (96.1 per cent) of them are not using the search engine WebCrawler.

Table 4.77 depicts the frequency of use of various search engines by the science doctoral students in University of Calicut. It is found that the most used Internet search engine by the science doctoral students in the University of Calicut is Yahoo. Majority (67.4 per cent) of the science doctoral students are using it often while 26.1 per cent of them are using it sometimes. The second most frequently used Internet search engine is Google and majority (65.2 per cent) of the scholars are using it often. About 21.7 per cent of them are using the search engine Google sometimes. Nearly 72 per cent of the science doctoral students are not using the search engine AltaVista while a few (26.1 per cent) of them are using it some times. Majority of them are not using the search engine Excite but a few of them are using it sometimes. Most of the scholars are not using the search engines WebCrawler, MetaEureka and WWW worm. A large majority of them are not using the search engines Lycos, WWW Virtual Library, HotBot and Infoseek.

TABLE 4.77 : Frequency of Use of Internet Search Engines by the Science Doctoral Students in University of Calicut

Search Engines	*Never*	*Sometimes*	*Often*
Alta vista	33(71.7%)	12(26.1%)	1(2.2%)
Excite	36(78.3%)	8(17.4%)	2(4.3%)
Yahoo	3(6.5%)	12(26.1%)	31(67.4%)
Google	6(13.1%)	10(21.7%)	30(65.2%)
Lycos	39(84.8%)	5(10.9%)	2(4.3%)
WebCrawler	46(100%)	–	–
WWW worm	44(95.7%)	–	2(4.3%)
WWW Virtual Library	41(89.1%)	4(8.7%)	1(2.2%)
HotBot	42(91.3%)	4(8.7%)	–
Infoseek	42(91.3%)	4(8.7%)	–
MetaEureka	44(95.7%)	2(4.3%)	–

It is found that the most frequently used Internet search engine by the science doctoral students in the University of Calicut is Yahoo. Majority (67.4 per cent) of them are using it often. The second most frequently used Internet search engine is Google and majority (65.2 per cent) of the scholars are using it often. Majority of the science doctoral students are not using the search engines AltaVista and Excite but a few of them are using it sometimes. Most of them are not using the search engines WebCrawler, MetaEureka and WWW worm. A large majority of the scholars are not using the search engines Lycos, WWW Virtual Library, HotBot and Infoseek.

Table 4.78 shows the frequency of use of various search engines by the science doctoral students in CUSAT.

TABLE 4.78 : Frequency of Use of Internet Search Engines by the Science Doctoral Students in CUSAT

Search Engines	*Never*	*Sometimes*	*Often*
AltaVista	40(58.8%)	24(35.3%)	4(5.9%)
Excite	49(72%)	15(22.1%)	4(5.9%)
Yahoo	3(4.4%)	18(25.5%)	47(69.1%)
Google	4(5.9%)	2(2.9%)	62(91.2%)
Lycos	55(80.9%)	7(10.3%)	6(8.8%)
WebCrawler	62(91.1%)	5(7.4%)	1(1.5%)
WWW worm	63(92.6%)	3(4.4%)	2(2.9%)
WWW Virtual Library	61(89.7%)	4(5.9%)	3(4.4%)
HotBot	63(92.6%)	5(7.4%)	–
Infoseek	65(95.6%)	1(1.5%)	2(2.9%)
MetaEureka	64(94.1%)	3(4.4%)	1(1.5%)

Analysis shows that in CUSAT also the most used Internet search engine by the science doctoral students is Yahoo. Majority (69.1 per cent) of them are using it often and about 27.9 per cent of the doctoral students are using it sometimes. The search engine Google is the second most used search engine and a large majority (91.2 per cent) of the science doctoral students is using it often. A good number (41.2 per cent) of them are using the search engine AltaVista and few of them are using it some times. Most (95.6 per cent) of the scholars are not using the search engine Infoseek. A large majority of them are not using the search engines MetaEureka (94.1 per cent), WWW worm (92.6 per cent), HotBot (92.6 per cent), WebCrawler (91.1 per cent), and WW Virtual Library (89.7 per cent). Majority of them are not using the search engines Lycos (80.9 per cent) and Excite (72 per cent).

It is found that in CUSAT, the most used Internet search engine by the science doctoral students is Yahoo; majority (69.1 per cent) of them are using it often. The search engine

Google is the second most used search engine and a large majority (91.2 per cent) of the scholars are using it often. Most of the science doctoral students are not using the search engine Infoseek. A large majority of them are not using the search engines MetaEureka, WWW worm, HotBot, WebCrawler, and WWW Virtual Library. Majority of them are not using the search engines Lycos, Excite and AltaVista.

Table 4.79 shows the frequency of use of various search engines by the science doctoral students in M. G. University. Analysis revealed that the most used Internet search engine by the science doctoral students in the M. G. University is Google. Most (96.8 per cent) of them are using it often. The second most frequently used Internet search engine is Yahoo and majority (61.3 per cent) of the scholars are using it often. About 29 per cent of them are using the search engine Yahoo sometimes. A good number of the doctoral students are using the search engines AltaVista (42 per cent) and Lycos (48.4 per cent) while a few of them are using it some times. Most of them are not using the search engines WWW worm, WWW Virtual Library, HotBot and MetaEureka. A large majority of them are not using the search engines Excite (87.1 per cent) and WebCrawler (87 per cent).

It is found that the most used Internet search engine by the science doctoral students in the M. G. University is Google. Most (99.8 per cent) of them are using it often. The second most frequently used Internet search engine is Yahoo and majority (61.3 per cent) of the scholars are using it often. A good number of them are using the search engines AltaVista and Lycos. Most of science doctoral students are not using the search engines WWW worm, WWW Virtual Library, HotBot and MetaEureka. A large majority of them are not using the search engines Excite and WebCrawler.

TABLE 4.79 : Frequency of Use of Internet Search Engines by the Science Doctoral Students in M. G. University

Search Engines	*Never*	*Sometimes*	*Often*
AltaVista	18(58%)	11(35.5%)	2(6.5%)
Excite	27(87.1%)	4(12.9%)	_
Yahoo	3(9.7%)	9(29%)	19(61.3%)
Google	_	1(3.2%)	30(96.8%)
Lycos	16(51.6%)	7(22.6%)	8(25.8%)
WebCrawler	27(87%)	2(6.5%)	2(6.5%)
WWW worm	31(100%)	_	_
WWW Virtual Library	30(96.8%)	1(3.2%)	_
HotBot	30(96.8%)	1(3.2%)	_
Infoseek	23(74.2%)	4(12.9%)	4(12.9%)
MetaEureka	30(96.8%)	1(3.2%)	_

9.2. Frequency of Use of Internet Search Engines according to Discipline

The Internet search engines used by the doctoral students in various science disciplines are given in Tables 4.80 to 4.85.

Table 4.80 shows the frequency of use of Internet search engines by the doctoral students in Bio Sciences. Analysis reveals that the most used Internet search engine among the doctoral students in Bio Sciences is Google. Most of them are using it often. The second most used Internet search engine is Yahoo and majority (74.4 per cent) of the doctoral students are using it often. Majority of them are not using the search engine AltaVista and few (37.2 per cent) of them are using it sometimes. A large majority of the doctoral students are not using the search engines WWW worm (93 per cent), WWW Virtual Library (90.7 per cent) and Excite (88.3 per cent). Most of them are not using the search engines HotBot (97.7 per cent), Infoseek (95.3 per cent), WebCrawler (95.3 per cent) and MetaEureka (95.3 per cent).

TABLE 4.80 : Frequency of Use of Internet Search Engines by the Doctoral Students in Bio Sciences

Search Engines	*Never*	*Sometimes*	*Often*
AltaVista	27(62.8%)	16(37.2%)	–
Excite	38(88.3%)	3(7%)	2(4.7%)
Yahoo	3(7%)	8(18.6%)	32(74.4%)
Google	1(2.3%)	–	42(97.7%)
Lycos	35(81.4%)	8(18.6%)	–
Web Crawler	41(95.3%)	2(4.7%)	–
WWW worm	40(93.0%)	3(7%)	–
WWW Virtual Library	39(90.7%)	4(9.3%)	–
HotBot	42(97.7%)	1(2.3%)	–
Infoseek	41(95.3%)	2(4.7%)	–
MetaEureka	41(95.3%)	2(4.7%)	–

It is found that most used Internet search engine among the doctoral students in Bio Sciences is Google. Most of the doctoral students are using it often. The second most used Internet search engine is Yahoo and majority (74.4 per cent) of the doctoral students are using it often. Majority of them are not using the search engine AltaVista and few of them are using it sometimes. A large majority of them are not using the search engines WWW worm, WWW Virtual Library and Excite. Most of them are not using the search engines HotBot, Infoseek, WebCrawler and MetaEureka.

The frequency of use of various Internet search engines by the doctoral students in Biological Sciences is given in Table 4.81.

The analysis revealed that the most used Internet search engine in Biological Sciences is Yahoo. Majority (75 per cent) of the doctoral students are using it often. The second most used Internet search engine is Google and about 76.7 per cent of the doctoral students are using it often.

Majority of them are not using the Internet search engine AltaVista and a few of them are using it sometimes. Majority of them are not using the Internet search engines Excite (83.3 per cent), Lycos (80 per cent), WWW worm (83.3 per cent) and WWW Virtual Library (81.7 per cent). A large majority of them are not using the search engines WebCrawler (93.3 per cent), Infoseek (90 per cent) and MetaEureka (93.3 per cent).

TABLE 4.81 : Frequency of Use of Internet Search Engines by the Doctoral Students in Biological Sciences

Search Engines	*Never*	*Sometimes*	*Often*
AltaVista	43(71.7%)	14(23.3%)	3(5%)
Excite	50(83.3%)	6(10%)	4(6.7%)
Yahoo	4(6.7%)	11(18.3%)	45(75%)
Google	6(10%)	8(13.3%)	46(76.7%)
Lycos	48(80%)	8(13.3%)	4(6.7%)
WebCrawler	56(93.3%)	2(3.3%)	2(3.3%)
WWW worm	50(83.3%)	2(3.3%)	8(13.3%)
WWW Virtual Library	49(81.7%)	6(10%)	5(8.3%)
HotBot	53(88.3%)	5(8.3%)	2(3.3%)
Infoseek	54(90%)	6(10%)	–
MetaEureka	56(93.3%)	4(6.7%)	–

It is revealed that most used Internet search engine in Biological Sciences is Yahoo. Majority (75 per cent) of the doctoral students are using it often. The second most used Internet search engine is Google and majority of the scholars are using it often. A large majority of them are not using the search engines WebCrawler, Infoseek and MetaEureka, and majority of them are not using the Internet search engines AltaVista, Excite, Lycos, WWW worm and WWW Virtual Library.

Table 4.82 depicts the use of various search engines

by the doctoral students in Computer Science. Analysis shows that all the respondents in Computer Science are using both the search engines Google and Yahoo. All of them are often using the search engine Google and about 50 per cent of them are often using the search engine Yahoo. About 50 per cent of the doctoral students are sometimes using the search engines AltaVista and Infoseek. No respondents are using the search engines Excite, WWW worm and WebCrawler and majority of them are not using the search engines Lycos, HotBot and WWW Virtual Library.

TABLE 4.82 : Frequency of Use of Internet Search Engines by the Doctoral Students in Computer Science

Search Engines	*Never*	*Sometimes*	*Often*
AltaVista	2(50%)	2(50%)	–
Excite	4(100%)	–	–
Yahoo	–	2(50%)	2(50%)
Google	–	–	4(100%)
Lycos	3(75%)	1(25%)	–
WebCrawler	4(100%)	–	–
WWW worm	4(100%)	–	–
WWW Virtual Library	3(75%)	1(25%)	–
HotBot	3(75%)	–	125
Infoseek	2(50%)	2(50%)	–
MetaEureka	3(75%)	1(25%)	–

It is found that all the respondents in Computer Science are using both the search engines Google and Yahoo and all of them are often using the search engine Google. About half numbers of the doctoral students are often using the search engine Yahoo. Nearly half of the doctoral students are sometimes using the search engines AltaVista and Infoseek. No respondents are using the search engines Excite, WWW worm and WebCrawler and majority of them are not using the search engines Lycos, HotBot and WWW Virtual Library.

Table 4.83 gives the use of various search engines by the doctoral students in Environmental science. Analysis shows that most used Internet search engine by the doctoral students in Environmental Science is Google. Majority (80.8 per cent) of them are using it often. The second most used Internet search engine is Yahoo and majority (80.8 per cent) of the scholars are using it often. Majority of them are not using the search engines AltaVista (76.9 per cent) and Excite (80.8 per cent), Lycos (88.4 per cent) and WWW Virtual Library (80.8 per cent). All the respondents are not using the search engines WebCrawler, WWW worm, HotBot, Infoseek and MetaEureka.

TABLE 4.83 : Frequency of Use of Internet Search Engines by the Doctoral Students in Environmental Science

Search Engines	*Never*	*Sometimes*	*Often*
AltaVista	20(76.9%)	6(23.1%)	–
Excite	21(80.8%)	4(15.4%)	1(3.8%)
Yahoo	3(11.5%)	2(7.7%)	21(80.8%)
Google	2(7.7%)	3(11.5%)	21(80.8%)
Lycos	23(88.4%)	3(11.5%)	–
WebCrawler	25(90.2%)	1(3.8%)	–
WWW worm	26(100%)	–	–
WWW Virtual Library	21(80.8%)	3(11.5%)	2(7.7%)
HotBot	26(100%)	–	–
Infoseek	26(100%)	–	–
MetaEureka	25(96.2%)	–	1(3.8%)

It is found that most used Internet search engine by the doctoral students in Environmental Science is Google. Majority of them are using it often. The second most used Internet search engine is Yahoo and majority of the doctoral students are using it often. Majority of them are not using the search engines AltaVista, Excite, Lycos and WWW Virtual Library. All the respondents are not using the search engines WebCrawler, WWW worm, HotBot, Infoseek and MetaEureka.

The frequency of use of Internet search engines by the doctoral students in Mathematical Science are analysed and given in Table 4.84

TABLE 4.84 : Frequency of Use of Internet Search Engines by the Doctoral Students in Mathematical Science

Search Engines	*Never*	*Sometimes*	*Often*
AltaVista	19(90.5%)	2(9.5%)	–
Excite	19(90.5%)	2(9.5%)	–
Yahoo	3(14.3%)	9(42.9%)	9(42.9%)
Google	4(19%)	2(9.5%)	15(71.4%)
Lycos	17(81%)	2(9.5%)	2(9.5%)
WebCrawler	19(90.5%)	2(9.5%)	–
WWW worm	18(85.7%)	1(4.8%)	2(9.5%)
WWW Virtual Library	19(90.5%)	2(9.5%)	–
HotBot	18(85.7%)	3(14.3%)	–
Infoseek	20(95.2%)	1(4.8%)	–
MetaEureka	18(85.7%)	3(14.3%)	–

Analysis shows that the most used Internet search engine by the doctoral students in Mathematics is Yahoo. A good number (42.9 per cent) of them are using it often. The second most used Internet search engine is Google and majority (71.4 per cent) of the doctoral students are using it often. Majority (81 per cent) of the scholars are not using the search engine Lycos and few of them are using it sometimes. A large majority of them are not using the search engines AltaVista (90.5 per cent), Excite (90.5 per cent), WebCrawler (90.5 per cent), WWW worm (85.7 per cent), WWW Virtual

Library (90.5 per cent), HotBot (85.7 per cent) and MetaEureka (85.7 per cent).

It is revealed that most used Internet search engine by the doctoral students in Mathematical Science is Yahoo. A good number (42.9 per cent) of them are using it often. The second most used Internet search engine is Google and majority of the doctoral students are using it often. Majority of the scholars are not using the search engine Lycos and a large majority of them are not using the search engines AltaVista, Excite, WebCrawler, WWW worm, WWW Virtual Library, HotBot and MetaEureka.

TABLE 4.85 : Frequency of Use of Internet Search Engines by the Doctoral Students in Physical Sciences

Search Engines	*Never*	*Sometimes*	*Often*
AltaVista	79(64.8%)	36(29.5%)	7(5.7%)
Excite	101(82.8%)	19(15.6%)	2(1.6%)
Yahoo	12(9.8%)	29(23.8%)	81(66.4%)
Google	6(4.9%)	6(4.9%)	110(90.2%)
Lycos	96(78.7%)	11(9%)	15(12.3%)
WebCrawler	115(94.3%)	4(3.3%)	3(2.5%)
WWW worm	117(95.9%)	3(2.5%)	2(1.6%)
WWW Virtual Library	103(84.4%)	10(8.2%)	9(7.4%)
HotBot	116(95.1%)	4(3.3%)	2(1.6%)
Infoseek	110(90.2%)	6(4.9%)	6(4.9%)
MetaEureka	114(93.4%)	3(2.5%)	5(4.1%)

Table 4.85 gives the frequency of use of various search engines by the doctoral students in Physical sciences. Analysis shows that most used Internet search engine by the doctoral students in Physical Sciences is Google. A large majority (90.2 per cent) of them are using it often. The second most used Internet search engine is Yahoo and majority (66.4 per cent) of the doctoral students are using it often. Majority

(64.8 per cent) of the scholars are not using the search engine AltaVista and few (29.5 per cent) of them are using it sometimes. Majority of them are not using the search engines Excite (82.8 per cent), Lycos (78.7 per cent) and WWW Virtual Library (84.4 per cent). A large majority of them are not using the search engines WebCrawler (94.3 per cent), Infoseek (90.2 per cent) and MetaEureka (93.4 per cent). Most of the doctoral students are not using the search engines WWW worm (95.9 per cent) and HotBot (95.1 per cent).

It is revealed that most used Internet search engine by the doctoral students in Physical Sciences is Google. A large majority of them are using it often. The second most used Internet search engine is Yahoo and majority (66.4 per cent) of the doctoral students are using it often. Majority of the scholars are not using the search engines AltaVista, Excite, Lycos and WWW Virtual Library and a large majority of them are not using the search engines WebCrawler, Infoseek and MetaEureka. Most of the doctoral students are not using the search engines WWW worm and HotBot.

10. PURPOSE OF CONDUCTING ELECTRONIC INFORMATION SEARCHES

The science doctoral students responses regarding the purpose of conducting searches are analysed university wise and discipline wise and given in Table 4.86 and 4.87.

10.1. Purpose of Conducting Electronic Information Searches according to University

Table 4.86 exhibits the purpose of conducting searches by the science doctoral students in the universities in Kerala. Analysis revealed that majority of the science doctoral students is searching electronic information resources for specific subject area (79 per cent), specific information (58.3 per cent) and abstracts of full text articles (56.9 per cent). A few numbers of them are conducting searches for library catalogues, full text articles and abstracts of citations.

Majority of the science doctoral students in the University of Kerala are conducting searches for finding specific subject area (78.1 per cent), specific information (64.8 per cent) and abstracts of full text articles (63.3 per cent). About 73.9 per cent of the science doctoral students in the University of Calicut are conducting searches for finding specific subject area. A good number (43.5 per cent) of them are conducting searches for specific information. Majority of the scholars in CUSAT are conducting searches for finding specific subject area (83.8 per cent), specific information (60.3 per cent), library catalogues (55.9 per cent) and abstracts of full text articles (51.5 per cent). A good number of them are searching for full text articles and abstracts of citations. In M. G. University, majority of the repondents are conducting searches for finding specific subject area (77.4 per cent),

TABLE 4.86 : Purpose of Conducting Electronic Information Searches According to University

Purpose of Conducting Searches	*Kerala*	*Calicut*	*CUSAT*	*M. G.*	*Grand Total*
Search library catalogue	29(22.7%)	10(21.7%)	38(55.9%)	13(41.9%)	90(32.6%)
Search specific information	83(64.8%)	20(43.5%)	41(60.3%)	14(45.2%)	158(58.3%)
Search specific subject area	101(78.9%)	34(73.9%)	57(83.8%)	24(77.4%)	216(79%)
Search only for full text articles	50(39.1%)	8(17.4%)	31(45.6%)	13(41.9%)	102(37.3%)
Browse abstracts of full text articles	81(63.3%)	15(32.6%)	35(51.5%)	23(74.2%)	154(56.9%)
Browse abstracts of citations	54(42.2%)	8(17.4%)	28(41.2%)	17(54.8%)	107(39.5%)

abstracts of full text articles (74.2 per cent) and abstracts of citations (54.8 per cent). A good number of them are searching for library catalogues, specific information and full text articles.

It is found that majority of the science doctoral students is searching electronic information resources for specific subject area, specific information and abstracts of full text articles. A few number of them are conducting searches for library catalogues, full text articles and abstracts of citations. Majority of the science doctoral students in the University of Kerala, University of Calicut, CUSAT and M. G. University are conducting searches for finding specific subject area. All the respondents in Kannur University are searching for specific information and abstracts of full text articles.

10.2. Purpose of Conducting Electronic Information Searches according to Discipline

Table 4.87 shows the purpose of conducting searches by the doctoral students in various science disciplines. Analysis revealed that 83.7 per cent of the doctoral students in Bio Sciences are conducting searches for finding specific subject area and 81.4 per cent of them are conducting searches for specific information. About 69.8 per cent of the doctoral students are browsing for abstracts of full text articles and 58.1 per cent of them searching for full text articles. Majority of the scholars in Biological Sciences are conducting searches for specific subject area (76.7 per cent) and specific information (53.3 per cent). All the respondents in Computer Science are conducting searches for specific subject area and majority of them are searching for specific information. About 80.8 per cent of the doctoral students in Environmental Science are conducting searches for specific subject area and specific information. Majority (61.9 per cent) of the doctoral students in Mathematical Science are conducting searches for specific subject area and a good number (47.7 per cent) of them are searching for specific information.

Majority of the scholars in Physical Sciences are conducting searches for specific subject area (80.3 per cent), abstracts of full text articles (60.7 per cent) and specific information (57.4 per cent).

TABLE 4.87 : Purpose of Conducting Electronic Information Searches According to Discipline

Discipline	*Purpose of Conducting Searches*					
	Search library catal-ogue	*Search spe-cific inform-ation*	*Search specific subject area*	*Search only for full text articles*	*Browse abstracts of full text articles*	*Browse abstracts of citations*
Bio Sciences	13 (30.20%)	35 (81.40%)	36 (83.70%)	25 (58.10%)	30 (69.80%)	23 (53.50%)
Biological Sciences	14 (23.30%)	32 (53.30%)	46 (76. 7%)	15 (25%)	29 (48.30%)	20 (33.30%)
Computer Science	1 (25%)	3 (75%)	4 (100%)	2 (50%)	2 (50%)	2 (50%)
Environmental Science	10 (38.50%)	21 (80.80%)	21 (80.80%)	6 (23.10%)	15 (57.70%)	12 (46.20%)
Mathematical Science	1 (4.80%)	10 (47.70%)	13 (61.90%)	8 (38.10%)	7 (33.30%)	1 (4.80%)
Physical Sciences	51 (41.80%)	70 (57.40%)	98 (80.30%)	47 (38.50%)	74 (60.70%)	51 (41.80%)
Grand Total	**90 (32.60%)**	**161 (58.30%)**	**218 (79%)**	**103 (37.30%)**	**157 (56.90%)**	**109 (39.50%)**

It is found that majority of the doctoral students in Bio Sciences, Biological Sciences, Environmental Science, Mathematical Science and Physical Sciences are conducting searches for specific subject area. All the respondents in Computer Science are conducting searches for specific subject area and majority of them are searching for specific information.

11. SEARCH METHODS USED

The search methods used by the science doctoral students for finding information from the electronic information resources is analysed and displayed in Table 4.88. Analysis shows that the most used search method among the science doctoral students is subject searches. Majority (76.1 per cent) of them are using it often. Nearly 85 per cent of the science doctoral students are using keyword searches. About 64.9 per cent of them are often conducting keyword searches while a few number of them are conducting it sometimes. Majority of the scholars are conducting author searches (67.4 per cent) and a good number (40.6 per cent) of them are using it sometimes. Search under journal title is carried out by 79.4 per cent of the respondents and majority (50.4 per cent) of them are using it often. Majority (77.2 per cent) of the doctoral students are searching under title of article and a good number (43.1 per cent) of them are using it often. A good number of them are using date of publication for searching the information while a few of them are using it often.

TABLE 4.88 : Search Methods Used by the Science Doctoral Students in Universities

Search Methods	*Never*	*Sometimes*	*Often*
Author	90(32.6%)	112(40.6%)	74(26.8%)
Keyword	42(15.2%)	55(19.9%)	179(64.9%)
Subject	25(9.1%)	41(14.9%)	210(76.1%)
Date of publication	152(55.1%)	76(27.5%)	48(17.4%)
Journal title	57(20.6%)	80(29.0%)	139(50.4%)
Title of article	63(22.8%)	94(34.1%)	119(43.1%)

It is found that the most used search method among the science doctoral students is subject searches. Majority (76.1 per cent) of them are using it often. The next most used search method is keyword searches and majority (64.9 per cent) of science doctoral students are often conducting keyword searches. Majority of them are conducting author searches and a good number of them are using it sometimes. Majority of the doctoral students are conducting searches under journal title and majority of them are using it often. Majority of the science doctoral students are searching under title of article and a good number of them are using it often. A good number of them are using date of publication for searching the information while a few of them are using it often.

11.1. Search Methods Used according to Universities

It is important to know the search methods used by the science doctoral students in different universities. The frequency of use of various search methods by the science doctoral students in the five universities in Kerala is represented in Tables 4.89 to 4.92. Table 4.89 shows the search methods used by the science doctoral students in University of Kerala for retrieving information from electronic information resources.

Table 4.89 : Search Methods Used in University of Kerala

Search Methods	*Never*	*Sometimes*	*Often*
Author	38(29.7%)	54(42.2%)	36(28.1%)
Keyword	17(13.3%)	18(14.1%)	93(72.7%)
Subject	9(7.1%)	19(14.8%)	100(78.1%)
Date of publication	68(53.1%)	34(26.6%)	26(20.3%)
Journal title	20(15.6%)	33(25.8%)	75(58.6%)
Title of article	24(18.8%)	39(30.5%)	65(50.8%)

Analysis shows that in University of Kerala, the most used search method is subject searches. Majority (78.1 per cent) of them are conducting it often. The second most used search method is keyword searches and nearly 72.7 per cent of the science doctoral students are using it often. A good number (42.2 per cent) of the scholars are conducting author searches sometimes and few (28.1 per cent) of them are using it often. Majority of them are often using journal title (58.6 per cent) and title of article (50.8 per cent) for searching the information. A good number (46.9 per cent) of them are searching under date of publication while a few of them are using it often.

It is revealed that in University of Kerala, the most used search method is subject searches. Majority (78.1 per cent) of the science doctoral students are conducting it often. The second most used search method is keyword searches and majority (72.1 per cent) of them are using it often. Majority of the scholars are conducting author searches and good number of them are using it sometimes. Majority of the science doctoral students are often using journal title and title of article for searching the information. A good number of them are searching under date of publication and a few of them are using it often.

The search methods used by the science doctoral students in University of Calicut are analysed and represented in Table 4.90. In University of Calicut also, the most used search method is subject searches. Majority (58.7 per cent) of the science doctoral students are using it often. A good number of them are often using keyword searches and few of them are using it sometimes. Majority of the scholars are conducting searches under author (50 per cent), journal title (65.3 per cent) and title of article (63.1 per cent) while a few number of them are using it often. Majority (69.6 per cent) of them are not using date of publication for searching the information.

It is found that in University of Calicut also, the most used search method is subject searches. Majority (58.7 per cent) of the science doctoral students are using it often. A good number of the scholars are often using keyword searches and few of them are using it sometimes. Majority of them are conducting searches under author, journal title and title of article and a few number of them are using it often. Majority of the scholars are not using date of publication for searching the information and few of them are using it sometimes.

TABLE 4.90 : Search Methods Used in University of Calicut

Search Methods	*Never*	*Sometimes*	*Often*
Author	23(50%)	18(39.1%)	5(10.9%)
Keyword	13(28.3%)	12(26.1%)	21(45.7%)
Subject	6(13%)	13(28.3%)	27(58.7%)
Date of publication	31(69.6%)	10(21.7%)	4(8.7%)
Journal title	16(34.7%)	17(37%)	13(28.3%)
Title of article	17(37%)	17(37%)	12(26.1%)

Table 4.91 illustrates the various search methods used by the science doctoral students in CUSAT. Analysis shows that large majority (86.8 per cent) of the science doctoral students in CUSAT are conducting subject searches and majority of them are using it often. Keyword search is the second most used search method and about 57.4 per cent of the science doctoral students are using it often. Majority of the scholars are conducting searches under author (66.2 per cent), journal title (70.6 per cent) and title of article (73.5 per cent). A good number of them are often conducting searches using journal title (47.6 per cent) and title of article

TABLE 4.91 : Search Methods Used in CUSAT

Search Methods	*Never*	*Sometimes*	*Often*
Author	23(33.8%)	26(38.2%)	19(27.9%)
Keyword	12(17.6%)	17(25%)	39(57.4%)
Subject	9(13.2%)	2(2.9%)	57(83.8%)
Date of publication	41(60.3%)	16(23.5%)	11(16.2%)
Journal title	20(29.4%)	16(23.5%)	32(47.1%)
Title of article	18(26.5%)	21(30.9%)	29(42.6%)

(42.6 per cent). Majority (60.3 per cent) of the science doctoral students are not using date of publication for searching the information.

It is revealed that large majority of the science doctoral students in CUSAT are conducting subject searches. Majority (83.8 per cent) of them are using it often. Keyword search is the second most used search method and majority of the doctoral students are using it often. Majority of them are conducting searches under author, journal title and title of article. A good number of them are often conducting searches using journal title and title of article. Majority of them are not using date of publication for searching the information and few of them are using it sometimes.

Table 4.92 depicts the different search methods used by the science doctoral students in M. G. University. Analysis shows that most used search method in M. G. University is keyword search. Majority (74.2 per cent) of the science doctoral students are often using it for searching information. Nearly 96.8 per cent of them are conducting searches using both subject and journal title. Majority of the scholars are often using subject searches (77.4 per cent) and searches using journal title (54.8 per cent). Large majority (87.1 per cent) of the science doctoral students are conducting searches using title of article, and majority (51.6 per cent) of them is using it sometimes. Majority of them are conducting searches using author (83.9 per cent) and date of publication (64.6 per cent), and a good number of them are using it sometimes.

It is found that most used search method in M. G. University is keyword search. Majority (74.2 per cent) of the science doctoral students are often using it for searching information. Most of them are conducting searches using both subject and journal title and majority of them are using it often. Large majority (87.1 per cent) of the doctoral students are conducting searches using title of article and majority of them are using it sometimes. Majority of the scholars are conducting searches using author and date of publication and a good number of them are using it sometimes.

TABLE 4.92 : Search Methods Used in M. G. University

Search Methods	*Never*	*Sometimes*	*Often*
Author	5(16.1%)	14(45.2%)	12(38.7%)
Keyword	–	8(25.8%)	23(74.2%)
Subject	1(3.2%)	6(19.4%)	24(77.4%)
Date of publication	11(35.4%)	14(45.2%)	6(19.4%)
Journal title	1(3.2%)	13(41.9%)	17(54.8%)
Title of article	4(12.9%)	16(51.6%)	11(35.5%)

11.2. Relation between the Use of Search Methods and the University

Table 4.93 shows the mean and standard deviations on the use of search methods for science doctoral students based on their university.

TABLE 4.93 : Relation between the Use of Search Methods and the University

Groups	*N*	*Mean*	*Standard Deviation*	*Minimum*	*Maximum*
University of Kerala	128	13.7109	2.85379	6.00	18.00
University of Calicut	46	11.4565	2.68913	6.00	17.00
CUSAT	68	12.9412	3.36746	6.00	18.00
M. G. University	31	14.2903	1.95267	10.00	18.00
Total	**273**	**13.2319**	**3.00736**	**6.00**	**18.00**

Table 4.94 shows the analysis of variance of the use of search methods based on the university of the science doctoral students.

TABLE 4.94 : **ANOVA Test of the Use of Search Methods based on the University**

Groups	*N*	*Mean*	*Standard Deviation*	*Minimum*	*Maximum*
Between Groups	232.623	4	58.156	6.990	.000
Within Groups	2254.536	271	8.319		
Total	2487.159	275			

The analysis of variance test indicates that the F value is 6.990 and the significance value is .000, which is less than 0.05. Hence, it is clear that there is significant difference in the use of search methods by the science doctoral students in different universities. The ANOVA test establishes that there is significant difference in the use of search methods between the science doctoral students in different universities.

11.3. Search Methods Used according to Discipline

It is important to assess the doctoral students' knowledge of various search methods to find out their information search pattern. The search methods used by the doctoral students in various science disciplines are given in Tables 5.95 to 5.100.

Table 4.95 describes the search methods used by the doctoral students in Bio Sciences for retrieving information from the electronic information resources. Analysis shows that the most used search method by the doctoral students in Bio Sciences is subject searches. Large majority (93 per cent) of them are using it often. The second most used search method is key word searches and majority (83.7 per cent) of the doctoral students are using it often. For searching information, large majority (90.7 per cent) of the scholars are using the journal title and majority (58.1 per cent) of them are using it often. Nearly 88.4 per cent of the doctoral students are using title of the article for searching and about 53.5 per cent of them are using it often. Majority of them are conducting searches using author (79.1 per cent) and date of publication

(69.8 per cent) and few of them are using it often.

TABLE 4.95 : Search Methods Used in Bio Sciences

Search Methods	*Never*	*Sometimes*	*Often*
Author	9(20.9%)	21(48.8%)	13(30.2%)
Keyword	1(2.3%)	6(14%)	36(83.7%)
Subject	–	3(7%)	40(93%)
Date of publication	13(30.2%)	19(44.2%)	11(25.6%)
Journal title	4(9.3%)	14(32.6%)	25(58.1%)
Title of article	5(11.6%)	15(34.9%)	23(53.5%)

It is found that the most used search method by the doctoral students in Bio Sciences is subject searches. Large majority (93 per cent) of them are using it often. The second most used search method is key word search and majority of the doctoral students are using it often. For searching information, large majority of them are using the journal title and title of the article, and majority of them are using it often. Majority of them are conducting searches using author and date of publication and a good number of them are using it sometimes.

The various search methods used by the doctoral students in Biological Sciences are given in Table 4.96.

TABLE 4.96 : Search Methods Used in Biological Sciences

Search Methods	*Never*	*Sometimes*	*Often*
Author	25(41.7%)	23(38.3%)	12(20%)
Keyword	10(16.7%)	11(18.3%)	39(65%)
Subject	9(15%)	14(23.3%)	37(61.7%)
Date of publication	39(65%)	11(18.3%)	10(16.7%)
Journal title	16(26.7%)	18(30%)	26(43.3%)
Title of article	20(33.3%)	18(30%)	22(36.7%)

Analysis revealed that the most used search method in Biological Sciences is subject searches. Large majority of the doctoral students are using subject searches and majority (61.7 per cent) of them are using it often. The second most used search method is keyword searches and majority (65 per cent) of them are using it often. Nearly 73.3 per cent of the doctoral students are using journal title for searching the information and a good number (43.3 per cent) of them are using it often. Majority of the scholars are conducting searches using author (58.3 per cent) and title of article (76.7 per cent) and few of them are using it often. Majority (65 per cent) of them are not using date of publication for searching the information.

It is revealed that the most used search method in Biological Sciences is subject searches. Large majority of the doctoral students are using subject searches and majority (61.7 per cent) of them are using it often. The second most used search method is keyword searches and majority of the doctoral students are using it often. Majority of them are using journal title for searching the information and a good number of them are using it often. Majority of the scholars are conducting searches using author and title of article and few of them are using it often. Majority of them are not using date of publication for searching the information while very few of them are using it often.

Table 4.97 shows the various search methods used by the doctoral students in Computer Science.

TABLE 4.97 : Search Methods Used in Computer Science

Search Methods	*Never*	*Sometimes*	*Often*
Author	–	2(50%)	2(50%)
Keyword	–	1(25%)	3(75%)
Subject	–	–	4(100%)
Date of publication	2(50%)	1(25%)	1(25%)
Journal title	–	–	4(100%)
Title of article	–	1(25%)	3(75%)

Analysis shows that all the respondents in the Computer Science are using author, keyword, subject, journal title and title of article for searching the information. All the respondents are often conducting searches using subject and journal title. Majority of them are often using key word (75 per cent), title of article (75 per cent) and author (50 per cent) for searching information. Nearly 50 per cent of the doctoral students are conducting searches using date of publication.

It is revealed that all the respondents in the Computer Science are using author, keyword, subject, journal title and title of article for searching the information. All of them are often conducting searches using subject and journal title. Majority of them are often using key word, title of article and author for searching information. Nearly half of the doctoral students are not conducting searches using date of publication.

The various search methods used by the doctoral students in Environmental Science are given in Table 4.98.

TABLE 4.98 : Search Methods Used in Environmental Science

Search Methods	*Never*	*Sometimes*	*Often*
Author	11(42.3%)	11(42.3%)	4(15.4%)
Keyword	4(15.4%)	7(26.9%)	15(57.7%)
Subject	4(15.4%)	2(7.7%)	20(76.9%)
Date of publication	19(73.1%)	4(15.4%)	3(11.5%)
Journal Title	8(30.8%)	6(23.1%)	12(46.2%)
Title of article	5(19.2%)	8(30.8%)	13(50%)

The analysis reveals that the most used search methods in Environmental Science are subject and keyword searches. Majority of the doctoral students are often using subject searches (76.9 per cent) and keyword searches (57.7 per cent). Nearly 80.8 per cent of the scholars are conducting searches using title of article and majority (50 per cent) of them are using it often. Majority (69.2 per cent) of the doctoral students are using journal title for searching information and a good number (46.2 per cent) of them are using it often. About 57.7 per cent of them are conducting author searches and a good number of them are using it sometimes. Majority of the doctoral students are not conducting searches using date of publication and very few of them are using it often.

It is revealed that the most used search methods in Environmental Science are subject and keyword searches. Majority of the doctoral students are often conducting subject searches and keyword searches. Majority of the scholars are conducting searches using title of article and majority of them are using it often. Majority of them are using journal title for searching information and a good number of them are using it often. Majority of the doctoral students are conducting author searches and a good number of them are using it sometimes. Majority of them are not conducting searches using date of publication and few of them are using it often.

Table 4.99 gives the various search methods used by the doctoral students in Mathematical Science. Analysis reveals that the most used search method in Mathematical Science is subject searches. A good number (47.6 per cent) of the doctoral students are using it often. Nearly 61.9 per cent of the scholars are using journal title and title of article for searching information and a good number of them are using it often. Majority (52.4 per cent) of the doctoral students are using key word and author for searching information, and few of them are using it often. Majority (66.7 per cent) of them are not conducting searches using date of publication and few of them are using it often.

TABLE 4.99 : **Search Methods Used in Mathematical Science**

Search Methods	*Never*	*Sometimes*	*Often*
Author	10(47.6%)	4(19%)	7(33.3%)
Keyword	10(47.6%)	5(23.8%)	6(28.6%)
Subject	4(19%)	7(33.3%)	10(47.6%)
Date of publication	14(66.7%)	4(19%)	3(14.3%)
Journal title	8(38.1%)	4(19%)	9(42.9%)
Title of article	8(38.1%)	4(19%)	9(42.9%)

It is found that most used search method in Mathematical Science is subject searches. A good number of the doctoral students are using it often. Majority of the scholars are using journal title and title of article for searching information and a good number of them are using it often. Majority of the doctoral students are using key word and author for searching information, and few of them are using it often. Majority of them are not conducting searches using date of publication and very few of them are using it often.

The various search methods used by the doctoral students in Physical Sciences are given in Table 4.100. The analysis revealed that in Physical Sciences, the most used search method by the doctoral students is subject searches. Majority (81.1 per cent) of them are using it often. The second most used search method is keyword searches and about 65.6 per cent of the doctoral students are using it often. Nearly 82.8 per cent of the respondents are using journal title for searching information and majority (51.6 per cent) of them are using it often. Majority (79.5 per cent) of them are using title of article for searching information and a good number (40.5 per cent) of them are using it often. Nearly 71.3 per cent of the doctoral students are using author name for searching information and a good number (41.8 per cent) of them are using it sometimes. Majority of them are not using date of publication for searching information.

TABLE 4.100 : Search Methods Used in Physical Sciences

Search Methods	Never	Sometimes	Often
Author	35(28.7%)	51(41.8%)	36(29.5%)
Keyword	17s(13.9%)	25(20.5%)	80(65.6%)
Subject	8(6.6%)	15(12.3%)	99(81.1%)
Date of publication	65(53.3%)	37(30.3%)	20(16.4%)
Journal title	21(17.2%)	38(31.1%)	63(51.6%)
Title of article	25(20.5%)	48(39.3%)	49(40.5%)

It is found that the most used search method by the doctoral students in Physical Sciences is subject searches. Majority (81.1 per cent) of them are using it often. The second most used search method is keyword searches and majority of the doctoral students are using it often. Majority of the scholars are using journal title for searching information and majority of them are using it often. Majority of the scholars are using title of article for searching information and a good number of them are using it often. Majority of the doctoral students are using author name for searching information and a good number of them are using it sometimes. Majority of them are not using date of publication for searching information.

11.4. Relation between the Use of Search Methods and the Discipline

Table 4.101 shows the mean and standard deviations on the use of search methods for doctoral students based on their discipline.

Table 4.102 shows the analysis of variance of the use of search methods based on the discipline of the doctoral students. The analysis of variance test indicates that the F value is 5.529 and the significance value is .000, which is less than 0.05. Hence, it is clear that there is significant difference in the use of search methods by the science doctoral students in different disciplines. The ANOVA test establishes that there is significant difference in the use search methods between the science doctoral students in different disciplines.

TABLE 4.101 : Relation between the Use of Search Methods and the Discipline

Groups	*N*	*Mean*	*Standard Deviation*	*Minimum*	*Maximum*
Bio Sciences	41	14.6977	2.80760	8.00	18.00
Biological Sciences	60	12.4500	2.66442	8.00	18.00
Computer Science	3	15.7500	2.06155	14.00	18.00
Environmental Science	26	12.6154	2.88551	6.00	18.00
Mathematical Science	21	11.5238	3.97013	6.00	18.00
Physical Sciences	122	13.4426	2.83149	6.00	18.00
Total	**273**	**13.2319**	**3.00736**	**6.00**	**18.00**

TABLE 4.102 : ANOVA Test of the Use of Search Methods for Science Doctoral Students Based on Discipline

Source of Variance	*Sum of Squares*	*d. f*	*Mean Square*	*F*	*Sig.*
Between Groups	230.999	5	46.200	5.529	.000
Within Groups	2256.160	270	8.356		
Total	**2487.159**	**275**			

12. USE OF ADVANCED SEARCH METHODS

In an electronic environment, it is necessary to know the use advanced search methods in order to narrow or broaden the search results. Table 5.103 depicts the use of advanced search methods by the science doctoral students in the universities in Kerala. The analysis shows that majority of the science doctoral students are using Boolean operators for searching the information. About 31.2 per cent of them are using it sometimes and a few (20.3 per cent) of them are using it often. Majority of the scholars are not using the truncation of search terms (71 per cent), field searching (52.9 per cent) and phrases (63.5 per cent) for searching the information. A good number (47.1 per cent) of the scholars are using the field searching and a few (29.3 per cent) of them are using it often.

TABLE 4.103 : Use of Advanced Search Methods by the Science Doctoral Students in the Universities in Kerala

Advanced Search Methods	*Never*	*Sometimes*	*Often*
Boolean operators	134(48.5%)	86(31.2%)	56(20.3%)
Truncation of search terms	196(71%)	62(22.5%)	18(6.5%)
Field searching	146(52.9%)	49(17.8%)	81(29.3%)
Phrases	175(63.5%)	56(20.3%)	45(16.3%)

It is found that majority (51.5 per cent) of the science doctoral students are using Boolean operators for searching the information and a few of them are using it often. Majority of them are not using the truncation of search terms, field searching and phrases for searching the information.

12.1. Use of Advanced Search Methods according to University

The frequency of use of advanced search methods by the science doctoral students in the five universities in Kerala is represented in Tables 4.104 to 4.113.

Considering the enormous growth of the amount of information that is available on the Internet, use of advanced search facilities will become increasingly necessary in order to limit the search results. Table 4.104 shows the use of advanced search methods by the science doctoral students in University of Kerala. Analysis revealed that the majority of the science doctoral students in the University of Kerala are using the field searching and 34.4 per cent of them are using it often. Majority of them are not using the advanced search methods such as truncation of search terms (75.7 per cent), searches using phrases (64 per cent) and Boolean operators (51.3 per cent). A good number (46.9 per cent) of the science doctoral students are using Boolean operators and few (21.9 per cent) of them are using it often.

TABLE 4.104 : Use of Advanced Search Methods by the Science Doctoral Students in University of Kerala

Advanced Search Methods	*Never*	*Sometimes*	*Often*
Boolean operators	68(53.1%)	32(25.0%)	28(21.9%)
Truncation of search terms	97(75.7%)	23(18.0%)	8(6.3%)
Field searching	62(48.4%)	22(17.2%)	44(34.4%)
Phrases	82(64%)	24(18.8%)	22(17.2%)

It is found that majority (51.6 per cent) of the science doctoral students in the University of Kerala are using the field searching and few of them are using it often. Majority of them are not using the advanced search methods such as truncation of search terms, searches using phrases and Boolean operators.

Table 5.105 shows the use of advanced search methods by the science doctoral students in University of Calicut.

TABLE 4.105 : Use of Advanced Search Methods by the Science Doctoral Students in University of Calicut

Advanced Search Methods	*Never*	*Sometimes*	*Often*
Boolean operators	33(71.7%)	10(21.7%)	3(6.5%)
Truncation of search terms	44(95.7%)	2(4.3%)	–
Field searching	27(58.7%)	11(23.9%)	8(17.4%)
Phrases	32(65.6%)	10(21.7%)	4(8.7%)

Analysis describes that in University of Calicut most of the science doctoral students are not using truncation of search terms (95.7 per cent) and majority of them are not using Boolean operators (71.7 per cent), phrases (65.6 per cent), and field searching (58.7 per cent) for finding information. Nearly 41.3 per cent of the science doctoral students are using field searching and few of them are using it often. It may be because of the reason that the science doctoral students in the University of Calicut are unaware of the use of advanced search methods.

It is found that in University of Calicut, most of the science doctoral students are not using truncation of search terms and majority of them are not using Boolean operators, phrases, and field searching for finding information.

The use of advanced search methods among the science doctoral students in CUSAT is analysed and given in Table 4.106. Analysis shows that in CUSAT, majority (58.8 per cent) of the science doctoral students are using the advanced search method Boolean operators. About 39.7 per cent of them are using it sometimes and 19.1 per cent respondents are using it often. Majority of them are not conducting searches using phrases (58.8 per cent), truncation of search terms (58.8 per cent), and field searching (54.4 per cent). Nearly 36.8 per cent of the science doctoral students are conducting searches using truncation of search terms and few (8.8 per cent) of them are using it often. About 27.9 per cent of them are often using field searching while 22.1 per cent of them are often conducting searches using phrases.

It is revealed that in CUSAT, majority (58.8 per cent) of the science doctoral students are using the advanced search method Boolean operators and few of them are using it often. Majority of them are not conducting searches using phrases, truncation of search terms and field searching.

TABLE 4.106 : Use of Advanced Search Methods by the Science Doctoral Students in CUSAT

Advanced Search Methods	*Never*	*Sometimes*	*Often*
Boolean operators	28(41.2%)	27(39.7%)	13(19.1%)
Truncation of search terms	37(54.4%)	25(36.8%)	6(8.8%)
Field searching	40(58.8%)	9(13.2%)	19(27.9%)
Phrases	40(58.8%)	13(19.1%)	15(22.1%)

Table 4.107 illustrates the various advanced search methods used by the science doctoral students in M. G. University. Analysis shows that in M. G. University majority (83.9 per cent) of the science doctoral students are using Boolean operators. A good number (48.4 per cent) of them are sometimes using Boolean operators and few (35.5 per cent) of them are using it often. Majority of them are not using phrases (64.5 per cent), truncation of search terms (58 per cent), and field searching (54.8 per cent) for searching information. A few of them are sometimes using truncation of search terms (32.3 per cent), field searching (22.6 per cent), and phrases (25.8 per cent) for searching information.

TABLE 4.107 : Use of Advanced Search Methods by the Science Doctoral Students in M. G. University

Advanced Search Methods	*Never*	*Sometimes*	*Often*
Boolean operators	5(16.1%)	15(48.4%)	11(35.5%)
Truncation of search items	18(58%)	10(32.3%)	3(9.7%)
Field searching	17(54.8%)	7(22.6%)	7(22.6%)
Phrases	20(64.5%)	8(25.8%)	3(9.7%)

It is found that in M. G. University, majority (83.9 per cent) of the science doctoral students are using Boolean operators and a good number of them are using it sometimes. Majority of the scholars are not using phrases, truncation of search terms and field searching for finding information and few of them are using it sometimes.

12.2. Use of Advanced Search Methods according to Discipline

The frequency of use of advanced search methods by the doctoral students in various science disciplines are analysed and represented in Tables 4.108 to 4.113.

Table 4.108 shows the use of advanced search methods in Bio Sciences. Analysis revealed that nearly 74.4 per cent of the doctoral students in Bio Sciences are using Boolean operators for searching information. A good number (44.2 per cent) of them are using it sometimes and few (30.2 per cent) of them are using it often. Majority (58.2 per cent) of the scholars are using field searching and a good number (44.2 per cent) of them are using it often. Majority of the doctoral students are not using truncation of search terms (55.8 per cent) and phrases (55.8 per cent) for searching information while few number of them are using it sometimes.

TABLE 4.108 : Use of advanced search methods by the Doctoral Students in Bio Sciences

Advanced Search Methods	*Never*	*Sometimes*	*Often*
Boolean operators	11(25.6%)	19(44.2%)	13(30.2%)
Truncation of search terms	24(55.8%)	16(37.2%)	3(7%)
Field searching	18(41.8%)	6(14%)	19(44.2%)
Phrases	24(55.8%)	11(25.6%)	8(18.6%)

It is found that majority (74.4 per cent) of the doctoral students in Bio Sciences are using Boolean operators for searching information. A good number of them are using it sometimes and few of them are using it often. Majority (58.2 per cent) of the doctoral students are using field searching and a good number of them are using it often. Majority of them are not using truncation of search terms and phrases for searching information while few number of them are using it sometimes.

Table 4.109 describes the frequency of use of various advanced search methods by the doctoral students in Biological Sciences. Analysis shows that a good number (46.7 per cent) of the doctoral students in Biological Sciences are using field searching for searching information and few (20.6 per cent) of them are using it often. Majority of them are not conducting searches using Boolean operators (70 per cent) and phrases (68.3 per cent), and few of them are using it sometimes. A large majority (90 per cent) of the respondents are not conducting searches using truncation of search terms.

TABLE 4.109 : Use of Advanced Search Methods by the Doctoral Students in Biological Sciences

Advanced Search Methods	*Never*	*Sometimes*	*Often*
Boolean operators	42(70%)	12(20%)	6(10%)
Truncation of search terms	54(90%)	6(10%)	–
Field searching	32(53.3%)	12(20%)	16(26.7%)
Phrases	41(68.3%)	15(25%)	4(6.7%)

It is revealed that a good number of the doctoral students in Biological Sciences are using field searching and few of them are using it often. Majority of them are not conducting searches using Boolean operators and phrases while few of them are using it sometimes. A large majority of the doctoral students are not conducting searches using truncation of search terms.

The frequency of use of advanced search methods by the doctoral students in Computer Science is given in Table 4.110.

TABLE 4.110 : Use of Advanced Search Methods by the Doctoral Students in Computer Science

Advanced Search Methods	*Never*	*Sometimes*	*Often*
Boolean operators	_	_	4(100%)
Truncation of search terms	1(25%)	1(25%)	2(50%)
Field searching	_	_	4(100%)
Phrases	1(25%)	1(25%)	2(50%)

The analysis shows that in Computer Science, all the doctoral students are often using the Boolean operators and field searching for finding the information. Majority (75 per cent) of them are using truncation of search terms and phrases for searching information and about 50 per cent of them are using it often.

It is revealed that in Computer Science, all the respondents are often using the Boolean operators and field searching for finding the information. Majority of the doctoral students are using truncation of search terms and phrases for searching information and about half of them are using it often

Table 4.111 shows the frequency of use of advanced search methods by the doctoral students in Environmental Science. Analysis revealed that nearly 50 per cent of the doctoral students in Environmental Science are using Boolean operators for searching information and few (26.2 per cent) of them are using it often. Majority of them are not conducting searches using truncation of search terms (84.6 per cent), field searching (69.2 per cent) and phrases (61.5 per cent) while few of them are using it often.

TABLE 4.111 : Use of Advanced Search Methods by the Doctoral Students in Environmental Science

Advanced Search Methods	*Never*	*Sometimes*	*Often*
Boolean operators	13(50%)	6(23.1%)	7(26.9%)
Truncation of search terms	22(84.6%)	3(11.5%)	1(3.8%)
Field searching	18(69.2%)	5(19.2%)	3(11.5%)
Phrases	16(61.5%)	5(19.2%)	5(19.2%)

It is found that nearly half of the doctoral students in Environmental Science are using Boolean operators for searching information and few of them are using it often. Majority of them are not conducting searches using truncation of search terms, field searching and phrases while very few of them are using it sometimes.

The use of advanced search methods by the doctoral students in the Mathematical Science is given in Table 4.112. Analysis revealed that majority of the doctoral students in Mathematical Science are not using Boolean operators (66.7 per cent) and field searching (71.4 per cent) for finding information while few of them are using it sometimes. Most of the scholars are not using truncation of search terms (85.7 per cent) and phrases (90.5 per cent) for searching information.

TABLE 4.112 : Use of Advanced Search Methods by the Doctoral Students in Mathematical Science

Advanced Search Methods	*Never*	*Sometimes*	*Often*
Boolean operators	14(66.7%)	6(28.6%)	1(4.8%)
Truncation of search terms	18(85.7%)	3(14.3%)	_
Field searching	15(71.4%)	3(14.3%)	3(14.3%)
Phrases	19(90.5%)	1(4.8%)	1(4.8%)

It is found that majority of the doctoral students in

Mathematical Science are not using Boolean operators and field searching for finding information while a very few of them are using it sometimes. A large majority of them are not using truncation of search terms and Phrases for searching information.

Table 4.113 shows the frequency of use of advanced search methods by the doctoral students in Physical Sciences. Analysis reveals that majority of the doctoral students in Physical Sciences are using Boolean operators for searching information and about 35.2 per cent of them are using it sometimes. A good number (48.4 per cent) of the scholars are using field searching and few (29.5 per cent) of them are using it often. Majority of them are not using truncation of search terms (63.1 per cent) and phrases (60.7 per cent) for searching information while few of them are using it sometimes.

TABLE 4.113 : Use of Advanced Search Methods by the Doctoral Students in Physical Sciences

Advanced Search Methods	*Never*	*Sometimes*	*Often*
Boolean operators	54(44.3%)	43(35.2%)	25(20.5%)
Truncation of search terms	77(63.1%)	33(27%)	12(9.8%)
Field searching	63(51.6%)	23(18.9%)	36(29.5%)
Phrases	74(60.7%)	23(18.6%)	25(20.5%)

It is revealed that majority (55.7 per cent) of the doctoral students in Physical Sciences are using Boolean operators for searching information and few of them are using it often. A good number (48.4 per cent) of the scholars are using field searching and few of them are using it often. Majority of them are not using truncation of search terms and Phrases for searching information while few of them are using it sometimes.

13. DIFFICULTIES IN OBTAINING INFORMATION FROM ONLINE SEARCH

The science doctoral students were requested to indicate the major obstacles they faced in online search and it is analysed university wise and discipline wise and represented in Table 4.114 and Table 4.115.

13.1. Difficulties in obtaining Information from Online Search according to University

Table 4.113 represents science doctoral students responses regarding the difficulties faced while conducting online search. Analysis shows that speed of access is the major obstacle in the online search. Majority (83.7 per cent) of the science doctoral students indicated speed of access as the major

TABLE 4.113 : Difficulties in obtaining Information from Online Search according to University

Obstacles in online search	*Kerala*	*Calicut*	*CUSAT*	*M. G.*	*Grand Total*
Unfamiliarity with search methods	33 (25.8%)	24 (52.2%)	15 (22.1%)	9 (29%)	81 (29.3%)
Too much information available	46 (35.9%)	20 (43.5%)	46 (67.6%)	19 (61.3%)	131 (47.8%)
Lack of time for searching	75 (58.6%)	28 (60.9%)	27 (39.7%)	12 (38.7%)	142 (51.8%)
Speed of access	118 (92.2%)	30 (65.2%)	62 (91.2%)	20 (64.5%)	230 (83.7%)
Cost	86 (67.2%)	19 (41.3%)	32 (47.1%)	18 (58.1%)	155 (56.2%)
Lack of on line help	40 (31.3%)	12 (26.1%)	9 (13.2%)	5 (16.1%)	66 (24.3%)
Lack of subject specificity	29 (22.7%)	17 (37%)	45 (66.2%)	19 (61.3%)	110 (40.2%)

obstacle in the online search. Nearly 56.2 per cent of them mentioned cost and about 51.8 per cent of them pointed out lack of time for searching as the impediments faced in online search. A good number of the scholars indicated that too much information available (47.8 per cent) and lack of subject specificity (40.2 per cent) are the difficulties faced in online search.

A large majority (92.2 per cent) of the science doctoral students in University of Kerala indicted the 'speed of access' as the major obstacle in online search and majority (67.2 per cent) of them are mentioned cost as the second impediment faced in online search. The major obstacles faced by the science doctoral students in University of Calicut are speed of access (65.2 per cent), lack of time for searching (60.9 per cent) and unfamiliarity with search methods (52.2 per cent). A large majority (91.2 per cent) of the scholars in CUSAT indicated that speed of access as the major impediment in online search. Where as a majority of them has the opinion that too much information available (67.6 per cent) and lack of subject specificity (66.2 per cent) are the obstacles in online search. The major obstacles faced by the science doctoral students in M. G. University are speed of access (64.5 per cent), too much information available (61.3 per cent), lack of subject specificity (61.3 per cent) and cost (58.1 per cent). Majority of the science doctoral students in Kannur University are not facing any obstacles in online search.

It is found that majority (83.7 per cent) of the science doctoral students indicated speed of access as the major obstacle in the online search. A large majority of the doctoral students in University of Kerala indicted the speed of access and majority of them are mentioned cost as the impediments faced in online search. The major obstacles faced by the scholars in University of Calicut are speed of access, lack of time for searching and unfamiliarity with search methods. A large majority of the science doctoral students in CUSAT indicated that speed of access as the major impediment in online search while a majority of them has the opinion that too much information available and lack of subject specificity are the obstacles in online search. The major obstacles faced by the science doctoral students in M. G. University are speed of access, too much information available, lack of subject specificity and cost.

13.2. Difficulties in Obtaining Information from Online Search according to Discipline

Table 4.114 shows the difficulties faced by the doctoral students in different science disciplines while conducting online search. Analysis revealed that majority (74.4 per cent) of the doctoral students in Bio Sciences indicted the 'speed of access' as the major obstacle in online search and few (34.9 per cent) of them are mentioned that too much information available in online search. The major obstacles faced by the doctoral students in Biological Sciences are speed of access (83.3 per cent) and lack of time for searching (58.3 per cent). Nearly half of the doctoral students in Computer Science indicated that speed of access and cost are the major impediments in online search. A large majority (88.5 per cent) of the doctoral students in Environmental Science opined that speed of access as the major impediment in online search. Majority of them have the opinion that lack of time for searching (84.6 per cent), too much information available (73.1 per cent) and cost (76.9 per cent) are the obstacles in online search. Majority (76.2 per cent) of the doctoral students in Mathematical Science indicated that speed of access is the major impediment in online search. A large majority (90.2 per cent) of the doctoral students in Physical Sciences mentioned that speed of access as the major impediment in online search while majority of them have mentioned cost (54.1 per cent) as the obstacle in online search.

TABLE 4.114 : Difficulties in obtaining Information from Online Search according to Discipline

Obstacles in Online Search	*Bio Scie-nces*	*Bio-logical Scie-nces*	*Comp-uter Scie-nce*	*Environ-mental Scie-nce*	*Mathe-matical Scie-nce*	*Physical Scie-nces*
unfamiliarity with search methods	1 (2.30%)	11 (18.30%)	_	4 (15.40%)	3 (14.30%)	39 (32%)
Too much information available	15 (34.90%)	19 (31.70%)	_	19 (73.10%)	_	60 (49.20%)
Lack of time for searching	7 (16.30%)	35 (58.30%)	2 (50%)	22 (84.60%)	5 (23.80%)	39 (32%)
Speed of access	32 (74.40%)	50 (83.30%)	2 (50%)	23 (88.50%)	16 (76.20%)	110 (90.20%)
Cost	6 (14%)	25 (41.70%)	_	20 (76.90%)	4 (19%)	66 (54.10%)
Lack of on line help	4 (9.30%)	17 (28.30%)	1 (25%)	2 (7.70%)	4 (19%)	16 (13.10%)
Lack of subject specificity	8 (18.60%)	9 (15%)	1 (25%)	4 (15.40%)	4 (19%)	54 (44.30%)

It is found that majority (74.4 per cent) of the doctoral students in Bio Sciences indicted the 'speed of access' as the major obstacle in online search. The major obstacles faced by the doctoral students in Biological Sciences are speed of access (83.3 per cent) and lack of time for searching (58.3 per cent). Nearly half of the doctoral students in Computer Science indicated that speed of access and cost are the major impediments in online search. A large majority of the scholars in Environmental Science mentioned that speed of access as the major impediment in online search. Majority of them have the opinion that lack of time for searching, too much information available and cost are the obstacles in online search. Majority of the doctoral students in Mathematical Science indicated that speed of access is the major impediment in online search. A large majority of the respondents in Physical Sciences indicated that speed of access as the major impediment in online search while majority of them have mentioned cost as the obstacle in online search.

14. ABILITY IN USING ELECTRONIC INFORMATION RESOURCES

The science doctoral students rating regarding their overall ability in using electronic information resources are represented university wise and discipline wise in the Table 4.115 and Table 4.116 respectively.

14.1. Ability in Using Electronic Information Resources according to University

Table 4.115 shows the science doctoral students responses regarding their overall ability in using electronic information

TABLE 4.115 : Ability in Using Electronic Information Resources according to University

Ability in using Electronic Information Resources	*University of Kerala*	*University of Calicut*	*CUSAT*	*M. G. University*	*Grand Total*
Beginner	14 (10.90%)	10 (21.70%)	5 (7.40%)	–	29 (10.50%)
Below Average	6 (4.70%)	3 (6.50%)	4 (5.90%)	1 (3.20%)	14 (5.10%)
Average	73 (57%)	28 (60.90%)	34 (50%)	17 (54.80%)	152 (55.70%)
Above Average	24 (18.80%)	5 (10.90%)	23 (33.80%)	10 (32.30%)	62 (22.50%)
Expert	11 (8.60%)	–	2 (2.90%)	3 (9.70%)	16 (6.20%)
Grand Total	**128 (100%)**	**46 (100%)**	**68 (100%)**	**31 (100%)**	**273 (100%)**

resources. Analysis revealed that majority (55.7 per cent) of the scholars rated their overall ability in using electronic information resources as average.

The majority of the science doctoral students in University of Kerala (57 per cent), University of Calicut (60.9 per cent), CUSAT (50 per cent) and M. G. University (54.8 per cent) rated their overall ability in using electronic information resources as average. It is revealed that majority of the science doctoral students in the universities in Kerala rated their overall ability in using electronic information resources as average. It is also found that majority of the respondents in University of Kerala, University of Calicut, CUSAT, M. G. University and Kannur University rated their overall ability as average in using electronic information resources.

14.2. Ability in Using Electronic Information Resources according to Discipline

The doctoral students in different science disciplines were requested to rate their overall ability in using electronic information resources and the responses are given in Table 4.116. Analysis shows that majority (58.1 per cent) of the doctoral students in Bio Sciences are average and few (25.6 per cent) of them are above average in using the electronic information resources. In Biological Sciences, majority (58.3 per cent) of the doctoral students are average and about 20 per cent of them are above average in using the electronic information resources. About 50 per cent of the scholars in Computer Science indicated that they are experts and 50 per cent of them are above average in using electronic information resources. Nearly 65.4 per cent of the doctoral students in Environmental Science rated their overall ability in using electronic information resources as average and few (15.4 per cent) of them are beginners in using the electronic information resources. Majority (52.4 per cent) of the scholars in Mathematical Science rated their overall ability as average and about 28.6 per cent of them indicated that they are beginners in using electronic information resources. Nearly 54.1 per cent of the doctoral students in Physical Sciences rated their overall ability in using electronic information resources as average and few (27.9 per cent) of them are above average in using the electronic information resources.

TABLE 4.116 : Ability in Using Electronic Information Resources according to Discipline

Discipline	*Overall Ability in Using Electronic Information Resources*				
	Beginner	*Below Average*	*Average*	*Above Average*	*Expert*
Bio Sciences	2 (4.70%)	_	25 (58.10%)	11 (25.60%)	5 (11.60%)
Biological Sciences	6 (10%)	5 (8.30%)	35 (58.30%)	12 (20%)	2 (3.30%)
Computer Science	_	_	_	2 (50%)	2 (50%)
Environmental Science	4 (15.40%)	3 (11.50%)	17 (65.40%)	2 (7.70%)	_
Mathematical Science	6 (28.60%)	3 (14.30%)	11 (52.40%)	1 (4.80%)	_
Physical Sciences	11 (9%)	3 (2.50%)	66 (54.10%)	34 (27.90%)	8 (6.60%)
Grand Total	**29 (10.50%)**	**14 (5.10%)**	**154 (55.80%)**	**62 (22.50%)**	**17 (6.20%)**

It is found that majority of the doctoral students Bio Sciences, Biological Sciences, Environmental Science, Mathematical Science and Physical Sciences rated their overall ability in using electronic information resources as average. About half of the respondents in Computer Science are experts and half of them are above average in using electronic information resources.

15. IMPACT OF ELECTRONIC INFORMATION RESOURCES ON RESEARCH

The university wise and discipline wise analysis of the science doctoral students' opinion about the impact of electronic information resources on research are given in Table 4.117 and Table 4.118 respectively.

15.1. Impact of Electronic Information Resources on Research according to University

The science doctoral students in the universities in Kerala were asked to indicate the impact of electronic information resources on research and the responses are given in Table 4.117. Analysis shows that the major impact of electronic information resources on research is fast research update, about 72.8 per cent of the science doctoral students indicated it. About 52.2 per cent of them mentioned that electronic information resources helped in saving time.

TABLE 4.117 : Impact of Electronic Information Resources on Research according to University

Impact of Electronic Information Resources	*University of Kerala*	*University of Calicut*	*CUSAT*	*M. G. University*	*GrandTotal*
Fast Research update	90 (70.30%)	30 (65.20%)	53 (77.90%)	25 (80.60%)	198 (72.80%)
Better co-operation with colleagues	23 (18.00%)	11 (23.90%)	34 (50%)	11 (35.50%)	79 (28.60%)
Fast access to databases	57 (44.50%)	14 (30.40%)	39 (57.40%)	17 (54.80%)	127 (46.70%)
Saving time	63 (44.50%)	22 (47.80%)	38 (55.90%)	20 (64.50%)	143 (52.20%)

In University of Kerala, the major impact of electronic information resources on research is fast research update, about 70.3 per cent of the science doctoral students have pointed out it. Nearly 44.5 per cent of them indicated that electronic information resources helped for the fast access to databases and in saving time. Majority (65.2 per cent) of the respondents in University of Calicut also indicated that electronic information resources helped them for fast research update. In CUSAT, the major impact of electronic information resources on research is fast research update. About 77.9 per cent of the science doctoral students have pointed out it. Majority of them indicated that electronic information resources helped in better co-operation with colleagues (50 per cent), fast access to databases (57.4 per cent) and saving time (55.9 per cent). Majority of the scholars in M. G. University indicated that electronic information resources helped them for fast research update.

It is revealed that majority of the science doctoral students indicated that the major impact of electronic information resources on research is fast research update. It is also found that majority of the science doctoral students in University of Kerala, University of Calicut, CUSAT and M. G. University have the opinion that electronic information resources helped them for fast research update.

15.2 Impact of Electronic Information Resources on Research according to Discipline

The doctoral students responses regarding the impact of electronic information resources on research is analysed discipline wise and given in Table 4.118. Analysis shows that majority (83.7 per cent) of the doctoral students in Bio Sciences have the opinion that electronic information resources helped them for fast research update and about 62.8 per cent of them indicated that it helped them for saving time. Nearly 71.7 per cent of the doctoral students in Biological Sciences indicated that electronic information resources helped them for fast research update and a good number (41.7 per cent) of them mentioned that it helped for saving time. In Computer Science, the major impact of electronic information resources on research is fast research update about 75 per cent of the respondents have pointed out it. Nearly 50 per cent of them indicated that electronic information resources helped for saving time and better co-operation with colleagues. Majority (76.9 per cent) of the doctoral students in Environmental Science also indicated that electronic information resources helped them for fast research update and for 61.5 per cent of them it helped for saving time. In Mathematical Science, the major impact of electronic information resources on research is fast research update about 52.4 per cent of the doctoral students have pointed out it. Majority (72.1 per cent) of the scholars in Physical Sciences have the opinion that electronic information resources helped them for fast research update and about 55.7 per cent of them indicated that it helped them for saving time.

TABLE 4.118 : Impact of Electronic information resources on Research according to Discipline

Discipline	*Impact of electronic information resources*			
	Fast Research update	*Better co-ope-ration with colleagues*	*Fast access to data-bases*	*Saving time*
Bio Sciences	36(83.7%)	10(23.3%)	24(55.8%)	27(62.8%)
Biological Sciences	43(71.7%)	13(21.7%)	20(33.3%)	25(41.7%)
Computer Science	3(75%)	2(50%)	1(25%)	2(50%)
Environmental Science	20(76.9%)	10(38.5%)	13(50%)	16(61.5%)
Mathematical Science	11(52.4%)	6(28.6%)	7(33.3%)	6(28.6%)
Physical Sciences	88(72.1%)	38(31.1%)	64(52.5%)	68(55.7%)
Grand Total	**201(72.8%)**	**79(28.6%)**	**129(46.7%)**	**144 (52.2%)**

It is found that majority of the doctoral students in all the science disciplines indicated that the major impact of electronic information resources on research is fast research update. Majority of the doctoral students in Bio Sciences, Computer Science, Environmental Science and Physical Sciences also pointed out that electronic information resources helped them for saving time.

16. USE OF PRINTED DOCUMENTS WHILE USING ELECTRONIC INFORMATION RESOURCES

It is important to know whether the use of electronic information resources diminished the use of printed documents among the science doctoral students in the universities in Kerala. The scholars' responses regarding the use of printed documents while using electronic information resources are represented university wise and discipline wise in Table 4.119 and Table 4.120 respectively.

16.1. Use of Printed Documents While Using Electronic information resources according to University

Table 4.119 gives the university wise analysis of the science doctoral students' responses regarding the use of printed documents while using electronic information resources.

TABLE 4.119 : Use of Printed Documents While Using Electronic Information Resources according to University

Use of Printed Documents	*University of Kerala*	*University of Calicut*	*CUSAT*	*M. G. University*	*Grand Total*
Decreased	48(37.5%)	9(19.6%)	24(35.3%)	13(41.9%)	94(34.8%)
Increased	24(18.8%)	7(15.2%)	12(17.6%)	4(12.9%)	47(17%)
No change	56(43.8%)	30(65.2%)	32(47.1%)	14(45.2%)	132(48.2%)
Grand Total	**128(100%)**	**46(100%)**	**68(100%)**	**31(100%)**	**273(100%)**

Analysis revealed that a good number (48.2 per cent) of the science doctoral students have the opinion that there is no change in the use of printed documents while using electronic information resources. A few number (34.8 per cent) of them indicated a decrease in the use of printed documents while using electronic information resources. Nearly 17 per cent of the doctoral students indicated an increase in the use of printed documents while using electronic information resources.

It is found that majority of the science doctoral students in University of Calicut (65.2 per cent) have the opinion that there is no change in the use of printed documents while using electronic information resources. Few of them indicated a decrease in the use of printed documents. A good number of the scholars in University of Kerala (43.8 per cent), CUSAT (47.1 per cent) and M. G. University (45.2 per cent) have the opinion that there is no change in the use of printed documents while using electronic information resources.

It is revealed that a good number of the science doctoral students have the opinion that there is no change in the use of printed documents. A few number (34.8 per cent) of them indicated a decrease in the use of printed documents while using electronic information resources. It is also found that majority of the science doctoral students in University of Calicut, and a good number of science doctoral students in University of Kerala, CUSAT and M. G. University have the opinion that there is no change in the use of printed documents while using electronic information resources.

16.2. Use of Printed Documents While Using Electronic Information Resources according to Discipline

Table 4.120 shows the doctoral students use of printed documents while using the electronic information resources in various science disciplines. Analysis revealed that a good number (41.8 per cent) of the doctoral students in Bio Sciences has the opinion that there is no change in the use of printed documents while using electronic information resources. About 37.2 per cent of them indicated a decrease in the use of printed documents while using electronic information resources. Majority of the doctoral students in Biological Sciences indicated that there is no change in the use of printed documents while using electronic information resources and few of them indicated a decrease in the use of printed documents. Nearly 75 per cent of the respondents in Computer Science indicated that there is a decrease in the use of printed documents while using electronic information resources. Majority (53.8 per cent) of the doctoral students in Environmental Science have the opinion that there is an increase in the use of printed documents and few (26.9 per cent) of them indicated no change in the use of printed documents while using electronic information resources. In Mathematical Science, majority (71.4 per cent) of the scholars indicated that there is no change in the use of printed documents while using electronic information resources. A good number (43.4 per cent) of the doctoral students in Physical Sciences have the opinion that there is a decrease in the use of printed documents and about 41 per cent of them indicated no change in the use of printed documents while using electronic information resources.

TABLE 4.120 : Use of Printed Documents While Using Electronic Information Resources According to Discipline

Dicciplino	*Use of Printed documents*		
	Decreased	*Increased*	*No Change*
Bio Sciences	16(37.2%)	6(14%)	21(41.8%)
Biological Sciences	16(26.7%)	5(8.3%)	39(65%)
Computer Science	3(75%)	_	1(25%)
Environmental Science	5(19.2%)	14(53.8%)	7(26.9%)
Mathematical Science	3(14.3%)	3(14.3%)	15(71.4%)
Physical Sciences	53(43.4%)	19(15.6%)	50(41%)
Grand Total	**96(34.8%)**	**47(17%)**	**133(48.2%)**

It is found that majority of the doctoral students in Bio Sciences, Biological Sciences and Mathematical Science indicated that there is no change in the use of printed documents while using electronic information resources. A decrease in the use of printed documents while using electronic information resources is indicated by majority of the doctoral students in Computer Science and a good number of the scholars in Physical Sciences. Majority of the respondents in Environmental Science indicated that there is an increase in the use of printed documents while using electronic information resources.

17. CHARACTERISTICS OF AN IDEAL SEARCH ENGINE

The responses of the science doctoral students regarding the ideal features of a search engine are summarized in Table 4.121. Analysis shows that the most required feature of a search engine is Global classification, a good number (42.4 per cent) of the science doctoral students were suggested this feature. Nearly 37 per cent of the respondents suggested the feature such as type the search terms by themselves.

The ideal features of search engine suggested by the science doctoral students in University of Kerala are type the search terms by themselves (49.2 per cent), global classification- the ability to choose a subject from a menu (44.5 per cent) and search by author name (43.8 per cent). The suggested features of search engine in University of Calicut are global classification (43.5 per cent) and type the search terms by themselves (41.3 per cent). Global classification (42.6 per cent) and search by author name (42.6 per cent) are the ideal features of a search engine suggested by the respondents in CUSAT. The ideal features of search engine suggested by the respondents in M. G. University are global classification - the ability to choose a subject from a menu (35.5 per cent), restrict searches by certain types of organizations (35.5 per cent) and restrict searches before or after a certain date (35.5 per cent).

TABLE 4.121 : Characteristics of an Ideal Search Engine

Ideal Features of Search Engine	*University of Kerala*	*University of Calicut*	*CUSAT*	*M. G. University*	*Grand Total*
Global classification	57 (44.50%)	20 (43.50%)	29 (42.60%)	11 (35.50%)	117 (42.40%)
To type in search terms yourself	63 (49.20%)	19 (41.30%)	25 (36.80%)	7 (22.60%)	114 (37%)
Search by author name	56 (43.80%)	9 (19.60%)	29 (42.60%)	8 (25.80%)	102 (41.30%)
Restrict search to resource stored(Date)	27 (21.10%)	7 (15.20%)	18 (26.50%)	11 (35.50%)	63 (23.20%)
Restrict search to resource stored (Organizations)	31 (24.20%)	6 (13.00%)	20 (29.40%)	11 (35.50%)	68 (24.60%)
Restrict search to certain documents	38 (29.70%)	10 (21.70%)	17 (25.00%)	6 (19.40%)	71 (25.70%)
Concept searching	33 (25.80%)	12 (26.10%)	19 (27.90%)	8 (25.80%)	72 (26.40%)
Fuzzy searching	39 (30.50%)	9 (19.60%)	19 (27.90%)	6 (19.40%)	73 (26.80%)
Meta searching	49 (38.30%)	10 (21.70%)	14 (20.60%)	8 (25.80%)	81 (27.70%)

It is found that the most required feature of a search engine is Global classification, a good number of the science doctoral students were suggested this feature. A good number of the science doctoral students in University of Kerala are suggested the features such as type the search terms by themselves, global classification- the ability to choose a subject from a menu and search by author name. A good number of the science doctoral students in University of Calicut, CUSAT and a few number of them in M. G. University suggested global classification- the ability to choose a subject from a menu as the ideal features of a search engine.

18. CONCLUSION

The survey revealed that the science doctoral students in the universities in Kerala are using various types of electronic information resources related to their research and Internet resources are the most widely used resources followed by electronic journals. Among the Internet tools/resources, e-mail is the most frequently used tool followed by online search. Majority of the science doctoral students are unaware of the major search engines and they lack proper knowledge regarding the various advanced search methods using in online search. Majority of them indicated that the major obstacle in the online search is the speed of access. As far as the purpose of conducting online search is concerned, search for specific subject area is the major purpose followed by search for specific information. Majority of the science doctoral students rated their overall ability to use electronic information resources are average. Majority of them opined that electronic information resources helped them for fast research update. A good number of the science doctoral students have the opinion that there is no change in the use of printed documents while using electronic information resources. The suggested features of an ideal search engine are global classification, the ability to choose a subject from a menu and search by author name.

5
Summary

THIS CHAPTER summarises the findings of the analysis of the case study, information search pattern of the science doctoral students in the electronic environment discussed in detail in the Chapter 4, suggestions and the conclusion.

5.1. MAJOR FINDINGS THE CASE STUDY

The knowledge about the information search pattern of the science doctoral students in the electronic environment is very important for designing library and information system: The present investigation has achieved its objectives, and it provides a delineation of the information search pattern of the science doctoral students in the universities in Kerala. The major findings of the study are following:

General Information

1. Majority (64.2 per cent) of the science doctoral students in the universities in Kerala are between 25-30 years of age. A few scholars are below 25 years and only very few of them are above 30 years of age. Majority (60.1 per cent) of the respondents in the universities in Kerala are female.
2. Majority (65.6 per cent) of the science doctoral students in the universities in Kerala have only post graduation. Majority of the respondents in the University of Calicut,

CUSAT and M. G. University possess only post graduation. Where as majority of the scholars in University of Kerala are M. Phil holders.

3. A few number (36.2 per cent) of the science doctoral students in the universities in Kerala are in the beginning stage of their research work and a few number of them are in the analysis stage of research work. Some of them are in the data collection and report writing stage of the research. A few number of the science doctoral students in University of Kerala are in the beginning stage and few (32 per cent) of them are engaged in analysis stage of the research work. A good number of the scholars in University of Calicut and M. G. University are in the beginning stage of research. A good number of the respondents in CUSAT are in the analysis stage of the research work.

4. A good number (41.7 per cent) of the respondents in the universities in Kerala have up to one-year experience in using the electronic information resources. A good number of the scholars in University of Kerala, University of Calicut and CUSAT have up to one-year experience in using electronic information resources. Where as a good number of the science doctoral students in M. G. University have more than two and half years experience in using the electronic information resources.

Places of Accessing Electronic Information Resources

5. Most (97.1 per cent) of the science doctoral students in the universities in Kerala are accessing Internet resources. Majority of them are accessing electronic journals, network based services and CD/DVD databases related to their research. Where as majority of them are not accessing audio/video recordings. Majority of them are accessing Internet resources from

both the departments (69.9 per cent) and university libraries (61.6 per cent). Majority of the scholars are accessing electronic journals from the university libraries and a good number (46 per cent) of them are accessing it from the departments. A good number (47.1 per cent) of the science doctoral students are accessing network based services from the university libraries and few of them are accessing CD/DVD databases from the departments.

6. Most (96.1 per cent) of the science doctoral students in the University of Kerala are accessing Internet resources. Majority of them are accessing electronic journals, network based services and CD/DVD databases related to their research. Where as majority of them are not accessing audio/video recordings. Majority of the scholars are accessing Internet resources (67.2 per cent) and electronic journals (51.6 per cent) from the university library. A good number of them are accessing network based services and a few of them are accessing CD/DVD databases from the departments.

7. In University of Calicut also, large majority (93.5 per cent) of the science doctoral students are accessing Internet resources. Nearly half of them are accessing it from the departments. Majority of the respondents are not accessing audio/video recordings, CD/DVD databases, electronic journals and network based services related to the research work. A few number of them are accessing network based services and electronic journals from the university library. A few of them are accessing CD/DVD databases from the departments.

8. In CUSAT, all the science doctoral students are accessing Internet resources. Large majority of them are accessing electronic journals (86.8 per cent) and

network based services (85.3 per cent) related to the research. Majority (75 per cent) of them are accessing CD/DVD databases. Majority of them have no access to audio/video recordings. Large majority (89.7 per cent) of the science doctoral students are accessing Internet resources from the departments. Majority of them are accessing network based services, electronic journals and CD/DVD databases from the departments.

9. In M. G. University, all the respondents are using Internet resources. Large majority (93.5 per cent) of them are accessing electronic journals related to their research. Majority of the doctoral students are using CD/DVD databases and network based services. Where as a large majority of them are not accessing audio/video recordings. Large majority (87.1 per cent) of them are accessing electronic journals from the university library. Majority of them are accessing Internet resources (83.9 per cent), CD/DVD databases (67.7 per cent) and network based services (64.5 per cent) from the university library.

10. All the respondents in Bio Sciences are using Internet resources and large majority (93 per cent) of them are using electronic journals related to their research. Majority of them are using network based services, CD/DVD databases and audio/video recordings. Large majority (86 per cent) of the scholars are accessing Internet resources from the departments. Majority of them are accessing electronic journals (83.7 per cent), network based services (65.1 per cent) and CD/DVD databases (55.8 per cent) from the departments. A good number of them are also accessing audio/video recordings from the departments.

11. Most (98.3 per cent) of the doctoral students in Biological Sciences are using Internet resources. Majority of them are accessing electronic journals (55

per cent) and network based services (58.3 per cent) related to their research. Majority of the doctoral students are not using CD/DVD databases and audio/ video recordings. Majority (73.3 per cent) of them are accessing Internet resources from the departments. A few number of the scholars are accessing electronic journals and network based services from the university libraries. Few of them are using CD/DVD databases and audio/video recordings from the departments.

12. In Computer Science, all the respondents are accessing Internet resources, network based services, electronic journals and CD/DVD databases related to their research. All of them are accessing electronic journals and CD/DVD databases from the departments. Majority of them are accessing Internet resources, network based services and audio/video recordings from the departments.
13. Most (96.2 per cent) of the doctoral students in the Environmental Science are accessing Internet resources. Majority of them are accessing CD/DVD databases, electronic journals and network based services related to their research. Where as majority of them are not accessing audio/video recordings. Majority of the scholars are accessing Internet resources (80.8 per cent), electronic journals (53.8 per cent) and network based services (57.7 per cent) from the university libraries. Few of them are using CD/DVD databases from both home and the university libraries.
14. Most (95.2 per cent) of the respondents in Mathematical Science are accessing Internet resources and majority (52.4 per cent) of them are accessing electronic journals related to their research. Large majority of the scholars are not accessing audio/video recordings. Majority of them are not accessing CD/DVD databases and network based services. Large majority (85.8 per cent)

of them are using Internet resources and a good number (42.9 per cent) of them are accessing electronic journals from the departments. A few number (38.1 per cent) of them are accessing network based services from the university libraries.

15. In Physical Sciences, most (95.9 per cent) of the doctoral students are accessing Internet resources. Majority of them are using electronic journals, network based services and CD/DVD databases related to their research. Where as majority of the doctoral students are not accessing audio/video recordings. Majority of them are accessing Internet resources (70.5 per cent) and network based services (51.6 per cent) from the departments. Majority (59 per cent) of them are accessing electronic journals from the university libraries. A good number of them are accessing CD/DVD databases from the departments.

Frequency of Accessing Electronic Information Resources

16. Most frequently accessed electronic information resources by the science doctoral students in the universities in Kerala are Internet resources. Majority (59.4 per cent) of them are using it once in a day. Next most used electronic information resource is electronic journals and few of them are accessing it once in a day. Few number of the respondents are using network based services and very few of them are using CD/DVD databases once in a day. A few number of them are rarely using audio/video recordings.
17. The ANOVA test establishes that there is significant difference in the use of electronic information resources between male and female science doctoral students. It is also found that male doctoral students are using electronic information resources more than female doctoral students.

18. The ANOVA test indicated that there is no significant difference in the use of electronic information resources among the science doctoral students in different age groups.
19. The ANOVA test established that the use of electronic information resources is different among the science doctoral students based on their experience in using the electronic information resources.
20. The most used electronic information resources by the science doctoral students in the University of Kerala are Internet resources. A good number (48.4 per cent) of them are using it once in a day. Majority of them are accessing electronic journals and few (31.3 per cent) of them are using it once in a day. A few number of the doctoral students are accessing network based services once in a week and very few of them are accessing CD/DVD databases daily. A very few number of them are accessing audio/video recordings rarely.
21. In University of Calicut, also the most frequently accessed information resources are Internet resources. A good number (41.3 per cent) of the science doctoral students are using it once in a week and a few of them are using it once in a day. A few number of the scholars are accessing network based services and electronic journals once in a week. A very few number of them are accessing CD/DVD databases and audio/video recordings rarely.
22. Most frequently used electronic information resource by the doctoral students in CUSAT is Internet resources. Majority (80.9 per cent) of them are accessing it once in a day. Next most used electronic information resource is electronic journals. A good number of the doctoral students are using electronic journals (41.2 per cent) and network based services (44.1 per cent) once in a day. A very few of them are using CD/DVD databases

once in a week. Very few number of them are accessing audio/video recordings rarely.

23. Most frequently used electronic information resources by the science doctoral students in the M. G. University are Internet resources. Most (96.8 per cent) of them are using it once in a day. Next most frequently used electronic information resource is electronic journals and majority (58.1 per cent) of the respondents are accessing it once in a week. A few number of them are using network based services once in a week. A good number (41.9 per cent) of the doctoral students are accessing CD/DVD databases once in a month. Few number of them are accessing audio/video recordings rarely.
24. The ANOVA test establishes that there is significant difference in the use of electronic information resources among the science doctoral students in different universities.
25. The most used electronic information resources by the doctoral students in Bio Sciences are Internet resources. Majority (65.1 per cent) of them are using it once in a day. The second most used electronic information resources are electronic journals and majority (55.8 per cent) of them are using it once in a week. A good number of them are using network based services once in a week and few of them are accessing it once in a day. A few number of the doctoral students are using CD/DVD databases once in a week and a very few number of them are using audio/video recordings rarely.
26. In Biological Sciences, the most used electronic information resources by the doctoral students are Internet resources. A good number (43.3 per cent) of them are using it once in a day. The second most used electronic information resources are network based

services and few number of them are using it once in a day. A very few of them are using electronic journals once in a day. A very few number of them are using CD/DVD databases once in a week and very few them are using audio/video recordings rarely.

27. In Computer Science, all the respondents are using Internet resources and network based services once in a day. Majority of the doctoral students are using CD/DVD databases once in a day and few of them are using it once in a week. About half of them are using electronic journals and audio/video recordings once in a day.
28. Most used electronic information resources in Environmental Science are Internet resources. Few number (38.5 per cent) of the doctoral students are using Internet resources once in a day. A few (34.6 per cent) of them are using network based services once in a week and very few of them are using it once in a day. A few number of the scholars are using electronic journals once in a week and a very few number of them are using it once in a day. A few number (34.6 per cent) of them are using CD/DVD databases once in a month. Few number of them are using audio/video recordings rarely.
29. The most used electronic information resources by the doctoral students in Mathematical Science are Internet resources. A good number (42.9 per cent) of them are using it once in a week, and few of them are using it once in a day. The second most used electronic information resources are electronic journals and few number of them are using it once in a month. A few number of the doctoral students are using network based services once in a month and very few of them are using it once in a day. A very few number of them are using CD/DVD databases and audio/video

recordings rarely.

30. In Physical Sciences, the most used electronic information resources by the doctoral students are Internet resources. Majority (72.1 per cent) of them are using it once in a day. The second most used electronic information resources are electronic journals and few (36.9 per cent) of them are using it once in a day. A few number (32 per cent) of the doctoral students are using network based services once in a week and few of them are using it once in a day. A very few number of them are using CD/DVD databases once in a day.
31. The ANOVA test establishes that there is significant difference in the use of electronic information resources by the science doctoral students in different disciplines.

Ways of Identifying Electronic Information Resources for Research

32. For identifying the electronic information resources, nearly a large majority (84.1 per cent) of the science doctoral students in the universities in Kerala are using Internet search engines and majority of them are using personal communication. Majority of the scholars in University of Kerala, University of Calicut and M. G. University are using Internet search engines for finding electronic information resources for research. All the respondents in Kannur University and a large majority of the science doctoral students in CUSAT are also using Internet search engines for identifying electronic information resources related to research.
33. All the respondents in Computer Science and a large majority of the doctoral students in Bio Sciences and Environmental Science are using Internet search engines for finding the electronic information resources for research. Majority of the doctoral students in Biological Sciences, Mathematical Science and

Physical Sciences are also using Internet search engines for finding the electronic information resources for research.

Methods of Learning Internet

34. Majority of the science doctoral students in the universities in Kerala have learned to use the Internet through self-learning method (58.3 per cent) and by the assistance from friends and teachers (54.3 per cent). Majority of the scholars in CUSAT and M. G. University have learned the Internet through self-learning method. Majority of them in the University of Kerala and University of Calicut have learned the Internet with the assistance from friends and teachers.
35. Although a variety of methods are used to learn the Internet, majority of the doctoral students in Bio Sciences, Computer Science and Mathematical Science are used the assistance of friends and teachers. Majority of the doctoral students in Biological Sciences, Environmental Science and Physical sciences are used self-learning method for learning the Internet.

Frequency of Use of Internet Tools and Resources

36. The most frequently used Internet tool by the science doctoral students in the universities in Kerala is e-mail. Most (94.6 per cent) of them are using e-mail and a good number (48.9 per cent) of them are using it once in a day. The second most frequently used Internet service is online search and a good number (48.6 per cent) of the scholars are using it once in a day. Majority of them are using electronic journals, WWW resources, down loading facilities, external catalogue/databases, discussion list, news groups and document delivery services related to their research. A few number of them are using electronic journals and WWW resources once

in a day.

37. The most used Internet tool by the science doctoral students in University of Kerala is e-mail. Nearly most (94.5 per cent) of them are using e-mail and few of them are using it once in a day. The second most used Internet service is online search and a good number (48.4 per cent) of the respondents are using it once in a day. Majority of them are using electronic journals and a good number of them are using it once in a week. Majority of the scholars are using external catalogue/ databases, WWW resources and down loading facilities and few of them are using it once in a week. Majority of them are not using document delivery services related to their research.

38. In University of Calicut also the most used Internet tool is e-mail. Large majority (87 per cent) of the science doctoral student are using e-mail and few of them are using it once in a day. The second most used Internet service is online search and few number (30.4 per cent) of the scholars are using it once in a day. Majority of them are using WWW resources and electronic journals, and few of them are using it once in a week. Majority of the doctoral students are using external catalogue/databases while few of them are using it rarely. Majority of them are using down loading facilities and few of them are using it once in a week.

39. All the science doctoral students in CUSAT are using both e-mail and electronic journals related to their research. Majority (73.5 per cent) of them are using e-mail and a good number (47.1 per cent) of them are using the electronic journals once in a day. Most of the doctoral students are using online search and majority (58.8 per cent) of them are using it once in a day. Large majority of them are using WWW resources and majority of them are using it once in a day. Majority of

the science doctoral students are using down loading facilities and few of them are using it once in a week. Majority of them are using discussion list, newsgroups and document delivery services, and few of them are using it rarely.

40. The most used Internet service by the science doctoral students in M. G. University is online search. All the respondents are using online search and a good number (48.4 per cent) of them are using it once in a day. Most of the scholars are using electronic journals and majority (64.5 per cent) of them are using it once in a week. Most of them are using down loading facilities and a good number of them are using it once in a week. Large majority of the science doctoral students are using e-mail and majority (80.6 per cent) of them are using it once in a day. Majority of them are using external catalogue/ databases and few of them are using it once in a week. Majority of the doctoral students are using WWW resources and few of them are using it once in a day. Majority of them are using document delivery services and majority (54.8 per cent) of them are using it rarely. A good number of them are using discussion list, newsgroups and few of them are using it once in a week.

41. The ANOVA test establishes that there is significant difference in the use of electronic information resources between the science doctoral students based on their universities.

42. Most frequently used Internet services in Bio Sciences are electronic journals and online search. Majority (60.5 per cent) of doctoral students are conducting online search and a good number (44.2 per cent) of them are using electronic journals once in a day. The second most used Internet tool is e-mail and majority (55.8 per cent) of them are using it once in a day. Large majority

of the doctoral students are using external catalogue/ databases and a good number of them are using it once in a week. Majority of them are using WWW resources and few of them are using it once in a day. Majority of them are using discussion list, newsgroups and a few number of them are using it rarely. Majority of the doctoral students are using document delivery services and very few of them are using it once in a week.

43. In Biological Sciences, the most frequently used Internet tool by the doctoral students is e-mail. Large majority (93.3 per cent) of the doctoral students are using e-mail and a few number (36.7 per cent) of them are using it once in a day. The second most used Internet service is online search, a large majority (91.7 per cent) of the scholars are using online search and 43.3 per cent of them are using it once in a day. Large majority of them are using WWW resources and few of them are accessing it once in a day. Majority (75 per cent) of the doctoral students are using electronic journals and few number of them are using it once in a week. Majority of them are using external catalogue/ databases and down loading services and very few of them are using it once in a day. A good number of the doctoral students are using discussion list, newsgroups and document delivery services and a very few number of them are using it once in a day.

44. In Computer Science, all the respondents are using e-mail, external catalogue/ databases, electronic journals, WWW resources, down loading services and online search related to the research. All of them are using e-mail and online search once in a day. Majority of them are using electronic journals, WWW resources and document delivery services once in a day. Majority of them are using discussion list, newsgroups and external

catalogue/ databases once in a week.

45. Most used Internet tool by the doctoral students in Environmental Science is e-mail. Most (96.2 per cent) of the doctoral students are using e-mail and a good number (46.2 per cent) of them are using it once in a week. The second most used Internet service is online search. A large majority (92.3 per cent) of the scholars are using online search and few of them are using it once in a day. Majority (84.6 per cent) of them are using electronic journals and WWW resources and few number of them are using it once in a week. Majority of the doctoral students are using down loading services and few of them are using it once in a month. Majority of them are using discussion list, newsgroups and external catalogue/ databases, and few number of them are using it rarely.

46. Most used Internet tool by the doctoral students in Mathematical Science is e-mail. Most (95.2 per cent) of the doctoral students are using e-mail and a few number (33.3 per cent) of them are using it once in a week. The second most used Internet service is online search, a large majority of them are using online search and a few number (38.1 per cent) of them are using it once in a day. Majority of the respondents are using WWW resources and few number of them are using it once in a day. Majority of them are using electronic journals and down loading services and very few of them are using it once in a day. Majority of them are not using discussion list, newsgroups, external catalogue/ databases and document delivery services, and few of them are using it rarely.

47. In Physical Sciences, the most used Internet tools by the doctoral students are e-mail and online search. Majority (63.1 per cent) of the scholars are using e-mail and good number (49.2 per cent) of them are using

online search once in a day. Large majority (86.9 per cent) of the scholars are using electronic journals and a good number of them are using it once in a week. Majority of them are using down loading services and WWW resources, and few of them are using it once in a day. Majority of the respondents are using external catalogue/ databases and few of them are using it once in a week. Majority of them are using discussion list, newsgroups and document delivery services, and few of them are using it rarely.

48. The ANOVA test establishes that there is significant difference in the use of Internet tools and resources by the science doctoral students in different disciplines.

The Time Spent for Using Internet Tools and Resources

49. A few number (23.2 per cent) of the science doctoral students in the universities in Kerala are using e-mail for up to 1 hour and few of them are using it for 1-2 hours per week. Nearly 38 per cent of them are using online search for 2-5 hours per week while 32.6 per cent of them are using it or 1-2 hours. A few number of the scholars are using electronic journals (27.9 per cent) and WWW resources (21.7 per cent) for 1-2 hours. A few number of them are using discussion list, news groups (20.7 per cent), external catalogue/ databases (23.9 per cent) and document delivery services (19.9 per cent) for less than 30 minutes.

50. In University of Kerala, a good number (46.1 per cent) of the science doctoral students are using online search for 2-5 hours per week and few of them are using it for 1-2 hours. A few number (24.2 per cent) of the respondents are using e-mail for 1-2 hours per week and few of them are using it for less than 30 minutes. A few number (32 per cent) of the doctoral students are using electronic journals for 1-2 hours and very few of

them are using it for more than 5 hours. A very few number of them are using discussion list, newsgroups for less than 30 minutes. A few number (21.9 per cent) of the scholars are using WWW resources for more than 5 hours. A very few number of them are using document delivery services and down loading services for up to 1 hour.

51. In University of Calicut, few number (28.3 per cent) of the science doctoral students are using the e-mail up to 1 hour and few of them are using it for 1-2 hours per week. Nearly 37 per cent of the respondents are using online search for 1-2 hours and few of them are using it for 2-5 hours. A few number (26.1 per cent) of them are using electronic journals for 1-2 hours and very few of them are using it for 2-5 hours per week. A very few number of them are using WWW resources for 1-2 hours and very few of them are using it for less than 30 minutes. Few number (21.7 per cent) of the scholars are using down loading services up to 1 hour. Some of them are using discussion list, newsgroups, external catalogue/ databases and document delivery services for less than 30 minutes.

52. In CUSAT, a good number (39.7 per cent) of the science doctoral students are using online search for 2-5 hours per week and few of them are using it for 1-2 hours. A few number (30.9 per cent) of them are using electronic journals for 2-5 hours per week and few of them are using it for more than 5 hours. A few number (25 per cent) of the doctoral students are using e-mail for 2-5 hours and few (22.1 per cent) of them are using it for 1-2 hours. A few number of the respondents are using discussion list and newsgroups for less than 30 minutes while few of them are using it for up to 1 hour. A few number (29.4 per cent) of the science doctoral students are using WWW resources for 2-5 hours and few of

them are using it for 1-2 hours. Nearly a good number of them are using document delivery services for less than 30 minutes and very few of them are using it up to 1 hour. A few number (23.5 per cent) of them are using down loading services for up to 2-5 hours per week.

53. A few number (35.5 per cent) of the science doctoral students in M. G. University are spending 2-5 hours per week for using e-mail while few of them are spending less than 30 minutes for using it. A few number (32.3 per cent) of the scholars are using electronic journals for 1-2 hours and few of them are using it for 2-5 hours per week. A few number (32.3 per cent) of them are using online search for 1-2 hours. A very few number (19.4 per cent) of the doctoral students are using WWW resources for more than 5 hours and very few of them are using it for 2-5 hours. A good number (48.4 per cent) of them are using down loading services for less than 30 minutes and few of them are using it for 1-2 hours. A few number of the doctoral students are using external catalogue/ databases for less than 30 minutes and few of them are using it for 1-2 hours. A few number of them are using document delivery services for 1-2 hours.

54. The ANOVA test establishes that there is significant difference in the time spent for using Internet tools and resources among the science doctoral students in different universities.

55. In Bio Sciences, 27.8 per cent of the doctoral students are using e-mail for less than 30 minutes per week and 25.6 per cent of them are using it up to 1 hour. A good number (48.8 per cent) of them indicated 2-5 hours use of online search and 46.5 per cent of them are using it for 1 to 2 hours. A few number (37.2 per cent) of them are using electronic journals for 2 to 5 hours and few of them are using it for 1 to 2 hours.

About 23.3 per cent of the doctoral students are using WWW resources for 1 to 2 hours and 20.9 per cent of them are using it for 2 to 5 hours per week. A few number (25.6 per cent) of them are using down loading services up to 1 hour and 1 to 2 hour use is mentioned by 20.9 per cent of the respondents. Few of them are using discussions lists, newsgroups for less than 30 minutes. A few number of them indicated that they are spending 1 to 2 hours for external catalogue/databases. A very few number of them are using document delivery services for 1 to 2 hours per week.

56. In Biological Sciences, 25 per cent of the doctoral students are using e-mail for 1-2 hours per week and 23.3 per cent of them are using it up to 1 hour. A few number (36.7 per cent) of the scholars indicated 2-5 hours use of online search and very few of them are using it for more than 5 hours. A few number.(26.7 per cent) of the doctoral students are using electronic journals for 1 to 2 hours, and very few (15 per cent) of them are using it for 2-5 hours. About 21.7 per cent of them are using WWW resources for 1 to 2 hours and very few of them are using it for more than 5 hours. A very few number of them are using down loading services and discussions lists, newsgroups for up to 1 hour. Nearly 21.7 per cent of the scholars are spending less than 30 minutes for external catalogue/databases and 16.7 per cent of them are spending up to 1 hour for using it. A very few number of them are using document delivery services for less than 30 minutes.

57. All the respondents in Computer Science are using electronic journals and online search for more than 5 hours per week. Majority of them are using WWW resources and down loading services for more than 5 hours per week. One doctoral student is using e-mail, discussion list, newsgroups and document delivery

services for more than 5 hours. Nearly half of them are using external catalogue/ databases for 2-5 hours per week.

58. In Environmental Science, a few number (30.8 per cent) of the doctoral students are using e-mail for 1-2 hours per week and very few of them are using it for 2-5 hours. A few number of them are using electronic journals and online search for 2-5 hours, and very few of them are using it for 1-2 hours per week. A few number (38.5 per cent) of the doctoral students are using WWW resources for 1 to 2 hours and very few of them are using it for 2- 5 hours. Some of the scholars are using down loading services for 1-2 hours and few of them using it up to 1 hour. A few number of them are using discussions lists, newsgroups for 1-2 hours. Nearly 26.9 per cent of the doctoral students indicated that they are spending less than 30 minutes for external catalogue/databases. A very few number of them are using document delivery services for up to 1 hour.

59. A good number (42.9 per cent) of the doctoral students in Mathematical Science are spending less than 30 minutes per week for using e-mail and a few of them are using it for up to 1 hour. A few number (33.3 per cent) of the scholars are using online search for more than 5 hours and few of them are using it for 2-5 hours per week. A very few number of the doctoral students are using electronic journals and WWW resources for more than 5 hours. A very few of them are using down loading services for 2-5 hours. A very few number of the respondents are using discussion list, newsgroups, external catalogue/ databases and document delivery services for less than 30 minutes.

60. In Physical Sciences, few number (23 per cent) of the doctoral students are using e-mail for up to 1 hour per week and few of them are using it for 2-5 hours. A few

number (38.5 per cent) of them indicated 2-5 hours use of online search and 36.9 per cent of them are using it for 1-2 hours. A few number of them are using electronic journals for 1 to 2 hours and few of them are using it for more than 5 hours. A very few of the scholars are using WWW resources for 2-5 hours and 18.9 per cent of them are using it for 1-2 hours. A very few number of them are using down loading services for 1-2 hours and up to 1 hour use is mentioned by 16.4 per cent of the respondents. A very few number of the doctoral students are using discussions lists, newsgroups, document delivery services and external catalogue/databases for less than 30 minutes.

61. The ANOVA test establishes that there is significant difference in the time spent for using Internet tools and resources by the science doctoral students in different disciplines.

Internet Facilities Used for Communication

62. A large majority (89.8 per cent) of the science doctoral students in the universities in Kerala are using e-mail for communication. Most of the scholars in the University of Kerala and a large majority of them in CUSAT are using e-mail for communication. Majority of the science doctoral students in University of Calicut, and M. G. University are also using e-mail for communication.

63. Most of the doctoral students in Computer Science, Environmental Science and Mathematical Science, and a large majority of them in Bio Sciences, Biological Sciences and Physical Sciences are using e-mail for communication.

Frequency of Use of Internet Search Engines

64. The most frequently used Internet search engine by the science doctoral students in the universities in

Kerala is Google. A large majority (86.2 per cent) of them are using it often. The second most used Internet search engine is Yahoo and majority (68.8 per cent) of them are using it often. Majority of the respondents are not using the search engine AltaVista while few of them are using it sometimes. A large majority of them are not using the search engines WebCrawler, HotBot, MetaEureka, WWW worm, Infoseek, WWW Virtual Library, Excite and Lycos.

65. Most frequently used Internet search engine in the University of Kerala is Google. A large majority (88.3 per cent) of the science doctoral students are using it often. The second most frequently used Internet search engine is Yahoo and majority (71.1 per cent) of them are using it often. Majority of them are not using the search engine AltaVista while a few number of them are using it sometimes. A large majority of the scholars are not using the search engines HotBot, Infoseek, MetaEureka, Excite, WWW worm, Lycos and WWW Virtual Library. Most (96.1 per cent) of them are not using the search engine WebCrawler.

66. In University of Calicut, the most frequently used Internet search engine by the science doctoral students is Yahoo. Majority (67.4 per cent) of them are using it often. The second most frequently used Internet search engine is Google and majority (65.2 per cent) of the scholars are using it often. Majority of them are not using the search engines Alta vista and Excite but a few of them are using it sometimes. Most of the science doctoral students are not using the search engines WebCrawler, MetaEureka and WWW worm. A large majority of them are not using the search engines Lycos, WWW Virtual Library, HotBot and Infoseek.

67. In CUSAT, the most used Internet search engine by the science doctoral students is Yahoo. Majority (69.1

per cent) of them are using it often. Google is the second most used search engine and a large majority (91.2 per cent) of the scholars are using it often. Most of them are not using the search engine Infoseek. A large majority of the respondents are not using the search engines MetaEureka, WWW worm, HotBot, WebCrawler, and WWW Virtual Library. Majority of them are not using the search engines Lycos, Excite and AltaVista.

68. The most used Internet search engine by the science doctoral students in the M. G. University is Google. Most (96.8 per cent) of the science doctoral students are using it often. The second most frequently used Internet search engine is Yahoo and majority (61.3 per cent) of them are using it often. A good number of the scholars are using the search engines AltaVista and Lycos. Most of of the scholars are not using the search engines WWW worm, WWW Virtual Library, HotBot and MetaEureka. A large majority of them are not using the search engines Excite and WebCrawler.

69. Most used Internet search engine among the doctoral students in Bio Sciences is Google. Most (97.7 per cent) of them are using it often. The second most used Internet search engine is Yahoo and majority (74.4 per cent) of the doctoral students are using it often. Majority of them are not using the search engine AltaVista and few of them are using it sometimes. A large majority of the doctoral students are not using the search engines WWW worm, WWW Virtual Library and Excite. Most of them are not using the search engines HotBot, Infoseek, WebCrawler and MetaEureka.

70. In Biological Sciences, the most used Internet search engine is Yahoo. Majority (75 per cent) of the doctoral students are using it often. The second most used Internet search engine is Google and majority of the

scholars are using it often. A large majority of them are not using the search engines WebCrawler, Infoseek and MetaEureka and majority of them are not using the Internet search engines AltaVista, Excite, Lycos, WWW worm and WWW Virtual Library.

71. All the respondents in Computer Science are using both the search engines Google and Yahoo. All of them are often using the search engine Google. About half of them are often using the search engine Yahoo. Nearly half of the doctoral students are sometimes using the search engines AltaVista and Infoseek. No respondents are using the search engines Excite, WWW worm and WebCrawler and majority of them are not using the search engines Lycos, HotBot and WWW Virtual Library.

72. Most used Internet search engine by the doctoral students in Environmental Science is Google. Majority (80.8 per cent) of them are using it often. The second most used Internet search engine is Yahoo and majority of the doctoral students are using it often. Majority of them are not using the search engines AltaVista, Excite, Lycos and WWW Virtual Library. All the respondents are not using the search engines WebCrawler, WWW worm, HotBot, Infoseek and MetaEureka.

73. Most used Internet search engine by the doctoral students in Mathematics is Yahoo. A good number (42.9 per cent) of them are using it often. The second most used Internet search engine is Google and majority (71.4 per cent) of the doctoral students are using it often. Majority of them are not using the search engine Lycos and a large majority of them are not using the search engines AltaVista, Excite, WebCrawler, WWW worm, WWW Virtual Library, HotBot and MetaEureka.

74. In Physical Sciences, the most used Internet search

engine by the doctoral students is Google. A large majority (90.2 per cent) of them are using it often. The second most used Internet search engine is Yahoo and majority (66.4 per cent) of the doctoral students are using it often. Majority of them are not using the search engines AltaVista, Excite, Lycos and WWW Virtual Library and a large majority of them are not using the search engines WebCrawler, Infoseek and MetaEureka. Most of the doctoral students are not using the search engines WWW worm and HotBot.

Purpose of Conducting Electronic Information Searches

75. Majority of the science doctoral students are searching electronic information resources for specific subject area (79 per cent), specific information (58.3 per cent) and abstracts of full text articles (56.9 per cent). A few number of them are conducting searches for library catalogues, full text articles and abstracts of citations. Majority of the science doctoral students in the University of Kerala, University of Calicut, CUSAT and M. G. University are conducting searches for finding specific subject area.

76. All the respondents in Computer Science and majority of the doctoral students in Bio Sciences, Biological Sciences, Environmental Science, Mathematical Science and Physical Sciences are conducting searches for specific subject area.

Search Methods Used

77. The most used search method among the science doctoral students in the universities in Kerala is subject searches. Majority (76.1 per cent) of them are using it often. The next most used search method is keyword searches and majority (64.9 per cent) of the scholars are often conducting keyword searches. Majority (67.4 per cent) of them are conducting author searches and

a good number of them are using it sometimes. Majority of the science doctoral students are conducting searches under journal title and majority of them are using it often. Majority of them are searching under title of article and a good number of them are using it often. A good number of them are using date of publication for searching the information while a few of them are using it often.

78. In University of Kerala, the most used search method is subject searches. Majority (78.1 per cent) of the science doctoral students are conducting it often. The second most used search method is keyword searches and majority (72.1 per cent) of the scholars are using it often. Majority of them are conducting author searches and good number of them are using it sometimes. Majority of the science doctoral students are often using journal title (58.6 per cent) and title of article (50.8 per cent) for searching the information. A good number of them are searching under date of publication and a few of them are using it often.

79. In University of Calicut also, the most used search method is subject searches. Majority (58.7 per cent) of the science doctoral students are using it often. A good number (45.7 per cent) of them are often using keyword searches and few of them are using it sometimes. Majority of the scholars are conducting searches under author, journal title and title of article and a few number of them are using it often. Majority of the doctoral students are not using date of publication for searching the information and few of them are using it sometimes.

80. Large majority (86.8 per cent) of the science doctoral students in CUSAT are conducting subject searches. Majority (83.8 per cent) of them are using it often. Keyword search is the second most used search method and majority of the science doctoral students

are using it often. Majority of them are conducting searches under author, journal title and title of article. A good number of them are often conducting searches using journal title and title of article. Majority of the doctoral students are not using date of publication for searching the information and few of them are using it sometimes.

81. All the respondents in M. G. University are using keyword searches. Majority (74.2 per cent) of them are often using it for searching information. Most of the scholars are conducting searches using both subject and journal title and majority of them are using it often. Large majority (87.1 per cent) of them are conducting searches using title of article and majority of them are using it sometimes. Majority of them are conducting searches using author and date of publication and a good number of them are using it sometimes.

82. The ANOVA test establishes that there is significant difference in the use of search methods between the science doctoral students in different universities.

83. The most used search method by the doctoral students in Bio Sciences is subject searches. Large majority (93 per cent) of them are using it often. The second most used search method is key word and majority (83.7 per cent) of the doctoral students are using it often. For searching information, large majority of them are using the journal title and title of the article, and majority of them are using it often. Majority of the scholars are conducting searches using author and date of publication and a good number of them are using it sometimes.

84. In Biological Sciences, the most used search method is subject searches. Large majority (85 per cent) of the doctoral students are using subject searches and majority (61.7 per cent) of them are using it often. The

second most used search method is keyword searches and majority (65 per cent) of the doctoral students are using it often. Majority of the scholars are using journal title for searching the information and a good number (43.3 per cent) of them are using it often. Majority of the doctoral students are conducting searches using author and title of article and few of them are using it often. Majority of them are not using date of publication for searching the information while very few of them are using it often.

85. All the respondents in the Computer Science are using author, keyword, subject, journal title and title of article for searching the information. All of them are often conducting searches using subject and journal title. Majority of them are often using key word, title of article and author for searching information. Nearly half of the doctoral students are conducting searches using date of publication.

86. The most used search methods in Environmental Science are subject and keyword searches. Majority of the doctoral students are often conducting subject searches (76.9 per cent) and keyword searches (57.7 per cent). Majority (80.8 per cent) of them are conducting searches using title of article and half of them are using it often. Majority of the doctoral students are using journal title for searching information and a good number (46.2 per cent) of them are using it often. Majority of the scholars are conducting author searches and a good number of them are using it sometimes. Majority of them are not conducting searches using date of publication and very few of them are using it often.

87. In Mathematical Science, the most used search method is subject searches. A good number (47.6 per cent) of the doctoral students are using it often. Majority of them

are using journal title and title of article for searching information and a good number of them are using it often. Majority of the doctoral students are using key word and author for searching information, and few of them are using it often. Majority of them are not conducting searches using date of publication and very few of them are using it often.

88. The most used search method by the doctoral students in Physical Sciences is subject searches. Majority (81.1 per cent) of them are using it often. The second most used search method is keyword searches and majority (65.6 per cent) of the doctoral students are using it often. Majority of the scholars are using journal title for searching information and majority (51.6 per cent) of them are using it often. Majority of the scholars are using title of article for searching information and a good number of them are using it often. Majority of them are using author name for searching information and a good number of them are using it sometimes. Majority of them are not using date of publication for searching information.

89. The ANOVA test establishes that there is significant difference in the use search methods among the science doctoral students in different disciplines.

Use of Advanced Search Methods

90. Majority (51.5 per cent) of the science doctoral students in the universities in Kerala are using Boolean operators for searching the information and a few of them are using it often. Majority of them are not using the truncation of search terms, field searching and phrases for searching the information.

91. Majority (51.6 per cent) of the scholars in the University of Kerala are using the field searching and few of them are using it often. Majority of them are not using the

advanced search methods such as truncation of search terms (75.7 per cent), searches using phrases (64 per cent) and Boolean operators (53.1 per cent).

92. In University of Calicut, most of the science doctoral students are not using the advanced search method truncation of search terms (95.7 per cent) and majority of them are not using Boolean operators (71.7 per cent), phrases (65.6 per cent), and field searching (58.7 per cent) for finding information.
93. Majority (58.8 per cent) of the science doctoral students in CUSAT are using the advanced search method Boolean operators and few (39.7 per cent) of them are using it sometimes. Majority of them are not conducting searches using phrases (58.8 per cent), truncation of search terms (54.4 per cent), and field searching (58.8 per cent).
94. In M. G. University, majority (83.9 per cent) of the science doctoral students are using Boolean operators. A good number (48.4 per cent) of them are using it sometimes. Majority of them are not using phrases (64.5 per cent), truncation of search terms (58 per cent) and field searching (54.8 per cent) for finding information and few of them are using it sometimes.
95. Majority (74.4 per cent) of the doctoral students in Bio Sciences are using Boolean operators for searching information. A good number of the scholars are using it sometimes and few of them are using it often. Majority (58.2 per cent) of them are using field searching and a good number (44.2 per cent) of them are using it often. Majority of the scholars are not using truncation of search terms (55.8 per cent) and phrases (55.8 per cent) for searching information while few of them are using it sometimes.
96. A good number (46.7 per cent) of the doctoral students

in Biological Sciences are using field searching and few number (20.6 per cent) of them are using it often. Majority of the doctoral students are not conducting searches using Boolean operators (70 per cent) and phrases (68.3 per cent) while few of them are using it sometimes. A large majority (90 per cent) of them are not conducting searches using truncation of search terms.

97. In Computer Science, all the respondents are often using the Boolean operators and field searching for finding the information. Majority of them are using truncation of search terms and phrases for searching information and about half of them are using it often.

98. Nearly half of the doctoral students in Environmental Science are using Boolean operators for searching information and few of them are using it often. Majority of the scholars are not conducting searches using truncation of search terms (84.6 per cent), field searching (69.2 per cent) and phrases (61.5 per cent) while very few number of them are using it sometimes.

99. Majority of the doctoral students in Mathematical Science are not using Boolean operators (66.7 per cent) and field searching (71.4 per cent) for finding information while a very few of them are using it sometimes. A large majority of them are not using truncation of search terms (85.7 per cent) and phrases (90.5 per cent) for searching information.

100. Majority (55.7 per cent) of the doctoral students in Physical Sciences are using Boolean operators for searching information and few of them are using it often. A good number (48.4 per cent) of them are using field searching and few of them are using it often. Majority of the doctoral students are not using truncation of search terms (63.1 per cent) and phrases (60.7 per

cent) for searching information while few of them are using it sometimes.

Difficulties in Obtaining Information from Online Search

101. Majority (83.7 per cent) of the science doctoral students in the universities in Kerala indicated that speed of access as the major difficulty in the online search. A large majority of the science doctoral students in University of Kerala indicted the speed of access and majority of them are mentioned cost as the impediments faced in online search. The major obstacles faced by the scholars in University of Calicut are speed of access, lack of time for searching and unfamiliarity with search methods. A large majority of the science doctoral students in CUSAT indicated that speed of access as the major impediment in online search while a majority of them has the opinion that too much information available and lack of subject specificity are the obstacles in online search. The major obstacles faced by the doctoral students in M. G. University are speed of access, too much information available, lack of subject specificity and cost.

102. In Bio Sciences, majority (74.4 per cent) of the doctoral students indicted the speed of access as the major obstacle in online search and few of them are mentioned that too much information available in online search. The major obstacles faced by the scholars in Biological Sciences are speed of access (83.3 per cent) and lack of time for searching (58.3 per cent). Nearly half of the doctoral students in Computer Science indicated that speed of access and cost are the major impediments in online search. A large majority of the respondents in Environmental Science indicated that speed of access as the major impediment in online search. Majority of them have the opinion that lack of

time for searching, too much information available and cost are the obstacles in online search. Majority of the doctoral students in Mathematical Science mentioned that speed of access is the major impediment in online search. A large majority of the respondents in Physical Sciences indicated that speed of access as the major impediment in online search. Majority of them have mentioned cost as the obstacle in online search.

Ability in Using Electronic Information Resources

103. Majority (55.7 per cent) of the science doctoral students in the universities in Kerala rated their overall ability in using electronic information resources as average. Majority of the scholars in University of Kerala, University of Calicut, CUSAT and M. G. University rated their overall ability as average in using electronic information resources.

104. Majority of the doctoral students Bio Sciences, Biological Sciences, Computer Science, Environmental Science, Mathematical Science and Physical Sciences rated their overall ability in using electronic information resources as average. About half of the respondents in Computer Science indicated that they are experts and half of them are above average in using electronic information resources.

Impact of Electronic information resources on Research

105. Majority (72.8 per cent) of the science doctoral students in the universities in Kerala indicated that the major impact of electronic information resources on research is fast research update. Majority of the scholars in University of Kerala, University of Calicut, CUSAT and M. G. University have the opinion that electronic information resources helped them for fast research update.

106. Majority of the doctoral students in all the science

disciplines indicated that the major impact of electronic information resources on research is fast research update. Majority of them in Bio Sciences, Computer Science, Environmental Science and Physical Sciences also pointed out that electronic information resources helped them for saving time.

Use of Printed Documents While Using Electronic information resources

107. A good number (48.2 per cent) of the science doctoral students in the universities in Kerala have the opinion that there is no change in the use of printed documents while using electronic information resources. Majority of the scholars in University of Calicut and a good number of of them in University of Kerala, CUSAT and M. G. University have the opinion that there is no change in the use of printed documents while using electronic information resources.

108. Majority of the doctoral students in Bio Sciences, Biological Sciences and Mathematical Science indicated that there is no change in the use of printed documents while using electronic information resources. A decrease in the use of printed documents while using electronic information resources is indicated by majority of the scholars in Computer Science and a good number of the doctoral students in Physical Sciences. Majority of the respondents in Environmental Science indicated that there is an increase in the use of printed documents while using electronic information resources.

Characteristics of an Ideal Search Engine

109. The most required feature of a search engine is global classification, a good number of the science doctoral students were suggested this feature. A good number of the scholars in University of Kerala are suggested

the features such as type the search terms by themselves, global classification- the ability to choose a subject from a menu and search by author name. A good number of the science doctoral students in University of Calicut, CUSAT and a few number of the respondents in M. G. University suggested global classification- the ability to choose a subject from a menu as the ideal features of a search engine.

5.2. SUGGESTIONS FOR IMPROVING THE ACCESS AND USE OF ELECTRONIC INFORMATION RESOURCES

The progress of a nation depends on its research work, which in turn depends on the available information. Scientists have always sought information relevant to their research, information about research results and the methods used to obtain those results. Today so much information is available on-line, that scientific community is put in the sometimes enviable—but often frustrating—position of having too much information. Many researchers see the online information sources as a monster that has grown out of control and yearn for a managed, maintained, and friendlier source of information. As a result, libraries are facing new challenges, new competitors, new demands, new expectations and a variety of information services from users tailored to their wants and needs. In order to develop a library and information system for science doctoral students in the electronic environment, it is very important to investigate their use of electronic information resources and the search methods used to retrieve information from these sources. The science doctoral students in the universities are not fully utilizing the benefits of electronic information resources due to the unavailability of the electronic information resources and the unawareness of the advanced search methods. The investigator is offering the following suggestions for providing better services to the scientific community in the electronic environment.

Electronic Information Resources

Providing electronic information to the scientific community has become a common feature in the developed countries. The developing countries like India are also taken the challenges of the new emerging technologies and increasing demands of the scientific community by adopting electronic information resources and services. However, it is not reached its eventual stage due to the lack of information technology infrastructure and unawareness of the available electronic information resources. The libraries in the universities should develop a good collection of electronic information resources so that they can serve the science doctoral students more efficiently and effectively. They have to provide more CD-ROM books, CD/DVD databases, bibliographic databases, online/electronic journals etc to satisfy the needs of the science doctoral students.

Electronic Information Services

The universities should provide electronic information services to the science doctoral students to keep up to date in their field of knowledge and to save their valuable time. The databases available in the library should be digitised and all the information of the holdings of the library has to be made available electronically so that the science doctoral students can retrieve information very quickly and easily. The following services should be provided electronically apart from the manual system:

1. E-mailing of the list of subscribing electronic journals to the science doctoral students.
2. Weekly additions of the electronic information resources and research reports should be made available on the web page.
3. Downloading of the content pages of journals available in the Internet and e-mailing of this to the scholars.

4. Downloading of research reports and part of theses from the Internet, which is useful to the science scholars.

Internet Library Services

The Internet provides access to a wealth of information on countless topics contributed by people throughout the world. The exponential growth of the Web has drastically changed the availability of electronic information, but, somewhat paradoxically, this success has also made it increasingly difficult to find and organize information. There is a need to provide more Internet library services to the scientific community in order to maximize the use of Internet based tools and resources. The suggested library services are

1. Internet introduction courses
2. Presentation of Internet resources
3. Evaluation of Internet resources
4. Making available electronic journals via Internet
5. Making available databases via Internet
6. Inter library loan via Internet

Resource Sharing and Networking

In the present dynamic era of continuous changes due to information explosion, no library is self sufficient to provide comprehensive services to the customers. To overcome these shortcomings, sharing of resources through well-developed networks assumes greater need in these days. The government of India has initiated networking of libraries and information centers in the country. Currently the university libraries are functioning in isolation and there is no mechanism for the dissemination of valuable information in these universities. The library network system will enable the universities to share and transmit the electronic information resources among them. Therefore, to provide the needed information to the scientific community, resource sharing and networking among the university libraries are must.

Digital Library

A digital library is an infrastructure of standardized electronic information that allows for distributed data storage, searching, and retrieval over a wide geographical region through links and operations transparent to the end-user. Digital libraries are being pursued because they allow for a wide distribution of a vast amount of data and because they provide new ways of interacting with information and manipulating data. Therefore, there is a need to develop digital libraries in the universities for providing timely information to the scientific community. Digital libraries would ideally be able to store data at multiple sites and allow scientific community to search for information across these multiple repositories in a single step

Training in the Use of Search Strategies

The science doctoral students in the universities are lacking knowledge about the advanced search methods used for retrieving online information. It is a well-known fact that science doctoral students often become overwhelmed by the number of items retrieved by a simple query in a search engine, and that the precision of those results is in many cases inadequate, resulting in low effectiveness. There for the science doctoral students should be taught about the search strategies and the use of controlled vocabulary to make the online search process easier and precise and to make optimum utilization of the internationally available online information sources.

Virtual Library

The World Wide Web has changed the environment for information delivery and for representation of information; the explosion of electronic information resources underscores the need for professionals to research, review, evaluate, and select authoritative sources to assist users seeking information. Virtual reality is gradually opening up a completely new era of communication by immersing the communicators inside the information. A library is "virtual" in the sense that a number of different information resources can be brought to an end-user, rather than delivering the end-user to a physical set of resources. There is a need to develop University Virtual Library with a wide range of electronic information resources, digital content, and online information services organized in a coherent and cohesive manner that should be searched by the scientific community. Access to the University Virtual Library should be provided through an easy-to-use Web-based multilingual common user interface, and users can retrieve information from multiple sources by a single search.

5.3. SUGGESTIONS FOR FURTHER RESEARCH

Based on the findings of the study, the following areas are suggested for further research.

1. The information search pattern of the academic library users in the electronic environment.
2. The information seeking behaviour of the special library users in the electronic environment.
3. Search query analysis of the science doctoral students in the universities.
4. The impact of electronic information resources use on scholarly productivity.

5.4. CONCLUSION

In an electronic environment, the studies that focus on how the science doctoral students are searching information, the types of information sources needed, the services they used and their priorities in searching for information are highly relevant, because they provide a basis for reorganizing libraries and information centers and reshaping their information support activities. This investigation has imparted a delineation of the information search pattern of the science doctoral students in the universities. Majority of the science doctoral students are accessing various electronic information resources related to research and the most frequently accessed electronic information resources by the scholars are Internet resources. The use of electronic information resources is different among the science doctoral students based on their gender and experience in using the electronic information resources. There is significant difference in the use of electronic information resources between the science doctoral students based on their university and discipline. The science doctoral students in the universities in Kerala are aware about the major Internet tools and resources but they are not fully utilizing most of the Internet tools and resources related to their research. Majority of them have learned to use the Internet through self-learning method and by the assistance from friends and teachers. The assistance provided by the library staff in learning Internet is inadequate. Lack of orientation/training in the use of Internet affected the proper use of Internet tools and resources. The most used communication facility among the science doctoral students is e-mail. The science doctoral students are unaware of various Internet search engines. Majority of them are searching electronic information resources for specific subject area. The most used search method among the scholars is subject searches and majority of them are unaware about the use of advanced search methods. Majority of the science doctoral students indicated speed of access as the major obstacle in the online search. They opined that major impact of electronic information resources on research is fast research update. A good number of the science doctoral students indicated that there is no change in the use of printed documents while using electronic information resources.

The electronic information resources have the effect of democratizing the science research community.

Researchers in the developing and developed countries can interact with each other on the same footing. The result is that the science research community seems to moving towards a greater international homogeneity. However, in developing countries like India the science research community is not fully utilizing the benefit of the situation because they consider online electronic information resources as a disorganized, unmanaged monster, without a way to verify on-line information, and without more than elementary search tools. Therefore, there is a need to provide proper guidance and training to the scientific community in the use of electronic information resources. The present study concluded that the science doctoral students in the universities need proper training in the use of electronic information resources and information search tools.

QUESTIONNAIRE

This questionnaire is intended for obtaining data on Information Search pattern in Electronic Environment of Doctoral students in the Universities.

Please indicate your response with a '✓' (tick mark) in the appropriate column.

A. Background Information

1. Name of the University :
2. Department :
3. Age : Below 25 years ☐
   Between 25 - 30 years ☐
   Between 31 - 35 years ☐
   Between 36 - 40 years ☐
   Between 41 - 45 years ☐
   Above 45 years ☐
4. Gender : Male ☐ Female ☐
5. Qualification : P. G. ☐
   M.Phil ☐
   Any other (Please specify)
6. Please specify the stage of your research work:
   Beginning Data Collection ☐
   Analysis Report Writing ☐

B. Use of Electronic Information Resources

1a. Do you use any electronic information sources such as CD/DVD Databases, Electronic journals, Internet based resources for research?

Yes ☐ No ☐

1b. **If yes**, how many months/years you have been using electronic information sources? (Please fill the number of months/years).

———Months/Years

2. From where do you get access to the following electronic information resources?

Electronic Information Resources	*No access*	*Home*	*Depart-ment*	*University Library*	*Other Place (Please Specify)*
Audio/Video Recordings					
CD /DVD Databases					
Electronic Journals					
Network Based Services					
Internet Resources					
Others (Please specify) ________					

3. How often do you use the following electronic information resources for research?

Electronic Information Resources	Rarely	Once in a Month	Once in a Week	Once in a Day
Audio/Video Recordings				
CD /DVD Databases				
Electronic Journals				
Network Based Services				
Internet Resources				
Others (Please specify) ______________				

4. How do you identify electronic information resources for research?
   a) Personal communications ☐
   b) Attend seminars and conferences ☐
   c) Citations in e-sources ☐
   d) Bibliographical citations in printed sources ☐
   e) Use Internet search engines ☐
   f) Browse to some sites regularly ☐
   g) Subscribe mailing lists or newsgroups ☐
   h) Others (Please specify) ______________

C. Use of Internet

1. How did you learn to use the Internet? ☐
   a) A course given by the Library or computer center ☐
   b) Individual/orientation instruction by library staff ☐

c) Assistance from friends, teachers ☐

d) Self instruction, trial and error ☐

e) Literature (Manuals, computer magazines etc.) ☐

f) On line instruction on the Internet itself ☐

g) Others (Please specify) ______________

2. How often do you use the following Internet tools/resources for research?

Internet Tools/ Resources	*Never*	*Rarely*	*Once in a Month*	*Once in a Week*	*Once in a Day*
E-mail					
Discussion Lists, News Groups					
External catalogues/ Databases					
Document delivery Services					
Electronic Journals					
WWW Resources (Text, images, sound)					
Down Loading Services					
Online search					
Other services (Please specify) ______________					

3. On an average how much time per week do you spend using Internet facilities for research?

Internet Tools/ Resources	***< 30 Minutes***	***Up to one Hour***	***1 - 2 Hours***	***2 - 5 Hours***	***> 5 Hours***
E-mail					
Discussion Lists, News Groups					
External catalogues/ Databases					
Document delivery Services					
Electronic Journals					
WWW Resources (Text, images, sound)					
Down Loading Services					
Online search					
Other services (Please specify) ______________					

4. Which facility on Internet do you use most often for communication?

   a) E-mail ☐

   b) Chat ☐

   c) Net phone ☐

   d) None ☐

D. Searching of Information Resources

1. How often do you use the following search engines?

Search engines	*Never*	*Sometimes*	*Often*
AltaVista			
Excite			
Yahoo			
Google			
Lycos			
WebCrawler			
WWW worm			
WWW Virtual Library			
HotBot			
Infoseek			
MetaEureka			
Others (please specify)			

2. For what purpose do you conduct searches in electronic information sources?
   a) Search library catalogues ☐
   b) Search specific information ☐
   c) Search specific subject area ☐
   d) Search only for full text articles ☐
   e) Browse abstracts of full text articles ☐
   f) Browse abstracts of citations ☐
   g) Others (Please specify) ______________________

3. How often do you use the following search methods?

Search Methods	*Never*	*Sometimes*	*Often*
Author			
Keyword			
Subject			
Date of publication			
Journal title			
Title of article			
Others (Please specify) ______________			

4. How often do you use the following advanced search facilities?

Search Methods	*Never*	*Sometimes*	*Often*
Boolean operators			
Truncation of search terms			
Field searching			
Phrases (Two terms in a specific order)			

5. What are the difficulties in obtaining information from the online search?
   a) Lack of any online help ☐
   b) Unfamiliarity with the search methods ☐
   c) Too much information available ☐
   d) Lack of time required for searching for information ☐
   e) Speed of access ☐
   f) Cost ☐
   g) Others (please specify) ________________
6. How would you rate your overall ability to use electronic information sources?
   a) No use at all ☐
   b) Beginner ☐
   c) Below average ☐
   d) Average ☐
   e) Above average ☐
   f) Expert ☐
7. In what way have the electronic information sources improved your research?
   a) Fast research update ☐
   b) Better co-operation with colleagues ☐

c) Fast access to databases ☐

d) Saving time ☐

e) Others (Please specify) ________

8. After using electronic information sources what do you think about your usage of Printed documents?

a) Decreased ☐

b) Increased ☐

c) No change ☐

9. Which of the following features should an ideal Search Engine posses, according to you?

a) Global classification, the ability to choose a subject from a menu ☐

b) The possibility to type in search terms yourself ☐

c) The possibility of searching by author's names ☐

d) The possibility of restricting the search to resources stored on the Internet before or after a certain date ☐

e) The possibility of restricting searches to resources stored on the Internet by certain types of organizations for example Universities ☐

f) The possibility of restricting searches to certain document types, such as bibliographic databases or electronic journals ☐

g) The possibility of concept searching (a command 'find more like this' enables to find sources similar to a source (that you already have found) ☐

h) The possibility of Fuzzy searching (this facility lets you find sources even if the words being searched are spelled slightly differently) ☐

i) Meta searching (a search engine, which searches your query in various search engines simultaneously) ☐

j) Other features, if any (Please specify)

____

Select Bibliography

Abdul Rashid. (1997) Recent trends in library automation. IN: Library and Information Science Parameters and Perspectives. Prasher, R.G., ed. New Delhi, Concept Publishing, p. 51.

Abels, Eleen G., Liebscher, Peter. & Denman, Daniel W. (1996) Factors that influence the use of electronic networks by science and engineering faculty at small institutions. Part I. Queries. Journal of the American Society for Information Science, 47 (2), pp. 146– 158.

Abifarin, Abimbola. (1994) Information seeking behaviour of agricultural students in selected Nigerian Universities. Journal of Library and Information Science,19(2), pp.141-147.

Adeniran, Olatunde R. (1999) Library software in use in Southern Africa: A comparative analysis of search engines, database fine tuning and maintenance tools. The Electronic Library, 17(1), pp.27-36.

Agada, John. (1999) Inner city gatekeepers: an exploratory survey of their information use environment. Journal of the American Society for Information Science, 50 (1), pp.74 – 85.

Agarwal, Vibuti. (2000) Library networking: challenges and opportunities. New Delhi, Rajat Publications.

Ally Sornam, S. & Dhandapani. (2004) Ranking of search engines a study among Internet users. IN: Information Communication, Library And Community Development. Ramesh Babu, B. & Gopalakrishnan, S., ed. New Delhi, BRP. pp. 629-634.

Bajpai, S. K. (1999) Library information technology management. New Delhi, Ess Ess Publications.

Baldwin, Nancy Sadler. & Rice, Ronald E. (1997) Information seeking

behavior of securities analysts: individual and institutional

influences, information sources and channels, and outcomes. Journal of the American Society for Information Science, 48 (8), pp. 674 – 693.

Bavakutty, M. (1988) Libraries in higher education. New Delhi, Ess Ess Pubications.

Belecis, Deborah D., et al. (2001) The measurement of use of web based information resources: An early look at vendor supplied data. College and Research Libraries, 62 (4), pp. 434-453.

Berger, Kenneth W. & Hines, Richard W. (1994) What does the user really want? The library user survey project at Duke University. The Journal of Academic Librarianship, 20 (5), pp. 306-309.

Bhaskara Rao, P. (1998) Information network and resource sharing. New Delhi: Reliance Publishing House.

Biradar, B. S. & Sampath Kumar, B. T. (2000) Periodical use pattern by teachers and research scholars of Kuvempu University; A case study. SRELS Journal of Information Management, 37 (4), pp. 301-314.

Brown, Cecelia M. (1999) Information seeking behavior of scientists in the electronic information age: Astronomers, Chemists, Mathematicians and Physicists. Journal of the American Society for

Information Science, 50 (10), pp. 929 – 943.

Bruce, Harry. (1998) User satisfaction with information seeking on the Internet. Journal of the American Society for Information Science, 49 (6), pp. 541 – 545.

Byerley, Suzanne L. & Chambers, Mary Beth. (2002) Accessibility and usability of web based library databases for non visual users. Library Hi Tech, 20(2), pp.169-178.

Charles, Susan K. & Clark, Katharine E. (1990) Enhancing CD-ROM searches with online updates: An examination of end-user needs, strategies and problems. College and Research Libraries, 51(4), pp.321-328.

Chaya Devi, V. (1997) Attitude of the end-users towards on-line information retrieval – A case study of NSDRC Library, Visakhapattanam. Annals of Library Science and Documentation, 44(1), pp.18 – 31

Chowdhury, G. G. (1999) Introduction to modern information retrieval. London, Library Association Publishing.

Cogdill, Keith W., et al. (1997) First year medical students information needs and resource selection: responses to a clinical scenario. Bulletin of Medical Library Association, 85 (1), pp.51 – 54.

Cooper, Michael D. (2001) Use patterns of web based catalogues. Journal of the American Society for Information Science and Technology, 52 (2), pp. 137-148.

Costa, Sely. & Meadows, Jack. (2000) The impact of computer usage on scholarly communication among Social scientists. Journal of Information Science, 26 (2), pp. 255-262.

Cothey, Vivian. (2002) A longitudinal study of World Wide Web users' information seeking behaviour. Journal of the American Society for Information Science and Technology, 53(2), pp.67-78.

Cottrell, J. R. & Eisenberg, M. B. (2001) Applying an information problem-solving model to academic reference work: findings and implications. College and Research Libraries, 62(4), pp.334-347.

Crabtree, Anna Beth. & Crawford, Julia H. (1997) Assessing and addressing the library needs of health care personnel in a large regional hospital. Bulletin of Medical Library Association, 85 (2), pp.167 – 175.

Curtis, Karen L., et al. (1997) Information seeking behavior of Health Sciences faculty: the impact of new information technologies. Bulletin of Medical Library Association, 85 (4), pp.402 – 410.

D'Elia, George, et al. (2002) The impact of the Internet on public library use: An analysis of the current consumer market for library and Internet services. Journal of the American Society for Information Science and Technology, 53(10), pp. 802-820.

Dalgleish, Andrew & Hall, Robert. (2000) Uses and perceptions of the world wide web in an information seeking environment. Journal of Librarianship and Information Science, 32 (3), pp. 104-114.

Davis, P. M. & Cohen, S. A. (2001) The effect of the Web on undergraduate citation behavior 1996-1999. Journal of the American Society for Information Science, 52(4), pp.309-314.

Debowski, Shelda. (2001) Wrong: go back an exploration of novice search behaviours while conducting an information search. The Electronic Library, 19(6), pp.371-382.

D'Esposito, J. E. & Gardner, R. M. (1999) University students' perceptions of the Internet: an exploratory study. Journal of Academic Librarianship, 25 (6), pp.456-461.

Devarajan, G. (1996) Progress in Information Technology. New Delhi, Ess Ess Publications.

Drag, B.S. (2000) Information seeking patterns of users of engineering institutions in Rajsthan. Library Herald, 37(4), pp.229-239.

Fernandez, L. (1999) Scholarly communication in the sciences: a Third World perspective. Internet Reference Services Quarterly, 4 (4), pp.19-27.

Ford, Nigel., Miller, David. & Moss, Nichola. (2002) Web search strategies and retrieval effectiveness: An empirical study. Journal of Documentation, 58(2), pp.30-48.

Gaur, Ramesh C. (2003) Re-engineering Library and Information Services. Mumbai, Allied Publishers.

Geetha, P. (2004) Information needs and use pattern of pure scientists." IN: New frontiers of knowledge in Information Science. Devarajan, G., ed. New Delhi, ESS ESS Publications. pp. 320-382.

Gopal, Krishan. (2000) Digital libraries in electronic information era. Delhi, Authors Press.

Grag, B.S. (2000) Information seeking patterns of users of engineering institutions in Rajasthan. Library Herald, 37 (4), pp. 229 – 239.

Grimes, Deborah. & Boening, Carl H. (2001) Worries with the web: A look at student use of web resources. College and Research Libraries, 62(1), pp11-21.

He, P. W. & Jacobson, T. E. (1996) What are they doing with the Internet? A study of user information seeking behaviours. Internet Reference Services Quarterly, 1(1), pp.31-51.

Hewitson, Andrew. (2002) Use and awareness of electronic information services by academic staff at Leeds Metropolitan University: A qualitative study. Journal of Librarianship and Information Science, 34 (1), pp. 45-52.

Hsieh-Yee, I. (1996) Student use of online catalogs and other information channels. College and Research Libraries, 57(2), pp.161-75.

Ikhizama, B. O. & Oduwole, A. A. (2003) Pattern of usage of information sources by scientist in Nigerian Universities of Agriculture (UOA). Library Progress, 23 (1), pp. 1-6.

Jagga Rao, N. V. & Ramachander, M. (2000) Books to Bytes: Library information technology in the new millennium. New Delhi, Ess Ess Publications.

Jakobovits, Leon A. & Nahl-Jakobovits, Diane. (1990) Measuring information searching Competence. College and Research Libraries, 51(5), pp.448-461.

Jange, Suresh. & Maheswarappa, B. S. (1998) Information seeking behaviour of physical scientists: A case study with reference to Gulbarga University. Kelpro Bulletin, 2 (1), pp. 38-42.

Julien, Heidi. & Michels, David. (2000) Source selection among information seekers: Ideals and realities. Canadian Journal of Information and Library Science, 25 (1), pp. 2-17.

Kawatra, P.S. (2000) Text book of Information Science. New Delhi, APH Publishing Corporation.

Khan, M.T.M. (1997) Information organization and communication. New Delhi, Ess Ess Publications.

Kovacs, D. K., Robinson, K. L. & Dixon, J. (1995) Scholarly e-conferences on the academic networks: how library and information science professionals use them. Journal of the American Society for Information Science, 46(4), pp.244-253.

Kuffalikar, Chitra Rekha & Mahakulkar, Vaishali. (2003) A study of information seeking behaviour of the user in P. G. Departments of Bio Chemistry and Microbiology, Nagpur University. Indian Journal of Information Library & Society, 16, pp. 185-196.

Kumbar, I. N. (1999) Online services and their use in the library. IN: Library vision 2010: Indian libraries and librarianship. Sardana, J. L., ed. ILA, Delhi, pp. 379-389.

Kumbar, Mallinath. & Shirur, Shiddayya. (2003) Internet and its use in Sree Jayachamarajendra College of Engineering: A case study. SRELS Journal of Information Management, 40(2), pp. 169-176.

Lazinger, Susan S., Bar-Ilan, Judit. & Peritz, Bluma C. (1997) Internet use by faculty members in various disciplines: a comparative case study. Journal of the American Society for Information Science, 48(6), pp.508 – 518.

Lehnert, Wendy G. (2001) Internet 101. Singapore, Addison Wesley Longman.

Lenox, M. F. (1998) Intellectual participation in an information age: issues, values, and strategies. Journal of Academic Librarianship, 24 (1), pp.59-64.

Liebscher, Peter., Abels, Eileen G. & Denman, Daniel W. (1997) Factors that influence the use of electronic networks by science and engineering faculty at small institutions. Part II preliminary use indicators. Journal of American Society for Information Science, 48 (6), pp. 496 – 507.

Lucas, Wendy. & Topi, Heikki. (2002) Form and function: The impact of query term and operator usage on web search results. Journal of the American Society for Information Science and Technology, 53(2), pp.95-108.

Maheswarappa, B.S. & Ebnazar, C. Emmanual. (2003) Use of Internet resources and services in Gulbarga city: An exploratory study. SRELS Journal of Information Management, 40(4), pp. 404 – 420.

Majid, S. & Abazova, A. F. (1999) Computer literacy and use of electronic information sources by academics: a case study of International Islamic University Malaysia. Asian

Libraries, 8(4), p.110.

Manda, Paul A. (1991) Information seeking behaviour of sociologists. International Information Communication and Education, 10(1), pp.18-29.

Marcella, Rita & Baxter, Graeme. (1999) The information needs and the information seeking behaviour of a national sample of the population in the United Kingdom, with special reference to needs related to citizenship. Journal of Documentation, 55(2), pp.159-183.

Marchionini, Gary. (2002) Co-evolution of user and organizational interfaces: A longitudinal case study of WWW dissemination of national statistics. Journal of the American society for Information science & Technology, 53 (14), pp. 1192-1209.

Marghlani, Mohammad Amin & Hafez, Abdulrashid A. (1993) Online search service at the King Abdulaziz University Library, Jeddah, Saudi Arabia. International Information and Library Review, 25, pp.27-41.

Markusova, V.A., Giljarevskij, R.S. & Cherny, A.T. (1994) Communication among Russian scientists and between them and world science. International Forum on Information and Documentation, 19, pp. 17-27.

Marshall, Joanne Gard. (1990) Diffusion of innovation theory and end-user searching. Library and Information Science Research, 12(1), pp.55 – 69

Martin, William J. (1995) The Global Information Society. England, Aslib Gower.

Mc Murdo, G. & Meadows, A. J. (1996) Acceptance and use of computer mediated communication by information students. Journal of Information Science, 22 (5), pp. 335 – 348.

McKeown, Patrick G. (2003) Information Technology and the Networked Economy. Boston, Thomson.

Mendes, Helena. & Meadows, A. J. (1997) Personal information acquisition by health professionals in Brazilian and British hospitals: A comparative study. Journal of Librarianship and Information Science, 29 (4), pp. 189-193.

Mohammed Haneefa, K. & Bavakutty, M. (2001) Wireless networking in Libraries: a conceptual introduction. IN: Proceedings of the National Seminar on Library Co-operation in a Networked World. 25-26 May, University of Calicut. New Delhi, Ess Ess Publications, p.135.

Monopoli, Maria & Nicholas, David. (2001) A user evaluation of subject based information gateways: case study ADAM. Aslib Proceedings, 53, pp. 39 – 50.

Monopoli, Maria. & Nicholas, David. (2000) A user –centered approach to the evaluation of subject based information gateways: Case study SOSIG. Aslib Proceedings, 52 (6), pp. 218-231.

Monopoli, Mariya., et al. (2002) A user oriented evaluation of digital libraries: Case study of the electronic journals service of the library and electronic journals service of the library and information service of the university of Patras, Greece. Aslib Proceedings, 54 (2), pp. 103-117.

Moyo, Lesley M. (1996) Training needs for Internet usage in a learning environment: University of Botswana case. International Forum on Information and Documentation, 21(4), pp.25-33.

Munshi, Usha Mujoo & Manju Kant. (1997) Information seeking in electronic environments. Library Herald, 34(3-4), pp.100-110.

Nagar, B. R. et al. (2000) Surfing for Indian information on the internet: A case study. Annals of Library Science and Documentation, 47(2), pp.53-62.

Nahl, Diane. (1998) Learning the internet and the structure

of information behaviour. Journal of the American Society for Information Science, 49(11), pp.1017-1023.

Nicholas, D. & Dobrowolski, T. (2000) Re-branding and re-discovering the digital information user. Libri, 50 (3), pp.157-62.

Nicholas, David. & Martin, Helen. (1997) Assessing information needs: a case study of journalists. Aslib Proceedings, 49 (2), pp. 43 – 52.

Nicholas, David., Hunbington, Paul. & Williams, Peter. (2002) Evaluating metrics for comparing the use of websites: A case study of two consumer health websites. Journal of Information science, 28(1), pp. 63-75.

Nicolas, Vaughan. (1997) Intranets. Boston, AP Professional.

Nikam, Khaiser. & Rajashekara, N. (2003) Reading habits of public library users: A survey. SRELS Journal f Information Management, 40(4), pp. 337-363.

Nwali, L.O. (1991) Potential value of CD - ROM in Nigerian Libraries and information centers. Journal of Librarianship and Information Science, 23(3), p. 156.

Obst, Oliver. (1998) Use of internet resources by German medical professionals. Bulletin of Medical Library Association, 86(4), pp.528- 533.

Ockacha, Kingsley Ferewisky. (1995) Socio-cultural departments of the use and transfer of scientific information by agricultural scientists in South Eastern Nigeria. Information and Library Review, 27, pp. 301 – 316.

Olepors, Niels. (1990) Users, collection use and online searching: Investigation in Danish public libraries. International Journal of Information and Library Research, 2 (2), pp. 63-76.

Pajarillo, Edmund. (2002) The use and evaluation of search databases by professional nurses: A case study. The

Electronic Library, 19(5), pp.296-306.

Park, H. O. (1996) Use of the Internet via universal access workstation. Internet Reference Services Quarterly, 1(1), pp.69-87.

Pathak, Pragnya J. & Saroj Das. (2001) Utilization of electronic information at IPR Library: A case study. Information Studies, 7(2), pp.109-118.

Pawar, S. S. (1992) Impact of new information technology in development of Libraries and services. IN: Proceedings of Thirty Eighth All India Library Conference on Library and Information Technology: In Pursuit of Excellence: Delhi, ILA.

Pelzer, Nancy L., Wise, William H. & Leysen, Joan M. (1998) Library use and information seeking behavior of Veterinary Medical students revised in the electronic environment. Bulletin of Medical Library Association, 86 (3), pp. 346 – 355.

Pettigrew, Karen E., Durrance, Joan C. & Unruh, Kenton T. (2002) Facilitating community information seeking using the Internet: Findings from three public libraries–community network systems. Journal of the American Society for Information Science and Technology, 53 (11), pp. 894-903.

Philip, G. (1996) Use of leading-edge information systems by academic chemists in the UK: Part II constraints and the need for usability engineering. Journal of Information Science, 22 (2), pp. 93 – 106.

Popoola, S. O. (2000) Scanning the environment for competitive advantage: a study of corporate banking managers in Nigeria. Libri,50(3), pp.210-16.

Prasanna Kumar, H. E. & Mudhol, Mahesh V. (2002) Multimedia: Its application in library and information science. New Delhi, Ess Ess Publications.

Pullinger, David. (1999) Academics and the new information environment: the impact of local factors on use of electronic journals. Journal of Information Science, 25 (2), pp.164 – 172.

Raman Nair, R. (2002) Internet for Information Services. New Delhi, Ess Ess Publications.

Ramdas, G. (2003) Electronic library: services and products. IN: Proceedings of the Fourty Eighth ILA Conference on Electronic Information Environment and Library Services: A Conteporary Paradigm. Delhi, ILA, pp.122-123.

Ray, Kathelin L. & Lang, Mary S. (1997) Analysing search styles of patrons and staff: A replicative study of two university libraries. Library Trends, 41(3), pp.219-235.

Reneker, Maxine H. (1993) A qualitative study of information seeking among members of an academic community: methodological issues and problems. Library Quarterly, 63(4), pp.487-501.

Rogers, Sally A. (2001) Electronic journal usage at Ohio State University. College and Research Libraries, 62(1), pp. 25-33.

Rolinson, J., Al-Shanbari, H. & Meadows, A. J. (1996) Information usage by biological researchers. Journal of Information Science, 22(1), pp.47-53.

Rowland, Fytton. & Rubbert, Iris. (2001) An evaluation of the information needs and practices of part-time and distance learning students in the context of educational and social change through life long learning. Journal of Documentation, 57 (6), pp.741-762.

Rowley, Jennifer. (1998) The Electronic Library. London, Library Association Publishing.

Salem, Shawky. (1997) Artificial Intelligence (AI) and Expert Systems (ES) tools for development. IN: Library and

Information Science Parameters and Perspectives. Prasher, R.G., ed. New Delhi, Concept Publishing, p. 91.

Sanjeev Kumar & Mishra, Sanjaya. (1993) Use of National Institute of Fashion Technology Library: A survey. ILA Bulletin, 283 (3), pp.116-123.

Saunders - McMaster, Laverna. (1997) Internet 2: an overview of the next generation of the Internet. Computers in Libraries, March, p. 57.

Savolainen, Reijo. (1999) The role of the internet in information seeking putting the networked services in context. Information Processing and Management, 35, pp.765 – 782.

Sehgal, R. L. (2000) Intranet and Internet applications for libraries. New Delhi, Ess Ess Publications.

Shaw, D. (1995) Bibliographic database searching by graduate students in language and literature: search strategies, system interfaces, and relevance judgments. Library and Information Science Research, 17(4), pp.327-45.

Shewale, Nanaji & Shewale, Madhukar N. (1997) Hyper text and HTML tools and techniques to develop webpages. IN: Proceedings of Fourty Third All India Library Conference on Sustainable Library and Information Services. Delhi, ILA, pp. 214-215.

Siatri, Rania. (1999) The evolution of user studies. Libri, 49, pp.132-141.

Siddiqui, Moid A. (1996) A statistical study of online searches in an academic library. International Forum on Information and Documentation, 21(2), pp.3-20.

Sonal Singh. (1998) Universeof Knowledge. Jaipur, Raj Publishing House.

Spink, Amanda H., Ozmutlu, Cenk. & Ozmutlu, Seda. (2002)

Multitasking information seeking and searching process. Journal of the American Society for Information science and Technology, 53(8), pp.639-652.

Spink, Amanda., et al. (2002) Information seeking and mediated searching study. Part 3 successive searching. Journal of the American Society for Information Science and technology, 53(9), pp.716-727.

Sprague, Mary W. (1994) Information searching pattern of university administrators and non faculty professional staff members. The Journal of Academic Librarianship, 19(6), pp.378-383.

Sridhar, B.S., Sampath Kumar, B.T. & Anil Kumar. M. (2003) Information use pattern by Sericulture scientists: A case study of Karnataka state Sericulture Research and Development Institute Library, Bangalore. SRELS Journal of Information Management, 40 (3), pp. 255-265.

Stilwell, Christine. (1999) Community Information Services : A view of the theoretical foundations. Desidoc Bulletin of Information Technology, 19(1), pp.15-16.

Sugunavathy, C. (1999) Information needs of subject matter specialists in agricultural extension service. Library Science with slant to Documentation and Information Studies, 36(3), pp.165-173.

Suriya, M., & Abdul Raheem, A. (1998) Information and communication technology infrastructure and sustainable development in high middle and low-income countries. International Forum on Information and Documentation, 23 (2), pp. 3-10.

Swaroop Rani, B.S. (1992) Digitizing libraries with today's information technology. IN: Proceedings of the Thirty Eighth All India Library Conference on Library and Information Technology: In Pursuit of Excellence. Delhi, ILA, p.51.

Tadasad, P. G. & Metesheela, D. (2001) Use pattern of information sources by post graduate students in a university environment: A case study of Gulbarga University, Gulbarga. SRELS Journal of Information Management, 38 (3), pp. 231-254.

Tomney, Hilary. & Burton, Paul F. (1998) Electronic journals: a study of usage and attitudes among academics. Journal of Information Science, 24 (6), pp. 419 – 429.

Tripathi, Manorama. (2000) Information requirements in Physical Sciences and Social Studies: A comparative study. Library Herald, 38(2), pp. 91-103.

Upadhya, Padma V. (1998) Multimedia and virtual system: New media for information presentation. IN:Information Technology Issues and Trends. Satyanarayana, B. et al., ed. New Delhi, Cosmo Pubications, p.105.

Varghese, Rekha Rani & Bavakutty, M. (2001) Networking of public libraries in Kerala. In: Proceedings of the National Seminar on Library Co-operation in a Networked World. 25-26 May, University of Calicut. New Delhi, Ess Ess Publications, p.175-183.

Vaughan, J. (1999) Considerations in the choice of an Internet search tool. Library Hi Tech, 17 (1), pp.89-106.

Vaughan, Liwen. & Thelwall, Mike. (2003) Scholarly use of the web: What are the key inducers of links to journal websites. Journal of American society for information science and Technology, 54(1), pp. 29-38.

VijayaLakshmi, B. & Kannakachary, M. (1994) Information needs and use patterns in humanities: A survey and proposal for setting up a national documentation center for humanities. International Forum on Information and Documentation, 19, pp. 37-41.

Voorbij, Henkj. (1999) Searching Scientific information on the internet: a Dutch academic user survey. Journal of the American Society for Information Science, 50(7), pp.598 – 615.

Wiberley, Stephen E. & Jones, William G. (1989) Patterns of information seeking in the Humanities. College and Research Libraries, 50 (6), pp. 638-645.

Wilkins, Janie L. Hassard. & Leckie, Gloria J. (1997) University professional and managerial staff: Information needs and seeking. College and Research Libraries,58 (7), pp. 561-573.

Wilson, T.D. (1999) Models in information behaviour research. Journal of Documentation,55(3), pp. 249-270.

Winship, Ian R. (1986) The use of online information services in UK higher education libraries. British Journal of Academic Librarianship,1(3), pp. 191-205.

Wolfram, Dietmar. & Xie, Hong (Iris). (2002) Traditional IR for web users: A context for general audience digital libraries. Information Processing and Management, 38, pp.627-648.

Wood, Fred B., Wallingford, Karen T., & Siegel, Elliot R. (1997) Transitioning to the Internet: Results of a National Library of Medicine user survey. Bulletin of Medical Library Association, 85(4), pp.331 – 339.

Xie, Hong (Iris). & Wolfram, Dictmar. (2002) State digital library usability: contributing organizational factors. Journal of the American Society for Information Science and Technology, 53 (13), pp. 1085-1097.

Zhang, Xiangmin. (2001) Collaborative relevance judgment: a group consensus method for evaluating user search performance. Journal of the American Society for Information Science, 53(3), pp. 220-231.

Zhang, Yin. (1999) Scholarly use of internet based electronic resources: A survey report. Library Trends, 47(4), pp.746 – 770.

WEB REFERENCES

Ananthaswamy, Anil. Tele immersion [Internet] Available from: <*www.newscientist.com*> [Accessed December 2nd 2004]

Balas, Janet L. (2003) Does wireless really mean no more wires. Computers in Libraries [Internet] 23(3). Available from: <*http://www.infotoday.com/cilmag/mar03/balas.shtml* > [Accessed October 10th 2005]

Banwell, L. and Coulson, G. (2004) Users and user study methodology: the JUBILEE Project. Information Research [Internet] 9(2). Available from: <*http://InformationR.net/ir/9-2/paper167.html*> [Accessed October 10th 2005]

Barletta, Antonio. (2001) Java Applications in Digital Audio Broadcasting. EBU Technical Review [Internet] September (1 / 14) Available from: <*http://21cif.imsa.edu/resources/materials/difcore* > [Accessed December 12th 2004]

Bergman, M. K. (2001) The deep Web: surfacing hidden information. The Journal of Electronic Publishing [Internet] 7 (1). Available from: < *http://www.press.umich.edu/jep/07-01/bergman.html* > [Accessed January 18th 2004]

Brain, Marshall. How WiFi works. [Internet]. Available from: <*http://www.howstuffworks.com/wireless-network.htm*> [Accessed June 20th 2005]

Breeding, Marshall. (2004) Wireless networks connect libraries to a mobile society. Computers in Libraries [Internet] 23(9). Available from: <*http://www.infotoday.com/cilmag/oct04/breeding.shtml*> [Accessed June 17th 2005]

Brooks, Terrence A. (2003) Web Search: how the Web has changed information retrieval. Information Research [Internet] 8(3). Available from: <*http://InformationR.net/*

ir/8-3/paper154.html> [Accessed June 17th 2005]

Brown, Christine D. (2001) The role of computer-mediated communication in the research process of music scholars: an exploratory investigation. Information Research [Internet] 6(2). Available from: <*http://InformationR.net/ir/6-2/paper99.html*> [Accessed January 2nd 2005]

Champandard, Alex J. Artificial Intelligence [Internet] Available from: <*http://ai-depot.com* > [Accessed October 4th 2004]

Cleveland, Gary. (1998) Digital Libraries: definitions, issues and challenges [Internet] IFLANET. Available from: < *http://www.ifla.org/VI/5/op/udtop8/udtop8.htm*> [Accessed June 20th 2005]

Coggan, Donald A. Knowledge base sets expert systems apart [Internet]. Available from: < *http://www.coggan.com/expertsystems.html* > [Accessed July 14th 2004]

Eskola, Evea-Liisa. (1998) University students' information seeking behaviour in a changing learning environment. Information Research [Internet] 4(2). Available from: <*http://www.shef.ac.uk/is/publications/infres/isic/eeskola.html* > [Accessed February 2nd 2004]

Franklin, Brinley & Plum, Terry. (2004) Library usage patterns in the electronic information environment. Information Research [Internet] 9 (4). Available from:<*http://www.informationr.net/ir/9-4/paper187.html*>[Accessed December 10th 2005]

Franklin, Curt. How Internet search engines work [Internet] Available from: <*http://www.howstuffworks.com/search-engine.htm/printable*> [Accessed September 20th 2005]

Gross, Melissa (2001) Imposed information seeking in public libraries and school library media centers: a common behaviour. Information Research [Internet] 6(2). Available from: <*http://InformationR.net/ir/6-2/paper100.html*> [Accessed March 23rd 2005]

Hargittai, Eszter. (2002) Beyond logs and surveys in-depth measures of people's web use skills. Journal of the American Society for Information Science and Technology [Internet] 53(14), pp.1239-1245. Available from: <*http://www.asis.org/Publications/JASIS/vol53n14.html* > [Accessed June 10th 2005]

Hepworth, Mark. (1998) Investigating methods for understanding user requirements for information products. Information Research [Internet] 4(2) October. Available from: < *http://www.informationr.net/ir/4-2/isic/hepworth.html* > [Accessed January 15th 2005]

Jansen, Bernard J. (2000) The effect of query complexity on Web searching results. Information Research [Internet] 6(1). Available from: <*http://InformationR.net/ir/6-1/paper87.html*> [Accessed May 20th 2004]

Järvelin, K. and Wilson, T.D. (2003) On conceptual models for information seeking and retrieval research. Information Research [Internet] 9(1). Available from: <*http://InformationR.net/ir/9-1/paper163.html*> [Accessed March 23rd 2005]

Kaine-Krolak, Maureen & Novak, Mark E. An Introduction to Infrared Technology [Internet] Available from: <*http://trace.wisc.edu/docs/ir_intro/ir_intro.htm*> [Accessed June 20th 2005]

Khan, M. Shamim & Khor, Sebastian. (2003) Enhanced web document retrieval using automatic query expansion. Journal of the American Society for Information Science and Technology [Internet] 55(1), pp.29-41. Available from: <*http://www.asis.org/Publications/JASIS/vol55n01.html*> [Accessed April 25th 2005]

Kling, Rob., McKim, Geoffrey & King, Adam. (2002) A bit more to it: scholarly communication forums as socio-technical interaction networks. Journal of the American Society for Information Science and Technology [Internet] 154(1), pp.47-67. Available from: <*http://www.asis.org/Publications/JASIS/vol54n01.html*> [Accessed January 15th 2005]

Koehler, W. (1999) Digital libraries and the World Wide Web sites and page persistence. Information Research [Internet] 4(4). Available from: <*http://www.informationr.net/ir/4-4/isic/hepworth.html* > [Accessed May 9th 2005]

Lamb, Roberta., King, John Leslie & Kling, Rob. (2002) Informational environments: organizational contexts of online information use. Journal of the American Society for Information Science and Technology [Internet] 154(2), pp.97-114.Available from: <*http://www.asis.org/Publications/JASIS/vol54n02.html*> [Accessed May 9th 2005]

Limberg, Louise. (1999) Experiencing information seeking and learning: a study of the interaction between two phenomena. Information Research [Internet] 5(1). Available from: < *http://informationr.net/ir/5-1/paper68.html*> [Accessed June 10th 2005]

Liu., Jian. (2001) Meta search engines [Internet]. Available from: <*http://www.indiana.edu/~librcsd/search*> [Accessed July 14th 2004]

Lynch, Clifford & Garcia-Molina, Hector. (1995) Interoperability, scaling, and the digital libraries research agenda: A report on the May 18-19, 1995 IITA Digital Libraries Workshop [Internet]. Available from: <*http://diglib.stanford.edu/diglib/pub/reports/iita-dlw/main.html#2.*> [Accessed March 5th 2005]

McMahan, Michael L., Khatzibadeh, Ali & Shah, Pradeep.

Wireless systems and technology overview [Internet]. Available from: <*http://www.ti.com/sc/data/wireless/panos1.pdf* > [Accessed March 7th 2005]

Meho, Lokman I. & Haas, Stephanie W. (2001) Information-seeking behavior and use of social science faculty studying stateless nations: a case study. Library & Information Science Research [Internet] 23(1), p.5-25. Available from: <*http://dois.mimas.ac.uk/DoIS/data/Articles/julibsqaby:2001:v:23:i:1:p:5-25.html*> [Accessed December 22nd 2004]

Mischo, William H. (2005) Digital libraries: challenges and influential work. D-Lib Magazine [Internet] 11(7/8). Available from: <*http://www.dlib.org/dlib/july05/mischo/07mischo.html* > [Accessed October 10th 2005]

Pettigrew, Karen E., Durrance, Joan C. & and Unruh, Kenton T. (2002) Facilitating community information seeking using the internet findings from three public library-community network systems. Journal of the American Society for Information Science and Technology [Internet] 53(11), pp.894-904. Available from: <*http://www.asis.org/Publications/JASIS/vol53n11.html* > [Accessed March 3rd 2005]

Pickard, Alison . (1998) The impact of access to electronic and digital information resources on learning opportunities for young people: A grounded theory approach. Information Research [Internet] 4(2). Available from: <*http://InformationR.net/ir/4-2/isic/pickard.html*> [Accessed January 25th 2004]

Robert Harris. (2000) Internet search tips and strategies [Internet]. Available from: < *http://www.virtualsalt.com/howlook.htm*> [Accessed April 2nd 2005]

Rodriguez, Luis German. Information and communication technologies (ICT): the administration of a positive social impact [Internet]. Available from: <*http://*

funredes.org/mistica/english/cyberlibrary/thematic/eng_doc_coord.html > [Accessed March 10th 2005]

Sicilia, Miguel Ángel, et al. (2003) A literature-based approach to annotation and browsing of Web resources. Information Research [Internet] 8(2). Available from: <*http://informationr.net/ir/8-2/paper149.html* > [Accessed December 12th 2004]

Smith, Alastair G. (2000) Search features of digital libraries. Information Research [Internet] 5(3). Available from: < *http://informationr.net/ir/5-3/paper73.html*> [Accessed December 12th 2004]

Sormunen, E & Pennanen, S. (2004) The challenge of automated tutoring in Web-based learning environments for IR instruction. Information Research [Internet] 9(2). Available from: < http://InformationR.net/ir/9-2/paper169.html> [Accessed April 14th 2005]

Spink, A., Bateman, J., & Jansen, B. (1998) Searching heterogeneous collections on the Web: behaviour of Excite users. Information Research [Internet] 4(2). Available from: <*http://InformationR.net/ir/paper53.html*> [Accessed August 30th 2004]

Waldman, Micaela. (2003) Freshmen's use of library electronic resources and self-efficacy. Information Research [Internet] 8(2). Available from: <*http://informationr.net/ir/8-2/paper150.html*]> [Accessed February 3rd 2005]

Ward, David & Reisinger, Sarah. (2000) Designing Internet research assignments: building a framework for instructor collaboration. Information Research [Internet] 6(1). Available from: <*http://InformationR.net/ir/6-1/paper86.html*> [Accessed March 10th 2005]

Watters, Carolyn & Amoudi, Ghada. (2002) Geosearcher: location-based ranking of search engine results. Journal of the American Society for Information Science and

Technology [Internet] 54(2), pp.140-151. Available from: <*http://www.asis.org/Publications/JASIS/vol54n02.html* > [Accessed April 23rd 2005]

Wilson, T. D. The cognitive approach to information-seeking behaviour and information use [Internet]. Available from: <*http://www.informationr.net/tdw/publ/papers/cogapp84.html*> [Accessed January 20th 2004]

Wilson, T.D. (2000) Recent trends in user studies: action research and qualitative methods. Information Research [Internet] 5(3). Available from: <*http://informationr.net/ir/5-3/paper76.html*> [Accessed January 20th 2004]

Whitley, Katherine M. (2002) Analysis of scifinder scholar and web of science citation searches. Journal of the American Society for Information Science and Technology [Internet] 53(14), pp.1210-1218. Available from: <*http://www.asis.org/Publications/JASIS/vol53n14.html* > [Accessed December 10th 2004]

Wouters, Paul., Hellsten, Iina. & Leydesdorff, Loet. (2004) Internet time and reliability of search engine [Internet] Available from: <*http://firstmonday.org/issues/issue9_10/wouters/index.html*> [Accessed September 25th 2004]

Yu, Byeong-Min & Roh, Seak-Zoon. (2002) The effects of menu design on information-seeking performance and user's attitude on the World Wide Web. Journal of the American Society for Information Science and Technology [Internet] 53(11), pp.923-934. Available from: <*http://www.asis.org/Publications/JASIS/vol53n11.html* > [Accessed December 6th 2004]

Index

A

Artificial Intelligence, 25

B

Bluetooth, 46
Boolean Search, 17
Broad Band Wireless, 34

C

CD Recorder, 29
CD Re-Writable, 29
CD-ROM, 28
Cellular Digital Pocket Data (CDPD), 55
Cellular Radio, 56
Code Division Mulliplo Access, 54
Codec, 38
Communication Devices, 44

D

Digital Audio Broadcasting (DAB), 50
Digital Information Fluency (DIF), 23
Digital Library, 56, 320
Digital Versatile Disc *see* DVD,
Digital Video Disc *see* DVD,
DVD, 30
DVD-Plus, 32
DVD-R, 31
DVD-RW, 31

E

Electronic Data Exchange, 32
Electronic Information, 12, 22
Electronic Information Resources, 318
Electronic Information Service, 90, 318
Electronic Publishing, 57
Expert Systems, 25
Extranet, 43

F

Fascimile Transmission, 33
Fax *see* Fascimile Transmission,
Field Search, 20
File Transfer Protocol, 38
Fixed Wireless System, 44

G

General Packet Radio Service, 53
Gopher, 38

H

Hyper LAN, 48

I

Information Needs, 110
Information Search Pattern, 64
Information Seeking Behaviour, 102
Infrared, 47
Input Devices, 24
Intranet, 42
Internet, 12, 37, 42, 79
Internet Library Service, 319
Internet Relay Chat, 40
Internet Search Engines, 14
Internet2, 42

L

Local Multi-point Distribution Service, 34

M

Meta Search Engines, 16
MMDS, 34
Mobitexs, 54
Mosaic, 38
Multimedia, 27

N

Networking , 36, 319

O

Online Search, 20
Output Devices, 24

P

Packet Radio, 55
Phrase Search, 19
Portable Wireless System, 45
Proximity Search, 19

R

Resource Sharing, 319

S

Search Engines, 13
Spider, 15
Subject Directories, 16

T

Tele Immersion, 40
Telnet, 38
Truncation, 18

U

Ultra-wide band, 37
Usenet, 38

V

Veronica, 38
Video Conferencing, 38, 39
Video Text, 34
Virtual Library, 320
Virtual Reality, 26, 40
Voice over Internet Protocol, 41

W

Wimax, 49
Wireless Application Environment, 52
Wireless Application Protocol, 51
Wireless Datagram Protocol, 52
Wireless Networking, 45, 49
Wireless Technology, 44
Wireless Transaction Layer Security, 52
Wireless Transaction Protocol, 52
World Wide Web (WWW), 13, 38
Wireless Wide Area Network (WWAN), 50